CATHOLIC THEOLOGICAL FORMATION SERIES

General Editor: Kevin Zilverberg

The Catholic Theological Formation Series is sponsored by The Saint Paul Seminary School of Divinity, the graduate school of theological formation for Roman Catholic seminarians and laity enrolled at the University of Saint Thomas in Saint Paul, Minnesota. As a premier institution of theological formation for the region and beyond, The Saint Paul Seminary School of Divinity seeks to form men and women for the task of fulfilling the specific call God has for them, a call grounded in their common baptismal vocation to serve one another in Christ.

As an institution of the Archdiocese of Saint Paul and Minneapolis, the school is intentional in its commitment to priestly and diaconal formation. As an institution of graduate theological education, the school prepares the laity for the equally compelling task of making Christ known and loved in the world. Although the students prepare for diverse ministries, all enroll in a curriculum of theological formation within the context of holistic and integrated Catholic formation.

It is this challenge of theological formation—the challenge to faithfully inform one's understanding—that serves as the focus of this series, with special attention given to the task of preparing priests, deacons, teachers, and leaders within the Roman Catholic tradition. Although the series is academic in tenor, it aims beyond mere academics in its integrative intellectual approach. We seek to promote a form of discourse that is professional in its conduct and spiritual in its outcomes, for theological formation is more than an exercise in academic technique. It is rather about the perfecting of a spiritual capacity: the capacity on the part of the human person to discern what is true and good.

This series, then, aims to develop the habits of mind required of a sound intellect—a spiritual aptitude for the truth of God's living Word and his Church. Most often, it will draw from the more traditional specializations of historical, systematic, moral, and biblical scholarship. Homiletics and pastoral ministry are anticipated venues as well. There will be occasions, however, when a theme is examined across disciplines and periods, for the purposes of bringing to our common consideration a thesis yet undeveloped.

Despite the variety of methodologies and topics explored, the series' aim remains constant: to provide a sustained reflection upon the mission and ministry of Catholic theological formation of both clergy and laity alike.

The general editor of the Catholic Theological Formation Series, Fr. Kevin Zilverberg, serves as assistant professor of Sacred Scripture and the founding director of Saint Paul Seminary Press at The Saint Paul Seminary School of Divinity.

CATHOLIC THEOLOGICAL FORMATION SERIES

Editor
Kevin Zilverberg

Editorial Board
Kelly Anderson
Matthew C. Briel
Paige Hochschild
Andrew Hofer, OP
Matthew Levering
Michael Monshau, OP
Christopher J. Thompson
Kevin Zilverberg

The Word of Truth, Sealed by the Spirit

Perspectives on the Inspiration and Truth of Sacred Scripture

Edited by

Matthew C. Genung and Kevin Zilverberg

SAINT PAUL, MINNESOTA • 2022

COVER IMAGE: Mosaic and tabernacle of the Immaculate Conception chapel
at Mount St. Mary's Seminary in Cincinnati
Photo by Matthew C. Genung
Cover design by Willem Mineur

© 2022 Matthew C. Genung and Kevin Zilverberg
Saint Paul Seminary Press is a registered trademark of The Saint Paul Seminary.
All rights reserved

Published 2022 by
Saint Paul Seminary Press
2260 Summit Ave., Saint Paul, Minnesota 55105

Library of Congress Control Number: 2022945888
LC record available at https://lccn.loc.gov/2022945888

Catholic Theological Formation Series
ISSN 2765-9283
ISBN 978-1-953936-09-7 (paperback)
ISBN 978-1-953936-59-2 (ebook)

spspress.com

Contents

Abbreviations		vii
Introduction *Matthew C. Genung and Kevin Zilverberg*		1
1.	The Inspiration and Truth of Scripture: Do They Still Matter? *Luis Sánchez-Navarro, DCJM*	7
2.	*The Inspiration and Truth of Sacred Scripture*: A Critical Appraisal of the Pontifical Biblical Commission's Document *Michael K. Magee*	22
3.	The Divine Voice of Sinai in Emended Scripture *Matthew C. Genung*	51
4.	Inspiration and Truth When Prophecy Fails: Ezekiel's Temple Vision *Anthony Pagliarini*	69
5.	Ratzinger on the Historicity of the Gospels: A Case Study of the Last Supper Narrative *Aaron Pidel, SJ*	84
6.	Changing Gender Roles and the Unchanging Message of 1 Corinthians 11:2–16 *Marcin Kowalski*	107
7.	The Old Testament as an Earthly Translation of an Inner-Trinitarian Dialogue: Implications for Inspiration *Kelly Anderson*	144
Contributors		165
Index of Names and Subjects		167
Index of Scripture References		173

Abbreviations

1QM	Milḥamah (War Scroll)
1QS	Serek Hayaḥad (Rule of the Community)
2 Fort.	*De fortuna* (Dio Chrysostom)
Abr.	*De Abrahamo* (Philo)
ABSt	Archeology and Biblical Studies
Am.	*Amores* (Pseudo-Lucian)
AnBib	Analecta Biblica
AncB	Anchor Bible
ANTC	Abingdon New Testament Commentaries
ArBib	The Aramaic Bible: The Targums (ed. Martin McNamara)
ASNU	Acta Seminarii Neotestamentici Upsaliensis
AYB	Anchor Yale Bible
BiSe	Biblical Seminar
BDAG	Walter Bauer, Frederick W. Danker, William F. Arndt, and F. Wilbur Gingrich, *A Greek-English Lexicon of the New Testament and Other Early Christian Literature*, 3rd edn. (Chicago: University of Chicago Press, 2000)
BEATAJ	Beiträge zur Erforschung des Alten Testaments und des antiken Judentums
BECNT	Baker Exegetical Commentary on the New Testament
BETL	Bibliotheca Ephemeridum Theologicarum Lovaniensium
BToSt	Biblical Tools and Studies
BTCB	Brazos Theological Commentary on the Bible
BTSK	Baptist Theological Seminary Kaduna

vii

ABBREVIATIONS

BZAR	Beihefte zur Zeitschrift für altorientalische und biblische Rechtsgeschichte
BZAW	Beihefte zur Zeitschrift für die Alttestamentliche Zeitscrift
C. Ap.	*Contra Apionem* (Josephus)
CBET	Contributions to Biblical Exegesis and Theology
CBQMS	Catholic Biblical Quarterly Monograph Series
CDF	Congregation for the Doctrine of the Faith
Clem.	*De clementia* (Seneca)
Conf.	*De confusione linguarum* (Philo)
Contempl.	*De vita contemplativa* (Philo)
CPhC	Cambridge Philosophy Classics
Crat.	*Cratylus* (Plato)
CTFS	Catholic Theological Formation Series
De or.	*De oratore* (Cicero)
DH	Peter Hünermann, Helmut Hoping, Robert L. Fastiggi, Anne Englund Nash, and Heinrich Denzinger, eds., *Compendium of Creeds, Definitions, and Declarations on Matters of Faith and Morals* (San Francisco: Ignatius, 2012)
Diatr.	*Diatribai* (Epictetus)
EKKNT	Evangelisch-Katholischer Kommentar zum Neuen Testament
EDNT	*Exegetical Dictionary of the New Testament,* ed. Horst Balz and Gerhard Schneider (Grand Rapids: Eerdmans, 1990–1993)
FAT	Forschungen zum Alten Testament
FAT.2	Forschungen zum Alten Testament – 2. Reihe
FRLANT	Forschungen zur Religion und Literatur des Alten und Neuen Testaments
GCS	Griechischen christlichen Schriftsteller der ersten drei Jahrhunderte
GPBS	Global Perspectives on Biblical Scholarship
GTS	Gettysburg Theological Studies
HBM	Hebrew Bible Monographs
HCOT	Historical Commentary on the Old Testament
Hom. 1 Cor.	*Homilies on First Corinthians* (John Chrysostom)
HThKAT	Herders theologischer Kommentar zum Alten Testament
ICC	International Critical Commentary
Inst.	*Institutio oratoria* (Quintilian)
Int.	Interpretation: A Bible Commentary for Teaching and Preaching
Inv.	*De inventione rhetorica* (Cicero)
JN1	Joseph Ratzinger, *Jesus of Nazareth: From the Baptism in the*

	Jordan to the Transfiguration, trans. Adrian J. Walker (San Francisco: Ignatius, 2007)
JN2	Joseph Ratzinger, *Jesus of Nazareth: Holy Week: From the Entrance into Jerusalem to the Resurrection*, trans. Philip J. Whitmore (San Francisco: Ignatius, 2011)
JN3	Joseph Ratzinger, *Jesus of Nazareth: The Infancy Narratives*, trans. Philip J. Whitmore (New York: Image, 2012)
JSNT	Journal for the Study of the New Testament
JSNTSup	Journal for the Study of the New Testament, Supplement Series
JSOTSup	Journal for the Study of the Old Testament, Supplement Series
LCL	Loeb Classical Library
Leg.	*Leges* (Plato)
LHB	The Library of Hebrew Bible/Old Testament Studies
LNTS	Library of New Testament Studies
LSJ	Henry George Liddell, Robert Scott, Henry Stuart Jones, *A Greek-English Lexicon*, 9th edn. with revised supplement (Oxford: Clarendon, 1996)
Met.	*Metaphysica* (Aristotle)
MNTC	Moffatt New Testament Commentary
MoBi(G)	Monde de la Bible (Geneva)
NAB	New American Bible
NABRE	New American Bible, Revised Edition
NAC	New American Commentary
NICNT	New International Commentary on the New Testament
NIGTC	New International Greek Testament Commentary
NT.S	Supplements to *Novum Testamentum*
NPNF	Nicene and Post-Nicene Fathers
NSK.AT	Neuer Stuttgarter Kommentar – Altes Testament
OBO	Orbis Biblicus et Orientalis
OBT	Overtures to Biblical Theology
Off.	*De officiis* (Cicero)
Opif.	*De opificio mundi* (Philo)
Or. 7	Oration 7, Euboean Discourse (Dio Chrysostom)
OTL	Old Testament Library
Part. or.	*Partitiones oratoriae* (Cicero)
PBC	Pontifical Biblical Commission
Phaed.	*Phaedo* (Plato)
Phaedr.	*Phaedrus* (Plato)
PilNTC	Pillar New Testament Commentary

ABBREVIATIONS

PreDi	Presencia y Diálogo
Ps-Phoc.	Pseudo-Phocylides
Rhet.	*Rhetorica* (Aristotle)
Rhet. Her.	*Rhetorica ad Herennium* (Cicero)
RSMS	Religious Studies Monograph Series
RSV2CE	Revised Standard Version, Catholic Edition (2nd ed.)
Sacr.	*De sacrificiis Abelis et Caini* (Philo)
SaPaSe	Sacra Pagina Series
Sat.	*Satirae* (Horace)
SBLMS	Society of Biblical Literature Monograph Series
SHBC	Smyth & Helwys Bible Commentary
SNTW	Studies of the New Testament and Its World
Spec.	*De specialibus legibus* (Philo)
StBM	Studia Biblica Matritensia
SubBi	Subsidia Biblica
SVF	*Stoicorum Veterum Fragmenta*
SWR	Studies in Women and Religion
TDNT	*Theological Dictionary of the New Testament*, ed. Gerhard Kittel and Gerhard Friedrich, trans. G. W. Bromiley (Grand Rapids: Eerdmans, 1964)
TDOT	*Theological Dictionary of the Old Testament*, ed. G. Johannes Botterweck and Helmer Ringgren, trans. John T. Willis et al. (Grand Rapids: Eerdmans, 1974–2006)
Thesm.	*Thesmorphoriazusae* (Aristophanes)
Tim.	*Timaeus* (Plato)
TNTC	Tyndale New Testament Commentaries
VT.S	Supplements to Vetus Testamentum
WBC	Word Biblical Commentary
WUNT	Wissenschaftliche Untersuchungen zum Neuen Testament

Introduction

"All Scripture is inspired by God" (2 Tim 3:16). This biblical truth, while on its face easy enough to understand, has taken on considerable strain under the weight of historical and literary criticism. Another Pauline passage teaches something similar, but with reference to the Gospel Paul proclaims: the Gospel is the word of truth that seals with the Spirit (cf. Eph 1:13). 1 John 1:1–4 indicates that the Gospel is also proclaimed in written form, which has the capacity to create fellowship between God and men. The Gospel, proclaimed by word and deed, is also proclaimed in writing, which has the power to transform in the Spirit because of its inspired nature. The strict relationship between Scripture, the Spirit, and truth is proclaimed by Scripture itself, yet needs to be reflected upon more fully in our day "in order to respond better to the necessity of interpreting the sacred texts in accordance with their nature."[1]

This book is a response to that necessity. It is the fruit of the sixth Quinn Biblical Conference, convened by Fr. Kevin Zilverberg at Christ the King Retreat Center in Buffalo, MN, June 27–30, 2021. The Monsignor Jerome D. Quinn Endowment for Biblical Studies generously funded the conference, under the auspices of The Saint Paul Seminary in Saint Paul, MN, and its Institute for Catholic Theological Formation. Zilverberg invited Catholic seminary professors of Sacred Scripture and other Catholic biblical scholars to gather

---

1. Pontifical Biblical Commission, *The Inspiration and Truth of Sacred Scripture: The Word That Comes from God and Speaks of God for the Salvation of the World*, trans. Thomas Esposito and Stephen Gregg (Collegeville, MN: Liturgical Press, 2014), General Introduction, §I.1.

INTRODUCTION

and study themes of contemporary importance in the field of biblical studies in order to equip them to carry out their service to the Church. Although the conference presenters chose their topics in light of the needs of Catholic seminaries, the reader will find that their appeal extends well beyond that context. We hope that this book finds an audience not only among Catholic seminary and university professors and their students, but also Protestant scholars and students, as well as catechized lay people of all Christian denominations.

The 2021 conference topic, "The Inspiration and Truth of Sacred Scripture," echoed the title of the Pontifical Biblical Commission's 2014 document that sought to present the Commission's work studying the relationship between inspiration and truth in Sacred Scripture, and specifically what the Sacred Scriptures themselves testify about their origin in God and their truth. This task was given to the Biblical Commission in order to penetrate more deeply and to advance the teaching of the Second Vatican Council promulgated in *Dei verbum*, an endeavor which Pope Benedict XVI specifically called for in his Post-Synodal Apostolic Exhortation *Verbum Domini*. The Quinn Conference, then, was a gathering of biblical scholars and theologians to consider this work of the Biblical Commission within the context of recent Magisterium and theological reflection, and to contribute to the same stream of reflection called for by the Church on the theme of biblical inspiration and truth.

The chapters in this volume are revisions of the papers presented at the conference, each of which underwent a double-blind peer review process that required two reviewers to approve their publication. The chapters are of two basic types. The first type, found in chapters 1–2, consists in analysis and reflection upon (1) the questions addressed by the Biblical Commission and (2) the product of the Biblical Commission's work, in *The Inspiration and Truth of Sacred Scripture*. The second type of contribution, chapters 3–7, responds to a particular aspect of the Biblical Commission's document within the larger context of the Magisterium on Sacred Scripture. Each of these chapters studies an exegetical or hermeneutical question arising from a particular biblical text, in order to advance the current dialogue on the questions of biblical inspiration and truth.

In the first chapter, "The Inspiration and Truth of Scripture: Do They Still Matter?," Luis Sánchez-Navarro asks the basic question regarding whether or not the topic of the PBC document is even relevant. He considers the history of the Church's teaching on the question of inspiration and truth treated in magisterial and theological documents leading up to the Second Vatican Council. This serves as a foundation for the discussion of the question in contemporary biblical studies. He investigates whether the inspired character of Scripture

2

affects the way one goes about interpreting them. To answer this he evaluates important theological and exegetical contributions of the postconciliar period in terms of their divergent presuppositions on the inspired status of the biblical texts. Finally, he shows what the consequences of these different hermeneutical positions bring to bear on the moral life. The author proposes that the relationship between revelation, biblical inspiration, and truth is not only the fundamental question which the interpreter of Scripture must face, it is also the basic question that needs to be addressed in order to understand how the Bible is relevant to the life of the Christian today.

In chapter 2, Michael Magee focuses specifically on the PBC document, and provides a critical analysis of it by situating it within the recent history of the Church's attempts to clarify the theology of biblical inspiration and truth and their interrelationship. He evaluates the document based upon its achievements in this regard. He scores the results of the PBC study in relation to the recommendations of the 12th Ordinary General Assembly of the Synod of Bishops, specifically its call for clarification of the concepts of biblical truth and inspiration. He also refers to magisterial pronouncements, including *Dei verbum*, and major nineteenth- and twentieth-century theology related to Catholic biblical hermeneutics.

The doctrine of biblical inspiration is founded upon an understanding of the nature of the Scriptures as originating in God. In chapter 3, "The Divine Voice of Sinai in Emended Scripture," Matthew Genung reflects on the PBC document's statement regarding the supreme importance of Exodus 19 in answering the question about what the Scriptures themselves say about their origin in God. He considers this statement in light of the historical-critical understanding of the redactional process of biblical authorship. He surveys evidence for understanding some of the redactional aspects of Exodus 19 within its larger context, seeking to show that not only does Scripture alert the reader to its divine origin, but it also indicates that its character as emended Scripture pertains to its inspiration. The redactional nature of the biblical text should not be ignored in the interpretation of either the literal or spiritual sense. Recognizing the redactional layers of an emended text allows greater penetration into the cadence of the divine voice, allowing one to be more attuned to what it means that God's voice is heard in Scripture.

In chapter 4, "Inspiration and Truth When Prophecy Fails: Ezekiel's Temple Vision," Anthony Pagliarini asks about the possibility of understanding the Book of Ezekiel as inspired Scripture given the non-fulfillment of Ezekiel's prophetic vision of the restored Jerusalem Temple. How can the discrepancy between prophecy and history be reconciled with the theology of biblical

INTRODUCTION

inspiration and truth? He approaches this question, in dialogue with critical scholarship, by first situating the Temple Vision within the rhetorical context of the Book of Ezekiel. Even here, the Vision at one level seems to amount to a failure of prophecy. When reexamined in light of the Church's theology of inspiration, specifically the teaching of *Dei verbum*, new vistas are opened for its interpretation. The major part of this contribution explores these vistas.

The issue of biblical truth, the inspired character of the Bible, and historicity is encountered in the New Testament as well as the Old, particularly in the Gospels. Chapter 5 addresses the question of a reliable methodology to determine the historicity of seemingly conflicting reports of the same events recounted in the canonical Gospels. This is the focus of "Ratzinger on the Historicity of the Gospels: A Case Study of the Last Supper Narrative" by Aaron Pidel. This chapter first identifies a set of four tests which Joseph Ratzinger employed in order to determine whether or not the devil is real or is a mythological construction, tests which allow the convergence of faith and reason on the historical data. Pidel then elaborates on the suitability of these tests to explore the extent of the historical grounding of events narrated in the Gospels, and to unveil the authorial intent within the context of a historical faith. Acknowledging with *Dei verbum* that the evangelists recounted historical events not according to standards of modern historiography, but imbuing them with theological symbolism, the author confronts the difficulty of determining the truth intended by the evangelists in their historical narratives. Ratzinger's analysis of the biblical accounts of the Last Supper is the case study for an explicit application of these tests, resulting in a methodologically explicit hermeneutic of faith and reason in exegesis.

If the truth claimed in a biblical text is historically and culturally contingent, the character of that text as inspired is undermined. This seems to be the case in some Pauline texts regarding the subordination of women to men. In chapter 6, "Changing Gender Roles and the Unchanging Message of 1 Corinthians 11:2–16," Marcin Kowalski addresses this difficulty raised in the PBC document. If Paul's letters originate in God, how can their teaching be superseded by cultural developments? Is Paul's teaching on sexuality and the relationship between men and women outdated in the twenty-first century or is it still relevant and even necessary for today's Church and society? These are the questions treated in this chapter through an exegetical study of 1 Corinthians 11:2–16. Kowalski uses rhetorical and socio-cultural analysis in his study of the pericope within the context of the entire letter. He frames its rhetorical *dispositio* to understand the thrust of the author's arguments, and carefully treats the exegetical difficulties in the text. The author accomplishes this in dialogue

4

with the best scholarship. He demonstrates the balanced relationship between theological truth based on Pauline arguments from biblical authority, ecclesial tradition, natural law, and advertence to transitory customs. These arguments are intertwined for a rhetorical force aimed at building up the fledgling church in Corinth. This Pauline strategy can help us to understand the nature of his letters as divinely inspired and communicating truth not only pertinent to the immediate first-century circumstances envisaged in the letter, but of perennial value and even of great importance for our day.

Rounding out the volume by bridging both Testaments, in chapter 7, "The Old Testament as an Earthly Translation of an Inner-Trinitarian Dialogue: Implications for Inspiration," Kelly Anderson evaluates a phenomenon encountered in certain Old Testament texts that depict a conversation between God and Wisdom, and/or within God himself. These "inner-Trinitarian dialogue" texts are taken up by other biblical texts in which human figures, animated by the Spirit and by divine Wisdom, become participants in the divine creative activity within the life of Israel. The author shows this phenomenon specifically in passages narrating the construction of the Tabernacle, the Temple in Jerusalem, and its symbolic portrayal in the Song of Solomon. The same phenomenon is shown in New Testament texts that apply Old Testament passages of divine dialogue to Christ, by which they communicate the identity and meaning of the life of Jesus. The author argues that this phenomenon serves as an analogy to understand the operation of biblical inspiration, as well as the relationship of inspired Scripture to the eternal dialogue of God.

Each of these chapters contributes to the question of the relationship between biblical inspiration and truth in its own way. Each pursues a unique line of inquiry or applies a different literary or historical-critical method. In this way, they show different facets of the nature of Scripture as the word of God in human language. We hope that this book, by showing the fruits of critical inquiry and the employment of a variety of methods, will promote further reflection and dialogue on the inspired Scriptures and the truth contained in them.

MATTHEW C. GENUNG
KEVIN ZILVERBERG
April 13, 2022

1. The Inspiration and Truth of Scripture: Do They Still Matter?

Luis Sánchez-Navarro, DCJM

Perhaps the question at the top of these pages is surprising, and all the more after the document of the Pontifical Biblical Commission dedicated some years ago precisely to the inspiration and truth of Scripture.[1] Does not this fact testify to the relevance of both categories in the Church? The divine inspiration of Scripture, by virtue of which the biblical writings remain sacred and canonical (cf. *Dei verbum*, §11), is the basis for its interpretation;[2] the Fathers of the Church lived this doctrine as a self-evident presupposition, to the point that those who disputed it (for example, the Gnostics) were excluded from the Christian faith.[3] However, there are elements in the Church that lead us today

1. Pontifical Biblical Commission, *The Inspiration and Truth of Sacred Scripture: The Word That Comes from God and Speaks of God for the Salvation of the World*, trans. Thomas Esposito and Stephen Gregg (Collegeville, MN: Liturgical Press, 2014). The topic had already been addressed by the PBC in a previous document: *The Interpretation of the Bible in the Church* (Vatican City. Libreria Editrice Vaticana, 1993); see Peter S. Williamson, "The Word of God in Human Language," 28–40 in *Catholic Principles for Interpreting Scripture. A Study of the Pontifical Biblical Commission's The Interpretation of the Bible in the Church*, SubBi 22 (Rome: Pontifical Biblical Institute, 2001).

2. See Denis Farkasfalvy, O.Cist., *Inspiration and Interpretation: A Theological Introduction to Sacred Scripture* (Washington, DC, Catholic University of America Press, 2010), who offers a survey from the New Testament and patristic times until the Second Vatican Council.

3. "No theory in this sense was elaborated or imposed upon reflection, the authority of the Bible was an indisputable fact": Jean Gribomont, "Scrittura (Sacra)," cols. 4791–97 in *Nuovo Dizionario Patristico e di Antichità Cristiane*, vol. 3, P–Z, ed. Angelo Di Bernardino, 2nd ed. (Rome: Institutum Patristicum Augustinianum; Marietti, 2008), 4794 (author's translation). For the patristic exegesis, whose first axiom is that the Bible is God's book, see the synthesis offered by Joseph A. Fitzmyer, *The Biblical Commission's Document "The Interpretation of the Bible in the Church": Text and Commentary,* SubBi 18 (Rome: Pontifical Biblical Institute, 1995), 145–50.

to raise the question: for a Catholic of the twenty-first century, is the divine inspiration of the Bible, from which its veracity springs, relevant?

Reasons for the Question

Much has happened since 1965, when the Council Fathers dedicated a section of the Dogmatic Constitution *Dei verbum* (§11) to divine inspiration and the truth of Sacred Scripture. In doing so, they intended to update a perennial certainty of the Church about the peculiarity of the books that make up the Christian Bible, a certainty that had recently been affirmed by Pius XII in the title of his great encyclical of 1943 on biblical studies, *Divino afflante Spiritu*. However, twenty years after the publication of this relevant document, the mainstream of Catholic exegesis, which had overwhelmingly embarked on the practice of the historical-critical method, considered this truth of faith as a mere theoretical presupposition without practical consequences for biblical interpretation. In his *ultima lectio* as professor at the Pontifical Biblical Institute in Rome (1989), Father Ignace de la Potterie expressed the problem openly:

> Let us then ask the question clearly, at least of exegetes who admit the divine inspiration of Scripture: What relation do they perceive between that which they call the "sense intended by the author" and the plan of God? This is the problem, almost ignored today, of the hermeneutic value of inspiration. To this question, the majority of exegetes would probably reply, "The fact that the text is inspired has nothing to do with the mode of interpreting Scripture, and it does not have to have anything to do with it, certainly not in scientific exegesis." Basically, for the practice of interpretation, inspiration is useless. But if this is the case, we can tranquilly abandon the doctrine of inspiration as a vestige of the past. At most we would attribute to it the merit of having heightened the authority of the text.[4]

The time that has elapsed since the Council, despite notable contributions in the deepening and updating of the traditional certainty of faith, has allowed us to speak of a wide diffusion in the life of the Church of this radical relativization of the divine origin of Scripture and of its vital implications; in the same year 1989 Antonio Artola affirmed that "our time is, without a doubt, the one that most acutely feels in Catholicism the temptation to dispense

---

4. Ignace de la Potterie, "Biblical Exegesis: A Science of Faith," 30–64 in *Opening Up the Scriptures: Joseph Ratzinger and the Foundations of Biblical Interpretation*, eds. José Granados, Carlos Granados, and Luis Sánchez-Navarro, Ressourcement (Grand Rapids: Eerdmans, 2008), at 39.

The Inspiration and Truth of Scripture: Do They Still Matter?

with inspiration. Critical exegesis is particularly prone to this practical indifference."[5] The passage of time has not brought about a change; and so in the year 2000, the Declaration *Dominus Iesus* (§4) included biblical inspiration among the elements that the theories on religious pluralism consider superseded.[6] Today, we see that in large sectors of the West the revealed Word has lost its impact on life. Not without paradox: on the one hand, the importance of Scripture for the life of Christians has never been so highly esteemed and praised in the Catholic Church. On the other hand, however, its power to shape that same life is blurred, and the Bible thus becomes a quasi-decorative element. A few examples are enough to illustrate this point with regard to the sacraments and morals. To many "committed Christians," that priestly ordination is reserved to men alone appears today to be an outdated practice, despite the overwhelming witness of the New Testament; on the other hand, there is a widespread awareness among Catholics of the legitimacy of divorce followed by remarriage, or of homosexual behavior. The overall witness of the Bible, so clear that it constitutes the foundation—corroborated by sacred Tradition—of these Catholic doctrines,[7] is thus rendered inoperative in the face of the new "canons" of modernity. Thus, even if not directly or openly questioned, divine inspiration and the truth of Scripture are ultimately rendered irrelevant and obsolete.

The teaching of the Bible thus appears—at best—as a starting point for a later development, or simply as a stage already passed in the history of human thought; it had its great importance, but it belongs irretrievably to the past. In fact, in the Christian academic sphere, voices are raised that openly question the biblical canon (a fact intimately linked to inspiration); we read in a relevant volume from the end of the twentieth century:

> The insight into the need to go beyond the limits of the canon in New Testament exegesis is relatively recent. It is grounded in the recognition that as far as the time of their composition is concerned, neither in content nor

---

5. Antonio M. Artola, "Treinta años de reflexión sobre la inspiración bíblica," *Estudios Bíblicos* 47 (1989): 363–415, at 414 (author's translation).

6. Congregation for the Doctrine of the Faith, Declaration *Dominus Iesus* (August 6, 2000) (Vatican City: Libreria Editrice Vaticana, 2000), §4. "The Church's tradition, however, reserves the designation of *inspired texts* to the canonical books of the Old and New Testaments, since these are inspired by the Holy Spirit" (§8).

7. Cf. Luis Sánchez-Navarro, "The Ecclesial Reading of Scripture," 72–86 in Carlos Granados and Luis Sánchez-Navarro, *In the School of the Word: Biblical Interpretation from the New to the Old Testament*, trans. Kristin Towle, CTFS (Saint Paul, MN: Saint Paul Seminary Press, 2021).

in form are the canonical writings in principle to be set apart from extra-canonical early Christian writings.[8]

In this situation, and in spite of what was said at the beginning of this essay, we cannot but ask: do the inspiration and truth of Scripture still matter, or are they really only "vestiges of the past"?

The Question in Postconciliar Theology

In the years following the Council, there was no lack of positive answers to the question (a); in this matter it is not difficult to discover an emotivist mentality (b). A recent exegete, Ulrich Luz, illustrates the consequences for exegesis (c).

a) Open Denial

The work published in 1974 by the Catholic exegete Oswald Loretz, in a prestigious publishing house that is also Catholic, was epoch-making; the title was eloquent: *The End of the Theology of Inspiration: Possibilities of a New Beginning.*[9] Although its radical nature can be understood as a consequence of the shift effected by the Second Vatican Council from the inerrancy of Scripture to its salvific truth,[10] the theological world clearly perceived it as a challenge to the faith itself: "the most demolishing book of the post-conciliar period on inspiration," Artola affirms; it had "the tone of a manifesto," considers De la Potterie.[11] This could be gathered from the first reactions; Fausto Perrenchio, who spoke of a title that was "presumptuous and problematic at the same time," discovered in Loretz's proposal a rupturist interpretation of Vatican II with the preceding tradition;[12] in a more thoughtful, but also critical analysis, Francis

---

8. Gerd Theissen and Annette Merz, *The Historical Jesus: A Comprehensive Guide*, trans. John Bowden (Minneapolis: Fortress, 1998), 23 (German original: 1996; 4th ed. 2010). The "critical edition" of Q equates the Coptic Gospel of Thomas with the Synoptics: James M. Robinson, Paul Hoffmann, John Kloppenborg, eds., *The Critical Edition of Q: Synopsis including the Gospels of Matthew and Luke, Mark and Thomas*, Hermeneia (Minneapolis: Fortress, 2000).

9. Oswald Loretz, *Das Ende der Inspirations-Theologie: Chancen eines Neubeginns*, vol. 1, *Untersuchungen zur Entwicklung der traditionellen theologischen Lehre über die Inspiration der Heiligen Schrift* (Stuttgart: Verlag Katholisches Bibelwerk, 1974).

10. "That 'charism to avoid error' into which inspiration had been converted by an apologetic theology concerned with the 'Biblical Question' lost almost all its interest." Artola, "Treinta años de reflexión," 363.

11. Artola, "Treinta años de reflexión," 380; De la Potterie, "Biblical Exegesis: A Science of Faith," 42.

12. Fausto Perrenchio, "Review to Loretz's *Das Ende der Inspirations-Theologie*," *Salesianum* 38 (1976): 191–92.

The Inspiration and Truth of Scripture: Do They Still Matter?

Schüssler Fiorenza criticized in Loretz the hasty identification ("too facile") between inspiration and absolute inerrancy, a defect that, according to him, affected his entire proposal, devalued also by the application to the New Testament of a radical opposition between Semitic and Greek culture.[13] Years later Artola completed a detailed and luminous critique of Loretz, bringing to light his presuppositions and his intention. For this purpose he started with a previous work of the author dedicated to the truth of Scripture, published by the Catholic Herder and promptly translated into English and French:[14]

> In the preface to the French edition, L. clearly expresses his intention to "refute" the doctrine of inerrancy. The refutation he wants to accomplish does not consist in reconsidering, from the new perspectives of DV, the immunity from error attributed to the Bible. What he intends is to undermine the authority of the Bible and the Church because they are based on an erroneous understanding of biblical truth.[15]

Artola's judgment on Loretz's next book, on inspiration, is, if possible, harsher:

> He is not interested in the subject of inspiration *per se*. What he intends is to refute the false support that the inspirational charism offers to the doctrine of the doctrinal authority of the Bible. In this endeavor he commits the same tactical error of the theologians so reviled by the author. If current theology had the obsession to defend inerrancy, he has the same obsession, only in the opposite direction. What interests him is to attack it. . . . The overall result of the investigation is reflected in the very title of the book: The End of Inspiration, that is, the death of inspiration. If the book on truth had sentenced the authority of the Bible to death, this new work reaches the same necrophiliac conclusion on inspiration.[16]

Some exegetes have taken this approach to its ultimate consequences; in our opinion, the radicalism of the Protestant exegete Ulrich Luz (†2019) stands out the most. The title of a 1998 essay, a rhetorical question whose answer is not difficult to guess, is in itself eloquent ("Can the Bible still be the foundation of the Church today?"). In it we read this conclusion:

---

13. Francis Schüssler Fiorenza, "Review to Loretz's *Das Ende der Inspirations-Theologie*," *Catholic Biblical Quarterly* 42 (1980): 126–28. "In short, L's book is much more helpful in explaining the emergence of the link between inerrancy and inspiration than in explaining the meaning of inspiration" (128).

14. Oswald Loretz, *Die Wahrheit der Bibel* (Freiburg: Herder, 1964); English translation by David J. Bourke, *The Truth of the Bible* (London: Burns and Oates, 1968); French translation Henri Rochais and Joseph Feisthauer, *Quelle est la vérité de la Bible?* (Paris: Le Centurion, 1970).

15. Artola, "Treinta años de reflexión," 384; for criticism of Loretz's works, 379–91.

16. Artola, "Treinta años de reflexión," 388–89.

LUIS SÁNCHEZ-NAVARRO, DCJM

> Today [exegesis] can no longer refer directly—along with the ancient Church—to the ἐνέργεια of the divine Logos and the divine Spirit in the texts. Nor can it compile from the Bible, with classical dogmatics, the foundation stones for the great ecclesial "metanarrative" [*métarécit*]. Perhaps it can, with the Reformers, point out that God has permanently become man, is permanently incarnated, and paradoxically remains with us under the mask of a crucified man. This exegesis will point out above all—this is the *conditio moderna*—that it itself cannot go beyond the limits of human history and human language, and that God could perhaps be the great hindrance [*Störung*] in the constructions of reality expressed in human language. But she does not know whether this is really the case.[17]

The biblical texts do not convey life, nor truth; they cannot ground the life of the Church. They are perhaps venerable, but in any case dispensable—or even harmful.

b) From the Modern Vision to "Emotivist Hermeneutics"

This mentality has its roots in the modern vision, which replaces tradition with progress,[18] and the divine Spirit with the human spirit. If truth lies in the future, what can the texts from the past offer us? If the supposedly divine binds us and imprisons us in a retrograde immobilism, what truth can there be in what is imposed from above, almost violently, on the enlightened spirit? Paraphrasing the psalm in an immanentist key, we would have to say that "truth springs from the earth" (cf. Ps 85:12)—and from nowhere else. The Bible is not made for the modern world: it belongs to an archaic age and has no place today. It is better to bury it respectfully. Unless we find an interpretative key appropriate to the times, which allows us to "recycle" it and thus put it at the service of better causes . . .

Postmodernity has rediscovered in the human subject the importance of emotions, understood as reactions of sensitivity. Emotionality thus understood has come to constitute the center of the conscious life of postmodern man, that which determines his ideas and actions: "The central thesis of emotivism . . . affirms that moral judgments do not describe properties (natural or otherwise) allegedly possessed by X, but express the emotions that X arouses in the

---

17. Ulrich Luz, "Kann die Bibel heute noch Grundlage für die Kirche sein? Über die Aufgabe der Exegese in einer religiös-pluralistischen Gesellschaft," *New Testament Studies* 44 (1998): 317–39, at 339 (author's translation).

18. Cf. Juan de Dios Larrú, "La virtud de la tradición y la tradición de las virtudes," 129–50 in *Tradición: Antídoto para no repetirse*, ed. José Noriega and Luis Granados, Didaskalos 56 (Madrid: Didaskalos, 2020), 131, 146.

one who formulates the judgment."[19] This is the new criterion of truth. With respect to Sacred Scripture, interpretative emotivism will accept as true that which arouses positive emotions in the subject, and as false (or simply unacceptable) that which arouses other kinds of emotional reactions. This is what we can call "emotivist hermeneutics." This is related to some basic currents of present-day Christianity. The Letter of the Congregation for the Doctrine of the Faith *Placuit Deo* (2018) has exposed two main deviations that, rooted in ancient heresies, threaten Christian life today: neo-Pelagianism and neo-Gnosticism.[20] Both tendencies, which obey two traits of modern man (individualism and intimism), are related to the crisis of the dogma of biblical inspiration. For if man can "save oneself, without recognizing that at the deepest level of being he or she derives from God and from others" (neo-Pelagianism); and if, on the other hand, this salvation is "merely interior, closed off in its own subjectivism," which consists in rising with the intellect "toward the mysteries of the unknown divinity" (neo-Gnosticism);[21] then any true instance of inspiration by God, objective and given to us from outside, lacks utility and meaning. Thus "a merely interior vision of salvation is becoming common, a vision that, marked by a strong personal conviction or feeling of being united to God, does not take into account the need to accept, heal and renew our relationships with others and with the created world."[22] In this context, "the figure of Christ appears" only "as a role model who inspires generous actions with his words and gestures": he is no longer the one "who transforms the human condition by incorporating us into a new existence, reconciling us with the Father and with one another through dwelling among us in the Spirit (cf. 2 Cor 5:19; Eph 2:18)."[23] The emotive hermeneutics of Scripture thus certifies the uselessness of the ancient dogma.

c) An Example from Matthew 23

This mentality is clearly reflected in biblical studies, where even at high academic levels we find a tendency to interpret Scripture according to the emotional reaction it provokes in the scholar. A significant case is the comprehensive

---

19. Angel Manuel Faerna García-Bermejo, "Emotivismo," p. 180 in *Diccionario Espasa Filosofía*, ed. Jacobo Muñoz (Madrid: Espasa, 2003).

20. Congregation for the Doctrine of the Faith, Letter *Placuit Deo* (March 1, 2018), §3; English translation *"Placuit Deo*: On Certain Aspects of Christian Salvation," in *Origins* 47, no. 41 (March 15, 2018): 649–54.

21. CDF, *Placuit Deo*, §3.

22. CDF, *Placuit Deo*, §2.

23. CDF, *Placuit Deo*, §2.

LUIS SÁNCHEZ-NAVARRO, DCJM

evaluation of Jesus' controversy with the teachers of Israel in Matthew 23 that, following Werner Georg Kümmel, Ulrich Luz—once again—makes. We read in his great commentary to the first Gospel:

> For me there is a fundamental contradiction between Jesus' command to love one's enemies and what happens in the woes with the scribes and Pharisees. It is a contradiction that cannot be explained away.[24]

And, later:

> Matthew 23 *is* a betrayal of Jesus' commandment to love one's enemies. Above all, however, this chapter is a betrayal of Jesus' proclamation of God's unearned and limitless love that according to Jesus applies especially, and almost exclusively, to Israel.[25]

The emotional key cannot understand Jesus' "woes" against the scribes and Pharisees as an expression of a strong love, a true *rîb* in the style of the great prophets;[26] it is too rough for modern sensibilities. The traditional criteria (expressed for example in *Dei verbum*, §12) are therefore no longer adequate to interpret these words in a reasonable and coherent way: it is in advance an enterprise doomed to failure. The same author cited above underlines the importance of the interpretation of this passage for one's understanding of the Bible.[27] For all these reasons, it is necessary to explain this passage by means of complex historical-psychological constructions that try to account for the way in which such deviant and misleading words have been put into the mouth of Jesus; according to Luz, "From a social-psychological perspective, what has led to the polemic of Matthew 23, which historically is unjust and theologically contradicts the message of Jesus, is in large measure understandable."[28] It follows, according to our author, that "Matthew 23 is an important theological text even today not because it reveals God's truth but because *it exposes human reality—yes, human sin*."[29]

In Jesus' mouth, then, the evangelist has put words that induce sin and

---

24. Ulrich Luz, *Matthew 21–28: A Commentary*, trans. James E. Crouch, Hermeneia (Minneapolis: Fortress, 2005), 138.

25. Luz, *Matthew 21–28*, 175; italics in original.

26. Cf. Mario Cucca, Benedetta Rossi, and Salvatore Maurizio Sessa, *"Quelli che amo io li accuso": Il rîb come chiave di lettura unitaria della Scrittura: alcuni esempi (Os 11,1; Ger 13,1–11; Gv 15,1–11/Ap 2–3)* (Assisi: Cittadella, 2012).

27. "In this sense how one deals with these woes will become a test case for every theologian of how one understands the Bible." Luz, *Matthew 21–28*, 138.

28. Luz, *Matthew 21–28*, 177.

29. Luz, *Matthew 21–28*, 177; italics in original.

The Inspiration and Truth of Scripture: Do They Still Matter?

that, therefore, are sin. The author is aware of what this statement implies; let us see how he tries to justify it:

> I have designated Matthew 23 as a human text, indeed as a document of sin. And now the text is canonized. . . . Canonical texts as documents of human reality—indeed, of human sin? Of course, that is not everything that is to be said about the canon. Matthew 23 is in the canon, however, and it cannot be removed from it by the prejudices of individual theologians or individual Christian churches. The canon was understood by the fathers of the ancient church as a divine-human writing that shared both in the divinity and in the humanity of Jesus. We could spin this thread further and say that Matthew 23 is one of those parts of the canon that in a great measure are human. Thus Matthew 23 also belongs to those parts of the canon that remind those who possess it—Christians and churches—of their own humanity as well and that may just keep them from self-righteously and arrogantly believing that they are the possessors of eternal truth.[30]

The emotional reaction they provoke in a representative of modernity forces one to see certain passages of the New Testament, including many words of Jesus himself, as negative elements that can even induce sin. How can God have inspired such texts? What kind of saving truth can there be in them? How can such an image of Jesus be affirmed as historically true? It is better to relegate these categories to the history of exegesis; what matters now is the text as an inspirer of positive emotions and feelings: the new criterion of truth.

The Response of Faith

However, as an author already cited said more than thirty years ago, "if Scripture is the soul of theology, inspiration is the soul of Scripture";[31] as Denis Farkasfalvy puts it (quoting Luis Alonso Schökel), "the general statement that God is the author of the biblical text is, indeed, an article of faith."[32] And this far from being an abstract or purely theoretical statement, affects the biblical text in a radical way. It is manifested by the testimony of Scripture (a), and is illuminated by the relationship of both concepts, inspiration and truth, with the concept—central to Christian theology—of revelation (b, c). Finally, we address the relevance of biblical inspiration for Christian life (d).

---

30. Luz, *Matthew 21–28*, 177.

31. Artola, "Treinta años de reflexión," 363.

32. Farkasfalvy, *Inspiration and Interpretation*, 216. See Luis Alonso Schökel, *The Inspired Word*, trans. Francis Martin (New York: Herder and Herder, 1967), 84.

LUIS SÁNCHEZ-NAVARRO, DCJM

a) The Testimony of Scripture

The New Testament passages that make explicit the doctrine of inspiration (2 Tim 3:16; 2 Pet 1:21) are certainly very important; but they are only the tip of an immense iceberg solidly compacted by a high number of OT and NT passages, and even more so, by Sacred Scripture in its entirety. That the Bible appears before us as the word of God is indisputable; the New Testament openly confirms this perspective.[33] Let us now turn our attention to the biblical quotations in the Gospels, particularly the very first of them.

The Gospel according to Matthew, which as we well know gives great relevance to the Scriptures of Israel, contains a series of quotations which, because of their number (ten, symbol of totality), their typology (always in the mouth of the narrator), their nature (illustrating a concrete aspect of the life of Jesus), and their literary features (a common introductory formula), have come to be called "fulfillment (or 'reflection') quotations": a veritable Decalogue of Christological prophecies.[34] As was said above, all of them are introduced by a formula that admits of minor differences of wording, but which is constant in its essentials; its most complete formulation appears in the first one, the oracle of Emmanuel, of incontestable theological relevance: "Now all this took place to fulfil what was spoken by the Lord through the prophet, saying . . ." (Matt 1:22 RSVCE). The prophetic oracle, then, does not come from the prophet but from YHWH; the prophet is only his qualified mediator. All these quotations from Scripture, therefore, refer not to their human authors, but to the Lord: God himself speaks through the prophet. From this fact flows the truth of that Scripture passage; in this regard, John's Jesus utters these words of controversy with his adversaries: "If [the Law] calls those to whom the Word of God was addressed gods—and Scripture cannot fail . . ." (John 10:35). "Scripture cannot fail": it is the supreme instance of truth for Israel—and for Jesus.

The result is that we understand that the New Testament relies on the presupposition, undisputed and indisputable, that in Israel's Scripture it is God himself who speaks: it has its origin in God. The reality that Paul makes explicit in the second letter to Timothy with the concept of inspiration, "all Scripture is God-inspired" (θεόπνευστος, 2 Tim 3:16), is active and operative in the New Testament's constant recourse to the Tanak. If we take into account the equalization in the apostolic Church of the New Testament with the Old in terms of

33. See the first part of *The Inspiration and Truth of Sacred Scripture*: "The Testimony of the Biblical Writings about Their Origin from God" (§§5–61).

34. Cf. Jean Miler, *Les citations d'accomplissement dans l'Évangile de Matthieu: Quand Dieu se rend présent en toute humanité*, AnBib 140 (Rome: Pontifical Biblical Institute, 1999).

Its origin and authority (cf. 2 Pet 3:16), we understand how the whole of these writings constitutes the most qualified testimony about God's will for man's life.

b) Inspiration and Revelation

As Aaron Pidel has shown, the young Joseph Ratzinger discovered in Saint Bonaventure a concept of inspiration that goes beyond that which would later become generalized in modern theology, to the point that in a certain sense it overlaps with that of revelation; the repercussions that this (re)discovery would have on the development of the Second Vatican Council, and in particular of the Constitution *Dei verbum*, are well known.[35] Consequently, it becomes possible to understand inspiration not as a charism limited to the mere production of a literary text (which remains, yes, a very singular moment),[36] but as an authentic mystical phenomenon that presides over the entire revelatory process: the great medieval doctor "used them both [*revelatio* and *inspiratio*] synonymously and more broadly, so as to include them under the twofold process of Scripture's composition and its reception in faith."[37] Divine revelation has a dialogical structure; therefore, the response to the Word is also guided by the inspiring Spirit of that Word. "Since Scripture remains a dead letter until its meaning has been mystically perceived, it follows that the believing subject belongs to the very concept of inspired Scripture."[38] According to medieval theology, therefore, the response of faith is the effect of divine inspiration. The risk of subjectivism is neutralized if we understand who is the true subject of that response: not the individual (the Protestant proposal) but the Church, and every member of it. Just as inspiration is a corporate process involving the ecclesial community,[39] so is its reception. As a consequence, Benedict XVI affirms, inspiration makes present a text from the past: "Scripture does not belong to the past, because its subject, the People of God inspired by God himself, is always the same, and therefore the word is always alive in the living

---

35. Cf. Peter Seewald, *Benedict XVI: A Life*, vol. 1, *Youth in Nazi Germany to the Second Vatican Council 1927–1965*, trans. Dinah Livingstone (London: Bloomsbury, 2020), 412–13.

36. Inspiration is absolutely necessary for the sacred author, a true human author, to write "everything and only those things" that God wills (cf. *Dei verbum*, §11).

37. Aaron Pidel, "*Christi Opera Proficiunt*: Ratzinger's Neo-Bonaventurian Model of Social Inspiration," *Nova et Vetera* 13, no. 3 (2015): 693–711, at 696.

38. Pidel, "Ratzinger's Neo-Bonaventurian Model," 697.

39. Pidel, "Ratzinger's Neo-Bonaventurian Model," 694–95. Cf. Luis Sánchez Navarro, *Un cuerpo pleno: Cristo y la personalidad corporativa en la Escritura*, StBM 4 (Madrid: Universidad San Dámaso, 2021), 146–47.

LUIS SÁNCHEZ-NAVARRO, DCJM

subject."[40] Thus, if tradition is "Scripture in the Church,"[41] then the whole process is framed by the dynamism of the Spirit: the Spirit makes Christ present in the community; he raises up in it (and not without it) the hagiographer who, through the singular charismatic influence of that Spirit, puts in writing the apostolic witness as the true author; and he moves the ecclesial community to recognize that witness in the writing, which thus becomes a precious object of life and transmission (*scriptura in ecclesia*).

This ecclesial vision of inspiration offers us a model capable of overcoming the great deficiency of modernity, which, as we have indicated, culminates in emotivist hermeneutics and, consequently, in "biblical emotivism." The receiving subject is an integral part of the process of inspiration; but that subject is the body of the Church and, within it, each of its members. This body is universal, not only from the synchronic point of view but also from the diachronic point of view, since it includes all Christians of all times:

> This communion, which we call "Church", does not only extend to all believers in a specific historical period, but also embraces all the epochs and all the generations. Thus, we have a twofold universality: a synchronic universality—we are united with believers in every part of the world—and also a so-called diachronic universality, that is: all the epochs belong to us, and all the believers of the past and of the future form with us a single great communion.[42]

Therefore, thanks to the Church's response of faith, every Christian can perceive and actualize the inexhaustible richness of Sacred Scripture, always open to new meanings precisely by virtue of that faith.

c) Truth and Revelation

If a certain real coincidence between revelation and inspiration can be postulated, with even greater reason do revelation and truth coincide. "I am the way and *the truth* and the life," says Jesus (John 14:6); as is well known, ἀλήθεια, "truth," has in Scripture, and consequently in John, the sense of "unveiling." According to the fourth Gospel "Jesus is the truth, *the fullness of revelation,*

---

40. Pope Benedict XVI, *Verbum Domini* (September 30, 2010) (Washington, DC: United States Conference of Catholic Bishops, 2010), §86.

41. "For [the Fathers], tradition is simply *scriptura in ecclesia*." Joseph Ratzinger to the German bishops (October 10, 1962), in Jared Wicks, "Six Texts by Prof. Joseph Ratzinger as Peritus before and during Vatican Council II," *Gregorianum* 89, no. 2 (2008): 233–311, at 275.

42. Pope Benedict XVI, General Audience "Communion in Time: Tradition" (April 26, 2006), English trans. in *L'Osservatore Romano* 39, no. 18 (May 3, 2006): 11.

because he reveals himself as the only begotten Son come from beside the Father (1:14)."[43] This truth presents a double dimension, for in Jesus the face of the Father is revealed ("he who has seen me has seen the Father": John 14:9, cf. 1:18) and, consequently, the face of man ("behold the man": John 19:5).

Therefore, the truth of Sacred Scripture is a necessary dimension of Scripture, insofar as it is inspired by God.[44] But the biblical notion itself suggests to us the way to understand it: it is not a kind of timeless and abstract truth, but a truth that is accessed in a living relationship, and which is ordered to the salvation of man (*salutis causa*). It is only within the framework of this relationship that the gift of truth can be accepted.

d) Inspiration, Grace, and Christian Life
The inspired Word is therefore also an inspiring Word. This must be understood in a strong sense: pregnant with the Holy Spirit who generated it, it communicates that Spirit to those who receive it. In his great magisterial teaching on the Word of God (*Verbum Domini*, 2010), Pope Benedict XVI speaks of the sacramentality of the Word read in the Church, in analogy with the real presence of Christ in the Eucharist (§56); and he insists on its performative character:

> By educating the People of God to discover the performative character of God's word in the liturgy, we will help them to recognize his activity in salvation history and in their individual lives (§53).[45]

This performativity is produced by virtue of the action of the Holy Spirit who communicates himself to the believer through the Word, eminently in the liturgical celebration. Through the Word received in the sacraments, the believer becomes a new creature, capable of living the Christian life to the full, as Saint John Paul II recalled in a vibrant argument:

> What are the "concrete possibilities of man"? And of *which* man are we speaking? Of man *dominated* by lust or of man *redeemed by Christ*? This is what is at stake: the *reality* of Christ's redemption. Christ has redeemed

---

43. Ignace de la Potterie, "Verità," 1655–59 in *Nuovo Dizionario de Teologia Biblica*, ed. Pietro Rossano, Gianfranco Ravasi, and Antonio Girlanda (Cinisello Balsamo: Paoline, 1988), 1658 (author's translation).

44. See the concluding reflection of Denis Farkasfalvy, O.Cist., *A Theology of the Christian Bible: Revelation, Inspiration, Canon* (Washington, DC: Catholic University of America Press, 2018), 213–23: "The Inspired Truth of the Holy Scripture."

45. Cf. Manuel Aroztegi Esnaola, "Una Palabra eficaz: Palabra y sacramento," 66–74 in *Escudriñar las Escrituras: Verbum Domini y la interpretación bíblica*, ed. Luis Sánchez Navarro, PreDi 32 (Madrid: Universidad San Dámaso, 2012).

us! This means that he has given us the possibility of realizing *the entire* truth of our being; he has set our freedom free from the *domination* of concupiscence. . . . God's command is of course proportioned to man's capabilities; but to the capabilities of the man to whom the Holy Spirit has been given; of the man who, though he has fallen into sin, can always obtain pardon and enjoy the presence of the Holy Spirit.[46]

Biblical inspiration is therefore not indifferent to Christian existence; on the contrary, the Spirit that this Word communicates makes man capable of a new life. As the Apocalypse affirms, "the witness of Jesus is the Spirit of prophecy" (Rev 19:10); the Spirit that animates prophecy is thus equated with the witness of the martyrs, who "as vehicles of divine revelation, deserve more than anyone else the name of servants of God. It is the Spirit of God, who inspires the prophets, who has raised them to such a high mission."[47]

Conclusion: Inspiration and Truth, or Nothing

"The Word of the Lord": the liturgical reading of Sacred Scripture concludes with this acclamation from the lector; then, the believing response of the assembly ratifies it: "Thanks be to God." Christian worship, in which the Word occupies a central place, is thus founded on the divine origin of this Word, an origin which constitutes it as a written witness to revealed truth. "It is in fact essential and fundamental for the life and mission of the Church that the sacred texts be interpreted in accordance with their nature: Inspiration and Truth are constitutive characteristics of this nature."[48] If it is not the Word of God, and, as such, pregnant with light and truth for the life of people today, then Scripture is nothing. Inspiration and truth, or nothing: this is the dilemma.

For if, as Loretz maintained, we are at "the end of the theology of inspiration," this means that we have reached the end of theology itself, which no longer has any foundation (Sacred Scripture in the Church). Let us therefore transform the Faculties of Theology into Faculties of Christian Religion, where we study not the mystery of the revealed God, but the evolution of our religious

---

46. Pope John Paul II, Encyclical Letter *Veritatis splendor* (August 6, 1993), 674–71 in *The Encyclicals of John Paul II*, ed. J. Michael Miller (Huntington, IN: Our Sunday Visitor, 1996), §103; italics in original.

47. Alfred Wikenhauser, *Offenbarung des Johannes* (Regensburg: Pustet, 1947), *ad locum* (author's translation).

48. Pope Benedict XVI, "Message for the Plenary Session of the PBC: The interpretation of the Bible in the unity of God's history" (May 2, 2011), English trans. in *L'Osservatore Romano* 44, no. 19 (May 11, 2011): 4.

The Inspiration and Truth of Scripture: Do They Still Matter?

beliefs. Let us replace the knowledge of reality with historical science. Let us replace life with erudition. And let us renounce a vision of man that, springing from faith, shapes our existence and our concrete relationships.

But if we want to continue doing theology, we must accept the gift of the inspiration of Scripture, which constitutes it as a witness to revealed truth. To do this, it will be necessary to understand inspiration in its intrinsic relationship with the Church. First, because this gift springs from her: it would be unthinkable for a hagiographer not to receive the charism of inspiration in the very heart of the community of faith! And second, because it is ordered to it: the purpose of biblical inspiration is the faith of the people of God (cf. John 20:31), a faith professed and lived "in truth" (cf. 2 John 4). Therefore, Holy Scripture remains as that Word which, coming from God and speaking of God (cf. *The Inspiration and Truth of Sacred Scripture*), illumines the truth about God, man, and the world. In this way, the "holy letter" becomes—thanks to the presence of the Spirit—a sure way to enter into a life-giving, life-transforming relationship with the living God. This is all the more relevant today because the effect of ideologies is all the more devastating for the Christian conscience. For this reason, the inspiration and truth of Scripture matter today more than ever.

2. *The Inspiration and Truth of Sacred Scripture*: A Critical Appraisal of the Pontifical Biblical Commission's Document

Michael K. Magee

During its Plenary Sessions from 2009 through 2013, the Pontifical Biblical Commission (PBC) devoted its meetings and work to the generation of a document on a topic entrusted to it by Pope Benedict XVI in the April 2009 session, namely the "Inspiration and Truth of the Bible." This assignment stemmed from the proposal of the 12th Ordinary General Assembly of the Synod of Bishops held in Rome from October 5 to 26 of the previous year, focusing on "The Word of God in the Life and Mission of the Church." Prominent among the final propositions of that gathering was the following, §12: "The Synod proposes that the Congregation for the Doctrine of the Faith clarify the concepts of the inspiration and truth of the Bible, as well as their reciprocal relationship, in order to bring about a better understanding of the teaching of *Dei Verbum* §11."[1] In light of the importance of these concepts for the teaching of Sacred Scripture and Fundamental Theology, especially in the context of religious and seminary formation, the purpose of the present paper is to raise the question of

1. My translation of the Italian text of the synodal proposition: "Il Sinodo propone che la Congregazione per la Dottrina della Fede chiarifichi i concetti di ispirazione e di verità della Bibbia, così come il loro rapporto reciproco, in modo da far capire meglio l'insegnamento della *Dei Verbum* §11," on the Synod of Bishops section of the Vatican site under "Sinodo dei Vescovi: XII Assemblea Generale Ordinaria, Elenco Finale delle Proposizioni," http://www.vatican.va/roman_curia/synod/documents/rc_synod_doc_20081025_elenco-prop-finali_it.html#Dalla_Costituzione_Dogmatica_Dei_Verbum, accessed April 8, 2021. The document begins by noting that while the text of propositions by its nature is confidential (*per la sua natura riservato*) because of the consultative nature of the Synod, it was being made public here in Italian-language version only as an unofficial working document.

22

A Critical Appraisal of the Pontifical Biblical Commission's Document

the degree to which the 2014 PBC document in question, *The Inspiration and Truth of Sacred Scripture,* does or does not prove helpful in clarifying them.

A critical appraisal of the document that the Biblical Commission articulated in response to this invitation cannot be undertaken in a vacuum. Indeed, the call for the clarification of these concepts has quite a long history, dating back at least to the years immediately preceding the Second Vatican Council, and perhaps even to the theories of inspiration and inerrancy proposed in the nineteenth century by various European theologians. Accordingly, it will be necessary to trace a sort of theological pedigree of the various proposals regarding these concepts in order to determine precisely what task had been bequeathed to the Commission not just by the Synod of Bishops but by this span of recent history, and thus to evaluate the adequacy or inadequacy of the Commission's document in meeting that task. Attention will be given here to the Synod's preparatory documents—which are most readily available online—since it is these documents that presumably reflect felt pastoral needs, including those relating to priestly formation, which bishops and others hoped to see addressed as a result of the Synod.

The *Lineamenta* prepared by the Synod's General Secretariat and sent out in 2007 to the various respondents had included in its questions at the end of chapter I on "Revelation, the Word of God and the Church" a challenge to "Describe the faithful's understanding of the charism of the inspiration and truth of the Scriptures."[2] This challenge had then spurred further proposals of a need to examine this subject, as reflected in the subsequent *Instrumentum Laboris* of May 11, 2008, five months before the start of the General Assembly:

> 14. One of the most persistent difficulties, cited by the Pastors, is Sacred Scripture's relation to the Word of [God, and in particular the] question of the Bible's inspiration and truth. This occurs on the following three levels:
>
> —some questions concern the Bible itself: "What does inspiration mean?", "What is the canon of Scripture?", "What kind of truth is attributed to the Scriptures?" and "What is the Bible's historic character?"
>
> —other questions regard the relation of Sacred Scripture to Divine Tradition and the Church's Magisterium;

---

2. Synod of Bishops, 12th Ordinary General Assembly, "The Word of God in the Life and Mission of the Church," *Lineamenta* (March 25, 2007), http://www.vatican.va/roman_curia /synod/documents/rc_synod_doc_20070427_lineamenta-xii-assembly_en.html, Question n. 4 for Chapter I.

MICHAEL K. MAGEE

—still others touch upon difficult parts of the Bible, especially in the Old Testament. In this case, the subject of the Word of God needs to be treated in catechesis.[3]

In thus proposing that the Synod discuss the topic of inspiration, the *Instrumentum Laboris* had also set forth several preliminary points that it affirmed "can be stated with certainty" based on existing magisterial teaching. In doing so, however, the Secretariat is already employing ambiguous language that would continue into the later preparation of the Synod document. While the *Instrumentum Laboris* seems intended to convey the magisterial data matter-of-factly, its wording seems somewhat less precise than the painstaking formulation devised earlier in the Dogmatic Constitution on Divine Revelation, *Dei verbum*, the principal source that it cites. The conciliar formula regarding the "truth that God, for the sake of our salvation, wanted to be put into the sacred writings" had created no basis for confining salvific truth to discrete *parts* of the text (and, as we shall see, had been crafted specifically to avoid such an implication). Even so, the text of the *Instrumentum Laboris*, while citing the text of *Dei verbum* outside of its full context, inexplicably does seem (whether inadvertently or deliberately) to open itself to such a limitation, even inserting the word "only":

—the charism of inspiration allows God to be the author of the Bible in a way that does not exclude humankind itself from being its true author. In fact, inspiration is different from dictation; it leaves the freedom and personal capacity of the writer intact, while enlightening and inspiring both;

—*with regards to what might be inspired in the many parts of Sacred Scripture, inerrancy applies only to "that truth which God wanted put into sacred writings for the sake of salvation" (DV 11);* [emphasis added: see footnote 4 below]

—in virtue of the charism of inspiration, the Holy Spirit constitutes the books of the Bible as the Word of God and entrusts them to the Church, so that they might be received in the obedience of faith;

—the totality and organic unity of the Canon of Sacred Scripture constitutes the criterion for interpreting the Sacred Book; and

—since the Bible is the Word of God recorded in human language, its interpretation is consonant with literary, philosophic and theological criteria,

---

3. Synod of Bishops, 12th Ordinary General Assembly, "The Word of God in the Life and Mission of the Church," *Instrumentum Laboris* (May 8, 2008), http://www.vatican.va/roman_curia/synod/documents/rc_synod_doc_20080511_instrlabor-xii-assembly_en.html, §14.

A Critical Appraisal of the Pontifical Biblical Commission's Document

always subject, however, to the unifying force of faith and the guidance of the Magisterium.[4]

The English version of the *Instrumentum Laboris* goes even further by using the limiting demonstrative adjective "*that* [truth]," which might be read as if intending to distinguish the Bible's truthful affirmations from other affirmations made within it and not directly concerned with salvation (cf. the previous footnote). Clearly, both *Dei verbum* and this *Instrumentum Laboris* are intended to call for an explanation of the fact that the Bible's articulation of truth is guaranteed and delimited by the specific purpose for which the text is intended (i.e., "for the sake of salvation"). Yet the wording of *Dei verbum* had carefully refrained from delimiting biblical truth only to certain *parts of the*

---

4. "The Word of God in the Life and Mission of the Church: *Instrumentum Laboris*," §15c. Unfortunately, the English text provided here also seems to render incorrectly the original text of the *Instrumentum Laboris*. Assuming that the working document was Italian, that text reads, "quantunque la Sacra Scrittura sia **ispirata** in tutte le sue parti la sua **inerranza** si riferisce solo alla «verità che Dio per la nostra salvezza volle fosse consegnata nelle sacre lettere» (DV §11)"— i.e., "Although the Sacred Scripture is **inspired** in all its parts, its **inerrancy** pertains only to the 'truth that God, for the sake of our salvation, wanted to be put into the sacred writings.'" First, the Italian text makes explicit reference to the inspiration of the whole of Scripture, which is absent in the English rendering of the same sentence (though not from the document as a whole). Second, the phrase rendered "for the sake of salvation" seems in the original to modify the verbal phrase "wanted to be put" instead of the noun "truth." Third, the Latin text of the *Instrumentum* (which despite its "official" status may not have been the actual working preparatory document) takes its wording directly from *Dei verbum*, §11 ("quamvis omnes Sacrae Scripturae partes divinitus **inspiratae** sint, tamen eius **inerrantia** pertinet tantummodo ad 'veritatem, quam Deus nostrae salutis causa Litteris Sacris consignari voluit'"), which certainly intends this sense as evidenced by its redaction history discussed later in this paper. The same sense is suggested or at least sustained by the French ("même si les Saintes Écritures sont **inspirées** dans leur totalité, leur **inerrance** se réfère uniquement à la 'vérité [. . .] que Dieu, en vue de notre salut, a voulu qu'elle [l'Écriture] fût consignée dans les Saintes Lettres'"), German ("obwohl die Heilige Schrift in allen ihren Teilen **inspiriert** ist, bezieht sich ihre **Irrtumslosigkeit** nur auf 'die Wahrheit [. . .], die Gott um unseres Heiles willen in heiligen Schriften aufgezeichnet haben wollte'"), Polish ("chociaż Pismo Święte jest **natchnione** we wszystkich swych częściach, jego **nieomylność** dotyczy jedynie 'prawdy, jaką z woli Boga została zapisana w księgach świętych dla naszego zbawienia'"), and Portuguese ("embora a Sagrada Escritura seja **inspirada** em todas as suas partes, a sua **inerrância** diz respeito apenas à 'verdade que Deus, para a nossa salvação, quis que fosse consignada nas sagradas letras'"). Finally, only in the English is the deliberately limiting demonstrative adjective "that"—i.e., "that truth" rather than simply "the truth"—inserted into the text, having no warrant either in the Latin nor in any of the other vernacular versions. Consequently, to the extent that the Synod Fathers might have been using their respective vernacular versions of the *Instrumentum Laboris* without comparing them with the others, they would not necessarily be starting out from the same set of presuppositions.

MICHAEL K. MAGEE

biblical text as such; the *Instrumentum Laboris*, on the other hand, seems effectively to omit any such caution.

A limitation of biblical inspiration and truth to certain parts of the Bible might seem to provide at least one way of freeing the exegete or theologian from the puzzling task of having to rescue biblical inerrancy from the challenges posed by numerous problematic passages in which the human authors' limited perspectives, divergences in details from known historical fact, and similar perennial conundrums render the claim of inerrancy particularly difficult. Even so, such a maneuver seems to sidestep without comment generations of papal teaching—as well as *Dei verbum*'s own teaching—regarding the truth of the Bible (at least in some sense) *in all its parts*. Discussion of the inerrancy of Sacred Scripture had long been preoccupied with the question of how it could be considered cogent to propose that the *truth* of the biblical text—depending as it does on his authorship—extends only to certain parts. Pope Leo XIII in his Encyclical *Providentissimus Deus*, §§20–21, had stated:

> It is absolutely wrong and forbidden, either to narrow inspiration to certain parts only of Holy Scripture, or to admit that the sacred writer has erred. . . . [S]o far is it from being possible that any error can co-exist with inspiration, that inspiration not only is essentially incompatible with error, but excludes and rejects it as absolutely and necessarily as it is impossible that God Himself, the supreme Truth, can utter that which is not true. . . . [T]hose who maintain that an error is possible in any genuine passage of the sacred writings, either pervert the Catholic notion of inspiration, or make God the author of such error.[5]

It is not impossible that those involved in the preparation for the 12th General Assembly of the Synod may have wished to reexamine and revise Leo's teaching on biblical inerrancy or, perhaps more fruitfully, at least to reexamine the adequacy of the terms in which it had been cast. If so, however, one does not find in these documents or deliberations any conscious intention to do so. In fact, at least twice since the publication of *Providentissimus Deus*—first by the Venerable Pius XII and then by the Second Vatican Council—such an explicit limitation of biblical truth to a subset of propositions within the Bible rather than to the whole had been explicitly rejected. Pius XII in *Divino afflante Spiritu* had gone further, mentioning in some detail certain of the earlier concrete proposals:

---

5. Pope Leo XIII, Encyclical Letter *Providentissimus Deus* (November 18, 1893), 325–39 in *The Papal Encyclicals*, vol. 2, *1878–1903*, ed. Claudia Carlen (Raleigh: McGrath, 1981), §§20–21.

26

A Critical Appraisal of the Pontifical Biblical Commission's Document

When ... some Catholic writers, in spite of this solemn definition of Catholic doctrine, by which such divine authority is claimed for the "entire books with all their parts" as to secure freedom from any error whatsoever, ventured to restrict the truth of Sacred Scripture solely to matters of faith and morals, and to regard other matters, whether in the domain of physical science or history, as "obiter dicta" and—as they contended—in no wise connected with faith, Our Predecessor of immortal memory, Leo XIII in the Encyclical Letter *Providentissimus Deus*, published on November 18 in the year 1893, justly and rightly condemned these errors and safe-guarded the studies of the Divine Books by most wise precepts and rules.[6]

The problem that lay in the background of such proposals was certainly a real one. God could not indeed be rightly regarded as intending and commanding genocide, conforming to the worldview of a faulty cosmology, setting forth faulty or mutually contradictory genealogies, proclaiming events according to chronologies contradicted by astrophysics or fossil records, or making errors of historical fact, all of which might be asserted in some sense of certain individual passages in the Bible, at least in regard to their verbal detail. Even so, the consistent hesitancy of the Magisterium—exemplified vividly by the teaching of *Providentissimus Deus* and *Divino afflante Spiritu*—to countenance any theory of partial inspiration or of merely occasional utterances of biblical truths interspersed among other affirmations lacking any such guarantee—seemed to invite consideration of other theories of inspiration allowing for an appreciation of ways in which every part of the biblical text might be seen as enlisted *in some way* into the service of some transcendent truth.

Such a problem of reconciling apparent discrepancies in the biblical text—whether between various parts of the Bible itself or between the Bible and human knowledge acquired through the natural sciences or otherwise—was far from new, dating even from the times of the Church Fathers. Over the centuries, there had been attempts to harmonize apparently divergent affirmations in the context of apologetics (as in Tatian's second-century *Diatessaron*); or to recognize the partial nature of certain earlier affirmations not as errors but as steps along the way toward a later fullness only gradually being revealed by a process of divine pedagogy; or to locate a diversity of possible senses within a configuration of the literal, allegorical, moral and anagogical senses.[7] And in

6. Pope Pius XII, Encyclical Letter *Divino afflante Spiritu* (September 30, 1943), 65–79 in *The Papal Encyclicals*, vol. 4, *1939–1958*, ed. Claudia Carlen (Raleigh: McGrath, 1981), §1.

7. Pietro Bovati, "Teologia biblica e ispirazione: Problemi e aperture," 289–95 in Peter Dubovský and Jean-Pierre Sonnet, eds., *Ogni Scrittura è ispirata* (Rome: Gregorian and Biblical Press, 2013). In the same article, Bovati also highlights the fact that any single part of the

MICHAEL K. MAGEE

response to the consternation unleashed by apparent discrepancies between the affirmations of Scripture articulated in terms of a primitive cosmology, on the one hand, and the findings of Copernicus, Galileo, and Kepler, on the other, the latter of these had articulated well the insight that biblical references to the movement of the sun around the earth were not being branded as *false* but retained their truth as expressions of true human experience in regard to these celestial events.[8] Much more recently, *Divino afflante* had undertaken a similar work of reconciliation of apparent discrepancies by its insistence on the ways in which different *literary genres* express the truth that they contain.[9]

It is certainly not surprising that the preparatory documents for the Synod of Bishops did not make reference to any such proposals regarding a theology of inspiration in their mere proposal that a clarification of the doctrines of inspiration and biblical truth should be taken up. But it would be disappointing indeed that neither the Synod itself nor the Commission entrusted with the further execution of such a task would attempt to do so.[10]

Scriptures can *only* effectively be interpreted as normative in light of the whole (p. 288). In such a perspective, clearly no part of the whole is expendable.

8. Oswald Loretz, *Das Ende der Inspirations-Theologie: Chancen eines Neubeginns,* vol. 1, *Untersuchungen zur Entwicklung der traditionellen theologischen Lehre* (Stuttgart: Verlag Katholisches Bibelwerk, 1974), 29. Loretz cites Kepler in the latter's Preface to his work *Astronomia Nova*: "Da wir mit dem Gesichtssinn die meisten und wichtigsten Erfahrungen in uns aufnehmen, ist es für uns nicht möglich, unsere Redeweise von diesem Gesichtssinn abzuziehen." An example of such a truth being articulated in terms of appearance would be the simple observation that "the sun came up" at a particular time. Even if one knows that the actual movement of the earth and the sun are otherwise from what is being expressed verbally, the statement is not false; rather it is true in the sense in which it is being articulated on the basis of appearances with respect to the observer.

9. Denis Farkasfalvy, O.Cist., *A Theology of the Christian Bible: Revelation, Inspiration, Canon* (Washington, DC: Catholic University of America Press, 2018), 123. Here Farkasfalvy offers the surprising but insightful observation: "Much too soon, however, Catholics realized that new challenges from the new approaches of literary criticism came with strong emphasis on the literary genre but threatened to subvert the foundations of the Christian message." Pointing out that much of German form criticism had made use of a strikingly similar exegetical methodology only to proceed to conclusions quite incompatible with Catholic faith, Farkasfalvy noted that "The similarities between literary criticism encouraged by *Divino Afflante* and Bultmann's movement of the *Formgeschichte* became a source of confusion."

10. Useful for outlining the *status quaestionis* of the theories of inspiration is the bibliography cited by Gianantonio Borgonovo, "Una proposta di rilettura dell'ispirazione biblica dopo gli apporti della Form- e Redaktionsgeschichte," 41–63 in *Interpretazione della Bibbia nella Chiesa: Atti del Simposio promosso dalla Congregazione per la Dottrina della Fede* (Rome: Libreria Editrice Vaticana, 1999), 41n2. Of particular note for English-language readers is the work of James T. Burtchaell, *Catholic Theories of Biblical Inspiration since 1810* (Cambridge: Cambridge University Press, 1969).

A Critical Appraisal of the Pontifical Biblical Commission's Document

Abbot Denis Farkasfalvy, up to the time of his death in March 2020, and even during the span of his term on the PBC during which the document on *The Inspiration and Truth of Sacred Scripture* was discussed and published, devoted a considerable amount of his research to the proposal that the conservative notions of biblical inspiration and truth needed to be reexamined. In this vein he was attempting to extend the study of biblical inspiration along a trajectory culminating in the research of important scholars just before the Council (including but not limited to the studies of Karl Rahner and Luis Alonso Schökel).[11] The concerns of such scholars had been taken up but not brought to a real resolution in the drafting, conciliar approbation, and promulgation of *Dei verbum*. In fact, the traces of Farkasfalvy's influence are discernible in the text of the final PBC document. Sadly, however, despite his participation in the Commission, the document does not seem to achieve much progress, if any, toward the objective that he had sought, nor indeed does it manifest a very clear awareness of such an intention.

In order to grasp better the kind of elucidation of the notion of the Bible's inspiration and truth for which scholars had been hoping since before the Second Vatican Council, as well as the unfortunate failure of the PBC document to achieve such an elucidation, it is necessary now to examine first the Commission's own conception of its task as distinguished sharply from the task that might seemed to have been bequeathed to it by the preconciliar scholarship and the conciliar deliberations and teachings. For this purpose we shall undertake a brief consideration of the elaboration of the problem in the successive drafts that became *Dei verbum* which left the problem still open despite the further insights affecting its composition. The trajectory thus established led eventually to the call for a reexamination of the matter at the Synod of Bishops almost half a century later. Finally, we shall consider the Commission's final document which seems, at least against this background, to signal a missed opportunity, at best.

How Did the Commission View Its Task?

The way in which the Pontifical Biblical Commission itself envisioned its mission to "clarify the concepts of the inspiration and truth of the Bible" (cf. Synod

---

11. Rahner's work, *Über die Schriftinspiration*, was translated into English and published as *Inspiration in the Bible*, Quaestiones Disputatatae, trans. Charles H. Henkey, SJ (New York: Herder and Herder, 1961); and Luis Alonso Schökel, *La Palabra Inspirada*, was translated as *The Inspired Word: Scripture in the Light of Language and Literature*, trans. Francis Martin, OCSO (London: Burns & Oates, 1967).

MICHAEL K. MAGEE

Proposition §12) is expressed in the concluding section of the Commission document in the following terms, at least as regards inspiration:

> The task of the Biblical Commission, charged with expressing itself on this matter, is not to formulate a doctrine of inspiration in competition with what is usually presented in manuals of systematic theology. The Commission, by means of this document, aims to show how Sacred Scripture itself points to the divine provenance of its assertions, thus becoming the messenger of God's truth.[12]

Regarding the "truth" of Sacred Scripture (the positive expression habitually and fruitfully adopted in preference to the negative concept of "inerrancy") the Commission helpfully specified that such truth should be understood "not as an aggregate of exact information on the various aspects of human knowledge but as a revelation of God himself and his salvific plan."[13] It is a truth that unfolds within history and finds expression in many different forms, ascertained not by absolutizing its discrete propositions one by one, but by grasping the integral totality revealed within the unified canon of both Testaments.

As it addresses itself to biblical scholars and readers today, what misguided tendencies or unbalanced theories of inspiration does the document seek to correct or to rule out? Rather inexplicably, it mentions only one such tendency as the object of its explicit critique:

> The duty of the interpreter is *to avoid a fundamentalist reading of Scripture* [emphasis added] so as to situate the various formulations of the sacred text in their historical context, according to the literary genres then in vogue. It is by embracing this characteristic of divine revelation that we are actually led to the mystery of Christ, the full and definitive manifestation of the truth in human history.[14]

The specific project that the Commission claims thus to have delimited for itself (for it does not seem to be one that this mandate was so delimited by anyone else) is striking for several reasons. First—except perhaps for reasons of personnel, time, and expertise—it is unclear why the task at hand would *not precisely* include, instead of explicitly eschewing, at least the initial building blocks of a theology of inspiration advancing beyond formulas "as presented in manuals of systematic theology." After all, generations of Bishops and experts

---

12. Pontifical Biblical Commission, *The Inspiration and Truth of Sacred Scripture: The Word That Comes from God and Speaks of God for the Salvation of the World*, trans. Thomas Esposito and Stephen Gregg (Collegeville, MN: Liturgical Press, 2014), §138.

13. *The Inspiration and Truth of Sacred Scripture*, §144.

14. *The Inspiration and Truth of Sacred Scripture*, §146.

A Critical Appraisal of the Pontifical Biblical Commission's Document

had already cited this framework as inadequate, as we shall show in the following section.

Second, it is puzzling that the Commission would regard the danger of *fundamentalism* envisioned in isolation as the sole or principal threat to an authentic understanding of the truth of Scripture. Admittedly a fundamentalist reading, despite all its overt deference to the supremacy of the divine word, can easily be seen to cloak instead a sort of fetishism of literality for the sake of the reader's *mastery* of the divine utterance, with the result that anything too difficult to understand or to reconcile with one's preconceived notions risks immediate rejection. For this reason, paradoxically, fundamentalism might be seen as psychologically akin to positivism, even if the data sets and conclusions of the two systems are diametrically opposed to one another. But even more closely akin to positivism—and therefore more potentially destructive to a reader's ability to grasp the divine message in all the sovereign freedom of its utterance and inexhaustible depth—is any tendency to absolutize or exaggerate the importance of scientifically reconstructing the various dimensions of the historical context in which the biblical text was written, even if such reconstruction is one helpful element of biblical interpretation. The danger of such a historical-critical reductionism is not only overlooked by the Commission; it seems to be exemplified by the Commission's own text. The Commission goes so far as to suggest that merely by situating "the various formulations of the sacred text in its historical situation, according to the literary genres then in vogue, . . . we are actually led to the mystery of Christ, the full and definitive manifestation of the truth in human history."[15]

In fairness it should be noted that the Commission in several different places quotes the principle articulated by *Dei verbum*, §12, according to which "Holy Scripture must be read and interpreted in the same spirit in which it was written"[16] and admits that "modern exegetical methods cannot take the place of faith."[17] Even so, this admonition is nowhere effectively integrated (beyond the citation of the wording of *Dei verbum*, §12 itself) into the document's own attempted clarification of the notions of biblical inspiration and biblical truth. To the extent that scientific reconstruction of the historical context is regarded as utterly indispensable for grasping the divine message, biblical interpretation is relegated to the province of experts, and the faithful

---

15. *The Inspiration and Truth of Sacred Scripture*, §146.

16. Second Vatican Council, *Dei verbum* (November 18, 1965) (Boston: Pauline Books & Media, 1965).

17. *The Inspiration and Truth of Sacred Scripture*, §53.

MICHAEL K. MAGEE

in general—including Fathers, Doctors and Saints—seem to be rendered mere beggars at their table.

The problem of biblical literalism had been confronted as early as the Council of Trent (in the form of the principle of *sola Scriptura* to the exclusion of the Magisterium's competency). Much more recently, by the late eighteenth or early nineteenth centuries, positivistic tendencies entailing an exaggerated and even exclusive reliance on diachronic methodologies were evident, reaching a crescendo only in the early twentieth. It was during this same period that various theories of inspiration had been articulated and an attempt made to explain the consequences of inspiration for the sacred character of the biblical text. The inadequacies perceived by the Council Fathers in recent manualistic theories of inspiration therefore seem arguably to have been due at least as much to their inability to address the challenges of the positivistic tendencies described above as to any fundamentalistic biblical literalism. We will proceed to a consideration, then, of the Council Fathers' expressed thoughts on the matter.

The Council's Consideration of Biblical Inspiration and Truth

Among the *consilia et vota* (in the case of the bishops) and the *proposita et monita* (in the case of the religious superiors) sent to the Holy See in view of the upcoming Second Vatican Council during the so-called "Antepreparatory Period," thirty-four of the respondents suggested in some form that the Council should treat of the doctrine of biblical inspiration, while eleven called for treatment of the doctrine of "inerrancy" (including eight that mentioned both).[18] Most frequently, the prospective Council Fathers simply mentioned the topic as worthy of consideration, while a great number also mentioned the need to delve further and uphold or reexamine some of the matters that the First Vatican Council had taught and that Popes Leo XIII and Pius XII had taught in their respective Encyclicals.[19] Also mentioned numerous times were

---

18. "Analyticus conspectus consiliorum et votorum quae ab Episcopis et Praelatis data sunt," Secretaria Pontificia Commissionis Centralis Praeparatoriae Concilii Vaticanii II, *Acta et Documenta Concilio Oecumenico Vaticano II Apparando*, Series I (*Antepraeparatoria*), Appendix Voluminis II (Typis Polyglottis Vaticanis, 1961), pars 1, pp. 16–18.

19. In this regard, it can be admitted that the teachings of Vatican I, Leo XIII, and Pius XII, while pointing to in various ways to the *truth* of the Sacred Scriptures, had always stopped short of affirming any absolute exclusion of error in the sacred writings (for example, as inherent in the manner of expression even if not in the directly intended message), thus leaving open a further articulation of the precise manner in which the *truth* contained within the Bible is to

A Critical Appraisal of the Pontifical Biblical Commission's Document

the specific issues found in biblical texts related to the creation of the world and the origin of humanity.[20]

On the other hand, several other *vota* provide more specific indications of the preoccupations of the prospective Council Fathers regarding these doctrines. Bishop Joseph Schoiswohl of Seckau, Austria, for example, raised the question of whether the notion of individual inspiration should perhaps be replaced with a collective one involving in some way the Church herself.[21] Bishop Michael Keller of Münster probed how the doctrine of inspiration might be impacted by form-critical studies, particularly because a tension between such studies and the doctrine of inspiration as currently developed seemed to have deleterious effects on the use of the Bible for preaching.[22] Several of the bishops raised the question not only of the nature but also of the limits of inspiration and inerrancy, seemingly in contrast to those aspects of the text that might be attributable exclusively to the human authors.[23] Evidently these

be affirmed. Vatican I (DH 3006) stated that the books of both Old and New Testaments in all their parts had been handed down *Spiritu Sancto dictante*. Leo XIII in *Providentissimus Deus* (DH 3291–92) had affirmed the incompatibility of inspiration with error and its extension to every part of Scripture, and had denied that the sacred writers had erred, but without clarifying in what respect or in what sense the truth of their affirmations was to be upheld, and in what sense not. The same affirmations could likewise be made of Benedict XV's *Spiritus Paraclitus* (DH 3652). And Pius XII in *Divino afflante* simply clarifies (§38) that biblical writers use figures of speech hastily branded by some as errors but evident on further examination to represent "nothing else than those customary modes of expression and narration peculiar to the ancients, which used to be employed in the mutual dealings of social life and which in fact were sanctioned by common usage." As such, they seem to elude any characterization as either true or false in any absolute sense, since they constitute the medium rather than the message of the biblical word.

20. An example is the *votum* of Bishop Maurice Schexnayder of Lafayette, Louisiana who wrote. *Magni momenti videtur ut, variis opinionibus modernis perpensis, natura 'Inspirationis' Sanctarum Scripturarum definiatur vel clarificetur. Aequalis momenti est quaestio de natura et significatione capitis 1–3 Genesis* (*Antepraeparatoria*, vol. II, pars 6, p. 356).

21. *Antepraeparatoria*, vol. II, pars 1, p. 67.

22. *Antepraeparatoria*, vol. II, pars 1, p. 631.

23. *Antepraeparatoria*, vol. II, pars 2, p. 115 (Bishop Arturo Tabera Araoz of Albacete, Spain). Similarly in the same part of vol. II pars 2, Bishop Angel Hidalgo Ibañez of Jaca, Spain (p. 193) who pointed out that the First Vatican Council had defined only the *fact* of inspiration, not its nature or the limits of the divine influence in it. Bishop Jose Eguino Trecu of Santander, Spain provides a summary view of this perspective, also considering it as a needed extension of previous conciliar and papal teaching: *Renovanda sunt decreta Conciliorum Tridentini et Vaticani atque ulterius complenda ita ut plenius definiatur divinae inspirationis natura et extensio intra diversa literaria sacrorum genera, adeo ut tuto discerni possint ea quorum Deus verus est auctor ab illis quae forte auctori humano tribui possint* (p. 293). It is noteworthy that this perspective

33

MICHAEL K. MAGEE

concerns were sometimes occasioned by tensions between various contemporary interpretations that seemed difficult to reconcile with biblical inerrancy.[24] One solution that seemed to find expression occasionally was a clarification of the distinction between the notions of *revelation*, on the one hand, and *inspiration*, on the other.[25]

A consensus of these bishops seemed thus to suggest that the doctrine of biblical inspiration had not yet been formulated with adequate precision in the face of the challenges of the moment, even if they seemed to envision the challenges in diverse ways. To some, the defense of a notional inerrancy of the various statements of Sacred Scripture seemed difficult when these touched upon matters then being subjected in new ways to scientific inquiry (such as the number of years since the creation of the world),[26] or when commands attributed to God seemed repugnant not only to modern sensibilities but to the natural law (such as acts of genocide during the conquest), or even when different biblical references to the same reality seemed to contradict each other (as for example, the factual discrepancies between Mark 2:26 and 1 Samuel 21:1ff, or the attribution in Matthew 27:9 to Jeremiah of a prophecy that seems actually to have been from Zechariah). These were some of the examples given in a notable intervention of Cardinal König of Vienna in which he asserted unabashedly that "there are in the Sacred Books historical and scientific statements that sometimes depart from the truth" (*in Bibliis Sacris notitias historicas et notitias scientiae naturalis a veritate quandoque deficere*).[27]

does seem to entail the sort of compartmentalization between the human and divine elements in Scripture, which the Council as such was careful to avoid in its final text.

24. *Antepraeparatoria*, vol. II, pars 2, p. 379 (Bishop Eduardo Martinez Gonzales of Zamora, Spain).

25. *Antepraeparatoria*, vol. II, pars 7, p. 383 (Bishop Carlos Guillermo Hartl de Laufen, OFMCap, Vicar Apostolic of Araucanía, Chile): *Clarius distinguendam esse puto inter inspirationem, quae revera pertinet ad totum textum ab hagiographo conscriptum, et revelationem quae spectat ad res fidei et morum et nostram salutem . . . . Ideo e. gr. geneologiae in quinto capite libri Genesis sunt sub inspiratione quidem scriptae, sed revelatum et id solum, quod ad fidem pertinet, id est omnes homines ab Adam et Eva originem ducere. Reliqua Spiritus Sanctus non intendit et sacer scriptor narrat secundum modum illo tempore consuetum. Chronologiam illam non posse veram esse scientia palaeontologica evidenter demonstrat.*

26. Loretz, *Das Ende der Inspirations-Theologie*, beginning in Chapter V treating of Johannes Kepler and Galileo Galilei, pp. 29–55, chronicles vividly the manner and degree to which new discoveries in the natural sciences proved to be the catalyst for a reexamination of the notions of biblical inerrancy and truth, and of their mutual correlation, affecting all subsequent writing on these matters.

27. Alois Grillmeier, "The Divine Inspiration and the Interpretation of Sacred Scripture," 199–246, chapter 3 of the section on the Dogmatic Constitution on Divine Revelation in Herbert

A Critical Appraisal of the Pontifical Biblical Commission's Document

Others such as Bishop Keller of Münster seemed more concerned about the detrimental effect on spirituality and preaching of theories of inspiration and inerrancy aligning the truth of the biblical message too rigidly with a scholarly, historical critical reconstruction of the intent of the human author. Even though these are very different concerns, both are categorized as reasons for needing a reexamination of the prevailing formulation of the notion of biblical inspiration, characterized by D. Farkasfalvy as "the traditional Thomistic model of 'double authorship.'"[28]

Meanwhile, in 1958, Karl Rahner had published the work that Farkasfalvy describes as "the most important book of the century on biblical inspiration."[29] It is interesting to note that his call for a reexamination of biblical inspiration addresses each of the seemingly disparate concerns articulated by the prospective Council Fathers, as outlined above. Rahner begins by presupposing what he regards as the binding content of the Church's teaching on inspiration, namely that:

> The . . . Scriptures have God as their originator; he is their originator in a literary sense, and therefore their "author". . . . [His] inspiration does not consist in the fact that the Scriptures have been accepted as canonical by the Church, nor solely in the fact that they inerrantly record the divine revelation. Rather, inspiration consists in God's supernaturally enlightening the human author's mind in the perception of the content and essential plan of the book, and his moving his will to write no more and no less than what

Vorgrimler, ed., *Commentary on the Documents of Vatican II*, vol. 3, trans. W. Glen-Doepel, H. Graef, J. M. Jakubiak, and S. and E. Young (New York: Herder and Herder, 1969), 205.

28. Farkasfalvy, *A Theology of the Christian Bible*, 2. Such a neo-Scholastic framework is precisely the model of biblical inspiration articulated unambiguously by the first schema *De fontibus revelationis*, which had been rejected by the Council Fathers, occasioning the composition of the new draft that would become the Dogmatic Constitution *Dei verbum*. In chapter 2, n. 8, the rejected preparatory schema described biblical inspiration in these terms: "*speciale quoddam charisma ad scribendum, quo Deus, in hagiographo et per hagiographum operando, mentem suam scripto hominibus manifestat, ideoque ipse nominatur veroque sensu est auctor principalis integri textus humanis, hagiographus autem, in complendo libro, est Spiritus Sancti 'organon,' seu instrumentum, idque vivum ac ratione praeditum, cuius proinde propria indoles ac veluti singulars notae ex libro sacro colligi possunt.*" Here the text cites Pius XII's *Divino afflante*. While not rejecting Pius's dichotomy between God as *auctor principals integri textus*, on the one hand, and the *hagiographi* (sacred writers) as *instrumenta*, the new draft would exercise caution both to say that the hagiographers are "true authors," and to avoid expressing God's role as if he were merely a *literary* author, albeit the principal one, on the same level as human authors who articulate arguments discursively. On this point, cf. the points that follow below concerning the background and history of the Council.

29. Farkasfalvy, *A Theology of the Christian Bible*, 1. Cf. Rahner, *Inspiration in the Bible*.

MICHAEL K. MAGEE

God himself wants written, God providing him the while with special assistance to ensure that the work, thus conceived and willed, be correspondingly carried into effect.[30]

Accordingly, Rahner seems to affirm effectively the main dogmatic tenets that could be characterized as settled regarding biblical inspiration. At the same time, he cites the need to distinguish between the divine and human causality in reference to any given text, so that God's intention is recognized as transcendent with respect to the intention of the human author. As Rahner puts it, "the divine authorship neither competes with, nor derogates from the human authorship; the latter is not diminished, it is not reduced to a mere secretarial function"; instead, the author's ingenuity is as fully engaged as that of any human author in the production of a literary product which God simultaneously "permeates" and "embraces."[31] But he points out a problem that he considers to vex existing theories of biblical inspiration, relying as they did largely on a notion of dual authorship: "God's acting as *literary* cause of the Bible, as its author, puts him, if we may so formulate it, on the level of the categorical, not transcendent, causality; that is, not only the thing caused, but also the causal operation itself, must be within the dimension of created existence and operation."[32]

It is well beyond the scope of the present paper to provide a full summary of Rahner's entire study of biblical inspiration, which is brief enough to be read without much difficulty. Further discussion of its meaning and importance is also provided by Farkasfalvy, who sees it as an important work signaling the need to move beyond a stifling neo-Scholastic framework of dual authorship that was actually less than a hundred years old and did not seem to characterize the relationship between the divine and human "authors" in as creative and rich a way as indicated in the Fathers and Doctors of the Church who had attempted to describe the sacred character of the biblical text.[33]

---

30. Rahner, *Inspiration in the Bible,* 10–13. The very fact that such a brief paragraph spans three pages of Rahner's text is due in part to the fact that he inserts numerous and voluminous footnotes into his brief text. He also uses two different German terms that are each compatible with the sense of the Latin term *auctor,* namely *Urheber* (translated here as "originator") and *Verfasser* (literally "composer," though it is frequently used in German for the writer of a text), in order to facilitate the distinction that he wishes to make in his study between the two types of "authorship."

31. Rahner, *Inspiration in the Bible,* 14–15.

32. Rahner, *Inspiration in the Bible,* 16.

33. Farkasfalvy, *A Theology of the Christian Bible,* 1–6, 29–31, 80–86. Farkasfalvy also helpfully points out that the neo-Scholastic theories being subjected to such criticism by Rahner

A Critical Appraisal of the Pontifical Biblical Commission's Document

Noteworthy in the present context is the likely influence on the prospective Council Fathers of Rahner's perception of the deficiencies of the neo-Scholastic framework of dual literary authorship. Whenever God's originating "authorship" was cast reductionistically into the same mold as that of the human authors—parallel to these even while superior to them—there arose precisely that array of problems signaled in the Antepreparatory *consilia et vota*. Such a framework seems to raise the question of how God himself could have directly intended, as the human author would, affirmations such as those that Cardinal König and others had cited as veering away from historical, scientific, or other verifiable truths. And on the other hand, whenever the intentionality of the divine author is identified too strictly with that of the human author, the ascertainment of Scripture's true meaning, thus envisioned, became a mere objective artifact of the remote past needing to be unearthed by historical-critical experts while impenetrable to the layman—more or less the concern that Bishop Keller had expressed.[34]

In his commentary on the conciliar debates, Joseph Ratzinger decries the largely "defensive spirit" of the *Schema Constitutionis dogmaticae de fontibus Revelationis* that had formed the basis of the discussion, and its espousal of "a largely verbalistic conception of the idea of inspiration" and "the narrowest interpretation of inerrancy ('*in qualibet re religiosa vel profana*')," compounded by an unrealistic "conception of the historicity of the Gospels that suggested that there were not problems."[35] After John XXIII's discarding of that draft following the negative assessment of it by a majority of Council Fathers, the new draft had contained some improvements.[36]

The initial *schema* had characterized God as *primarius Scripturarum Auctor*

and others were *not* from Saint Thomas himself, but from other writers attempting to build upon Saint Thomas's brief references to the notion of biblical inspiration as a form of prophecy, especially in questions 171–74 of the *tertia pars* of the *Summa*, cf. *A Theology of the Christian Bible*, 4/n13/.

34. A further analysis of the deficiencies of the neo-Scholastic framework can be found in Denis Farkasfalvy, O.Cist., "How to Renew the Theology of Biblical Inspiration?," *Nova et Vetera* 4, no. 2 (2006): 231–54, at 236–40.

35. Joseph Ratzinger, "Dogmatic Constitution on Divine Revelation. Origin and Background," 155–66 in Herbert Vorgrimler, ed., *Commentary on the Documents of Vatican II*, vol. 3, trans. W. Glen-Doepel, H. Graef, J. M. Jakubiak, and S. and E. Young (New York: Herder and Herder, 1969), 157–60.

36. Cf. the English-language Preparatory Note in Francisco Gil Hellín, *Concilii Vaticani II Synopsis in ordinem redigens schemata cum relationibus necnon patrum orations atque animadversiones: Constitutio Dogmatica de Divina Revelatione* Dei Verbum (Vatican City: Libreria Editrice Vaticana, 1993), xxiii n1.

and *auctor principalis integri sacri textus*, and the *hagiographus* (the human sacred writer—*not* author!) as *instrumentum, idque vivum ac ratione praeditum*, whose own personal traits and style could be noted within the text.[37] The new *schema* still characterized God as the "principal author" of Sacred Scripture (*Deum habet principalem auctorem*) and the human authors again as *hagiographi*, who committed to writing all of what God had "commanded" them to write, and nothing more (*ea omnia aeque sola quae Ipse iuberet*). At the request of a number of Council Fathers, the characterization of God as *principalis auctor* was changed to *auctor*, and the word "commanded" was changed to "willed" (*iuberet* to *vellet*), while still making clear God had been acting in them and through them, and a later text incorporating suggestions of the Fathers went further to characterize these "sacred writers" (*hagiographi*) as "true authors" (*veri auctores*).[38]

The new schema, presented to the Council Fathers in April 1963, was characterized by Ratzinger as having "avoided the controversial questions," being thus a "real step forward," and treating of the problems of inspiration and interpretation "in a relatively open way." Even so, he recounts, "no one was very happy with this new draft. It was too inadequate and vague, recognizable at first sight as a product of resignation," besides the fact that "The Church could not express itself before the world in this way on a subject which should have been a heartfelt concern."[39]

The concept of biblical inerrancy, on the other hand, remained closely tied throughout all the *schemata* with that of divine authorship. As proposed in the initial *schema* after its description of inspiration in the terms noted above, and after affirming the extension of inspiration to the whole of Scripture (as all of the drafts up to and including the final Dogmatic Constitution would do), the initial *schema* had baldly stated that "everything articulated by the sacred writer must be held as articulated by the Holy Spirit" (*omnia quae ab hagiographo enuntiantur, a Spiritu Sancto enuntiata retineri debent*), and therefore that the whole of Scripture is immune from all error "in all matters, whether religious or profane."[40] The new draft of April 1963, likewise basing its reasoning on inspiration itself, pared this statement back somewhat to "entirely immune from all error" (*ab omni prorsus errore immunem*), amended later to an affirmation that

---

37. Hellín, *Concilii Vaticani II Synopsis*, 183 (no. 8 in chapter II of the *schema*).

38. Hellín, *Concilii Vaticani II Synopsis*, 88–89.

39. Ratzinger, "Dogmatic Constitution on Divine Revelation: Origin and Background," 3:161–62.

40. Hellín, *Concilii Vaticani II Synopsis*, 184.

A Critical Appraisal of the Pontifical Biblical Commission's Document

the biblical text "teaches without any error" (*sine ullo errore docere*). The further drafts of 1964 and 1965, in response to the Fathers' proposals, had added the adverbs "solidly" (*inconcusse*) and "faithfully" (*fideliter*) before "without error" and added afterward the citation of 2 Timothy 3:16–17 regarding the truth and divine dependability of all Scripture.[41]

With these changes, the text now articulated the notions of inspiration and inerrancy as they would still be contained in the final approved Dogmatic Constitution *Dei verbum*, §11. Over the course of the deliberations and drafts, certain trajectories can be discerned. Within this context, the greatest distance traveled was in regard to the notion of authorship. From an initial preparatory draft that had characterized God as "primary author" while the human "sacred writers" (*hagiographi*) had been denied any characterization as "authors" at all, the final text of *Dei verbum* does characterize God as *auctor* (a broader term than the English word "author," and one that Rahner had rendered "originator"; i.e., *Urheber*), and the human writers as "true authors" (*veri auctores*) who did commit to writing "everything and only those things which [God] wanted" (*Dei verbum*, §11). Such a formulation does not exclude the neo-Scholastic notion of double authorship, but it does open the way for a consideration of God's authorial (i.e., originating) role in a transcendent manner, rather than regarding his authorship as merely a superior parallel to that of the human writer who merely thinks and writes discursive arguments in finite concepts, albeit protected from error. The successive drafts also move progressively toward an increasing appreciation (even beyond what had been found in *Divino afflante*) of the truly active role of the human authors, and away from any characterization of them as merely passive instruments.

Affirmations of the truth of Scripture as a corollary of its divine origin and of the extension of the guarantee of truth to the whole of the Bible remain throughout all the drafts into the Dogmatic Constitution. However, from the initial draft, which considers biblical truth as distributed among all the Bible's parts, with all affirmations of the writers equally guaranteed in their human intentionality by virtue of these precise affirmations' coming ultimately from God, the various drafts progressively made way for a global notion of biblical truth according to which the divine utterance takes place in and through the limited and time-bound concepts and words of the human writers even while remaining in some sense transcendent to these.

Compositely, then, the trajectory of the deliberations and drafts manifests a desire to move beyond and improve upon the neo-Scholastic framework of

41. Hellín, *Concilii Vaticani II Synopsis*, 92–93.

MICHAEL K. MAGEE

dual authorship entailing a notion of inerrancy aligned too tightly with each biblical writer's affirmations precisely as framed by each writer's finite and historically bound perspectives. But given the mark that such theories had left by virtue of their inclusion within the theological formation of so many of the Council Fathers themselves, it would not have been possible to formulate a text that would transcend the neo-Scholastic framework in a definitive way. In fact, it is not difficult to understand the persistent fear that casting God's originating role as anything other than a superior *literary* authorship might be seen as tying him too vaguely to a text attributed directly to the human writers alone, as some grand theme might be said colloquially to "inspire" a human author to write a work purely out of his own creativity. On the other hand, the idea that discrete affirmations of the Bible might be characterized in any sense as false might seem to place cannon fodder in the hands of secularists wishing to debunk the whole of Scripture as a quaint relic of past human aspirations, still "inspiring" on a spiritual level but wholly undependable in historical, cosmological, and moral terms.

Consequently, the final draft of *Dei verbum* constitutes a compromise text capable of leaving the framework of double literary authorship fully in place, but without giving it official conciliar sanction—avoiding some of its strictures while not moving definitively beyond it except to characterize the human writers as true authors with greater clarity and emphasis. This turn, in itself, did point toward a new area of exploration.[42] Even so, the thought-provoking questions posed by Rahner and others and their call for a renewed formulation of the doctrine of inspiration remained simply that, while the desire for an official ecclesial response to many questions such as those that had been raised by Bishop Keller and others remained unfulfilled. Such questions pertain, among other things, to the way an affirmation of biblical truth is to be reconciled with apparent divergences from known scientific or historical discoveries, and how assertions today considered morally reprehensible, especially in the Old Testament, are to be reconciled with God's goodness and a consideration of him as their source.

---

42. Loretz, *Das Ende der Inspirations-Theologie*, 169, emphasizes the importance of the new direction marked in this respect by *Dei verbum*: "Alle theologischen Theorien und Erklärungen der Inspiration, die das Zueinander des Göttlichen und Menschlichen in der Schrift verkürzt zur Darstellung bringen und das menschliche Element geleugnet oder so abgeschwächt haben, das sie die menschliche Sprache der Heiligen Schrift zu einer zeitlosen und irrtumsfreien erklärten, erfahren durch das *Vatikanum II* eine eindeutige Ablehnung."

The Pontifical Biblical Commission Enters the Discussion

In seeking to address questions that had been under discussion for so long by theologians and exegetes, the members of the Pontifical Biblical Commission between 2009 and 2013 were hampered by challenges of personnel as well as of a methodology crafted for individuals working at a distance from one another in relative isolation. The members were exegetes but, for the most part, not theologians, while biblical inspiration and inerrancy are essentially theological themes, pertaining to the discipline of fundamental theology. Besides the fact that none of the Commission's members were old enough to have been present at the Second Vatican Council, they did not manifest (except for Farkasfalvy and perhaps a few others) much familiarity with the theological background of the issue of biblical inspiration, or with the reasons that Rahner and others at the Council had been wishing for a reexamination of the issue. They seem instead to have been focused principally on a perceived challenge posed by a fundamentalist reading of Scripture that would minimize the contribution of the human authors while attributing to God, in an unnuanced way, affirmations reflecting the limited perspective of those human authors. The Commission's document manifests little if any awareness of the dangers that had been raised by some of the Council Fathers of limiting the scope of exegesis merely to what is ascertainable by historical-critical analysis.

As a Member of the Commission himself, Farkasfalvy is able to report that "when the wish of the pope was communicated to the PBC that it prepare a document on inspiration, there was an audible murmur in the meeting room: 'We are exegetes; we know little about this; this is a theological topic.'"[43] A major methodological flaw, cited by Farkasfalvy as having been devised to keep the worldwide membership of the commission on task and on schedule but justifiably criticized by him, was the plan for the document to begin with a survey of "what the biblical writings themselves say about their divine provenance."[44] Regarding the resulting section of the document (i.e., Part Two) Farkasfalvy is reminded of the famous statement of the Roman poet Horace: *Parturiunt montes, nascetur ridiculus mus* ("Mountains are in labor to give birth to a ridiculous mouse")[45]—specifically, in a disjointed list of various

---

43. Farkasfalvy, *A Theology of the Christian Bible*, 98.

44. *The Inspiration and Truth of Sacred Scripture*, General Introduction, §II.3.

45. Farkasfalvy, *A Theology of the Christian Bible*, 102, capping a critique that begins on p. 97. While usually avoiding carefully the mention of specific persons on the Commission, he does attribute this methodological decision exclusively to the decision of Father Klemens Stock, SJ, the Commission's Secretary (p. 98).

41

kinds of biblical assertions about God's influence on human writers. This way of proceeding may have been chosen under pressure not only of time but also of the fact that most of the members of the Commission were exegetes rather than theologians.

Since some parts of Scripture say almost nothing in explicit terms about their own divine origin, such a truncated methodology leads also at times to rather vague formulations such as the statement that "The personal relationship with the Lord Jesus, practiced with a living and informed faith in his person, constitutes the basic foundation for this 'inspiration' that makes the apostles capable of communicating in speech or in writing, the message of Jesus."[46] Such an affirmation, to which many similar ones could be added, seems somewhat reductionistic, inviting the question of how the same things might not be said of the writings of any Father or Doctor of the Church, or indeed any believer writing under the influence of divine grace.[47] In fact, in the concluding section of chapter I the document even goes so far as to point out that "Every literature has its classic books," and that "Many religions too have, so to speak, their classics," adding that "The same phenomenon occurred for the Jews," and that "The same happened among Christians of the first centuries, with the apostolic writings contained in the New Testament."[48]

Nor is it very helpful simply to identify and analyze those affirmations in the Scriptures manifesting an awareness that their message comes from God (as for example, concerning the Prophetic and Historical Books: "Indeed, these books declare insistently that the Lord is the author of their content")[49] since it would seem that anyone at all could make such a claim, authentically or inauthentically. Excluded from such an analysis in these terms of the

---

46. *The Inspiration and Truth of Sacred Scripture*, §8.

47. Similarly, in §10, "The respective biblical writing comes from God through its author's living faith in God and through the relationship of this author with a specific form (or with different forms) of divine revelation." And similarly, of the Book of Sirach (§20), "The careful and devout reading of the Sacred Scriptures, in which God speaks to the people of Israel, united the author with God, became the source of his wisdom, and led him to write his work. Thus one can clearly see a way in which the book comes from God." Also (§30), "Through their presentation of Jesus, the Word of God, the gospels themselves become the word of God." And finally, regarding the author of the Letter to the Hebrews (§43 who "presents himself as belonging to the second Christian generation," this is author is said to show "that he, and consequently his work, is linked to the Son and to God through the ministry of those witnesses who had heard the Lord." How, indeed, would this characterization of the author differ from what might be said of authentically Christian writers in every succeeding era?

48. *The Inspiration and Truth of Sacred Scripture*, §60.

49. *The Inspiration and Truth of Sacred Scripture*, §13.

A Critical Appraisal of the Pontifical Biblical Commission's Document

biblical text itself is the crucial notion of canonicity: Christians, after all, affirm the sacredness of the biblical texts not so much because the text itself affirms its divine origin, but because the Church's tradition—and in particular, her liturgy—vouches for their divine origin and sacredness. A methodology based only on the Scriptures' own attestation of their divine origin also sidesteps the question of how one might ascertain such the divine origin of the biblical books that make no such explicit claim. A clear biblical description of inspiration as such does emerge briefly in the consideration of 2 Timothy 3:15–16 and 2 Peter 1:20–21, but the resulting definition of inspiration is not integrated in any global way into the published document.[50]

In a final section claiming (unjustifiably, per Farkasfalvy[51]) to synthesize these biblical data, the essential description of inspiration that the Commission gives is that it "presents itself as a special relationship with God (or with Jesus) whereby he grants to a human author to relate—through his Spirit—that which he wishes to communicate to human beings." It then proceeds merely to repeat the relevant paragraph of the Dogmatic Constitution.[52] At its culmination, then, the document seems to offer little that is new and to fall short even of conveying in any comprehensive or compelling way what has already been articulated before it.

On the question of the inerrancy of Scripture, now rebranded as its "truth," Farkasfalvy recounts the Commission's debate while criticizing its misreading of *Dei verbum*, §11, seemingly to restrict biblical truth to certain affirmations made specifically "for the sake of our salvation," while arguing that the phrase *nostrae salutis causa* in the Latin text of *Dei verbum* clearly does not restrict the sense of *veritatem*, but modifies *consignari voluit*, thus expressing the intentionality of God's truth that is contained in the whole of Scripture.[53] Even if it locates the Bible's "truth" on a plane transcending the human authors' individual affirmations, *Dei verbum* therefore does not intend to confine biblical truth only to certain parts, as the PBC document suggests. Yet the PBC document suggests such a reading.[54]

Nowhere does the document address the problem of how such an apparent restriction of the Bible's "truth" is compatible with the divine inspiration of *all* Scripture, perhaps because the Commission's own articulation of the meaning

---

50. Farkasfalvy, *A Theology of the Christian Bible*, 56–57, 60–61.

51. Farkasfalvy, *A Theology of the Christian Bible*, 101–2.

52. *The Inspiration and Truth of Sacred Scripture*, §52.

53. Farkasfalvy, *A Theology of the Christian Bible*, 108–9.

54. *The Inspiration and Truth of Sacred Scripture*, §63; Farkasfalvy, *A Theology of the Christian Bible*, 108–9.

43

of inspiration is insufficiently precise to allow such a conflict to come into relief. Seemingly adhering to an understanding of biblical "truth" in the classical philosophical sense of *adaequatio mentis ad rem*—the correspondence of a proposition with some objective reality—it seeks to isolate those "true" affirmations of the salvific message from the broader context of a literary corpus where we also "encounter contradictions, historical inaccuracies, implausible narratives, and in the Old Testament, moral precepts and behavior in conflict with the teachings of Jesus."[55] The creation account in Genesis 1 is said to describe truthfully "not *how* the world came into being but *why* and *for what purpose* it is as it is."[56] Similarly, the Exodus account, it is said, "does not intend primarily to transmit a record of ancient events in the manner of an archival document but rather to call to mind a tradition which attests that today, as yesterday, God is present along with his people to save them."[57] Certainly, the purpose of the narrative does encompass all time and is addressed to readers of every era; but is not the reference to at least some truly historical kernel of the narrative also a necessary element? Without such, it would be difficult to ascertain the difference between historical revelation and pagan mythology.

While the plausible distinction between an actual historical nucleus and fictive narrative elements is left unspecified for the most part, in other instances it seems overstated—for example, when the figure of the Archangel Raphael in the Book of Tobit is rather boldly characterized as "a character of literary fiction."[58] Likewise, the destruction of Jericho by Joshua is dismissed as historically unreal.[59] Certainly, the correctness or incorrectness of this latter affirmation is a legitimate matter for debate, and various archaeological digs over some decades have yielded different conclusions in its regard. Even so, a casual dismissal of historicity without justification—ostensibly because such things do not happen "in a real war"—seems unhelpful and unnecessary for the purpose of suggesting that the perennial truth being affirmed here might lie on a different plane.

The document thus contents itself with a description of inerrancy designed primarily for ruling out a fundamentalist reading of the biblical text—i.e., one that could be described as "Monophysite" by analogy with Christology: that is, an interpretation ascribing uncritically to the divine author every affirmation

---

55. *The Inspiration and Truth of Sacred Scripture*, §104.
56. *The Inspiration and Truth of Sacred Scripture*, §1.
57. *The Inspiration and Truth of Sacred Scripture*, §108.
58. *The Inspiration and Truth of Sacred Scripture*, §109.
59. *The Inspiration and Truth of Sacred Scripture*, §128.

A Critical Appraisal of the Pontifical Biblical Commission's Document

precisely as intended by the human authors.[60] But the Commission seems to press this point at a considerable cost. Affirming the divine origin of the biblical text while seeking to avoid casting God as a "literary author" in a reductionistic sense, the attempt to describe inspiration as a function of the author's spiritual relationship with God also seems implausibly reductionistic in the opposite direction. One might say that in order to avoid a "Monophysite" notion of biblical inspiration and inerrancy, the document risks aligning itself instead with an analogically "Nestorian" manner, as if human authors enlisted as God's instruments accordingly only intermittently served as vehicles guaranteed to articulate propositions conforming objectively to the realities to which they refer.

Benedict XVI himself referred to the Christological analogy between the Incarnation and biblical inspiration in his Post-Synodal Apostolic Exhortation *Verbum Domini*. He wrote,

> Here too we can suggest an analogy: as the word of God became flesh by the power of the Holy Spirit in the womb of the Virgin Mary, so sacred Scripture is born from the womb of the Church by the power of the same Spirit. Sacred Scripture is "the word of God set down in writing under the inspiration of the Holy Spirit." In this way one recognizes the full importance of the human author who wrote the inspired texts and, at the same time, God himself as the true author.[61]

These words of Pope Benedict were written after he had already committed to the Commission the task of preparing the document, but early in the process of its elaboration. Such a notion of the analogy is found in the concluding section of *The Inspiration and Truth of Sacred Scripture*, albeit in a slightly different form:

> If we can restate the principle of incarnation, applying it analogously to the commitment to writing of divine revelation, it is also necessary to indicate how, in this very human weakness, the glory of the divine Word nonetheless shines forth.[62]

There is, however, an important difference between the application of the incarnational analogy by Benedict and by the Commission. The former applies it to the reality of the inspired word in its objective form, while the latter

---

60. This project is pursued with particular insistence in Part Three, "The Interpretation of the Word of God and its Challenges," the purpose of which is explicitly tied to the intention "to overcome fundamentalism: cf. *The Inspiration and Truth of Sacred Scripture*, General Introduction, §III.4.

61. Pope Benedict XVI, Post-Synodal Apostolic Exhortation *Verbum Domini* (September 30, 2010) (Washington, DC: United States Conference of Catholic Bishops, 2010), §19.

62. *The Inspiration and Truth of Sacred Scripture*, §149.

45

applies it to biblical inspiration in its subjective sense, to the *process* of "the commitment to writing of divine revelation." Even before the Synod began its work—indeed, even before Joseph Ratzinger had become Pope Benedict XVI—Farkasfalvy had pointed out that the elaboration of an adequate theology of inspiration would benefit greatly from the drawing of a clear "conceptual differentiation between the 'inspired authors' (subjective inspiration) and 'inspired texts.'"[63] He had observed that one weakness in *Dei verbum* itself had been that it "switches back and forth, meandering between inspired author and inspired texts," with the result that "the Christological analogy . . . becomes muddled, and we never know if it applies to the relationship of the two authors (divine and human) or to the inner layers of meaning in the scriptural text."[64] He pointed out in the same context that even though the application of the incarnational analogy to the "sacramental" or "theandric" structure of the *biblical word itself* as such has a rich history from patristic times, the usefulness of its application to the *relationship between the inspired human author and the Holy Spirit* remained to be seen. Indeed, the relative ineffectiveness of the analogy, thus applied, within the PBC document seems to bear out Farkasfalvy's doubts on the matter.

Conclusions

In summary, then: especially given many voices calling for a clarification of the Bible's inspiration and truth for more than half a century, the long-awaited discussion of these topics by the Pontifical Biblical Commission finally yielded a document that does not seem to add much to the previous discussion, or to provide needed nuance without contradiction of magisterial affirmations, noted above, regarding the inspiration of the whole of Scripture and the incompatibility of such inspiration with outright falsehood. Such would seem to have been precisely the task called for during the preparation of the Second Vatican Council and renewed in the 2008 Synod, and entrusted to the PBC. Even though none of the existing scholarly proposals regarding these concepts seems to have prevailed over the others in order to constitute real progress toward any sort of ecclesial consensus, the PBC document seems to proceed as if these proposals had never even existed.[65]

One avenue of thought within the existing literature that might have

63. Farkasfalvy, "How to Renew the Theology of Biblical Inspiration?," 242–43.
64. Farkasfalvy, "How to Renew the Theology of Biblical Inspiration?," 243.
65. Cf. footnote 10 above.

A Critical Appraisal of the Pontifical Biblical Commission's Document

provided a particularly promising invitation to the kind of nuance needed for clarifying the concepts of biblical inspiration and truth was the 1974 study of Oswald Loretz entitled *Das Ende der Inspirations-Theologie: Chancen eines Neubeginns*.[66] Perhaps the noteworthiest aspect of Loretz's contribution is his manner of characterizing the "pseudo-problem of the absolute inerrancy of Holy Scripture." Loretz's language regarding the "end of inspiration theology" and this "pseudo-problem" of inerrancy seems consciously intended to shock, but the interest thus aroused is not disappointed as one realizes that the "end" heralded by him is for the sake of a fresh new beginning, and that the problem of biblical truth is a "pseudo-problem" only insofar as it continues to be cast uncritically in terms alien to the Bible's own world of thought. What he is asserting in this regard emerges from his observation that

> In the Semitic culture of the Ancient Near East and among the Israelites, the opposition of truth/error plays no essential role. The Semitic-biblical concept of truth highlights instead the opposition between truth and lie.
>
> For the Semites of the Ancient Near East that which is *true* (*'emeth*) is something constant, loyal, dependable. In opposition and contradiction to truth stands therefore what is *passing, changing, deceitful*, or a lie. In accordance with this understanding of truth, the Holy Scripture would be *untrue* if it were uttered by a disloyal, fickle God who did not stand behind his own word. . . . In this perspective of the biblical notion of truth, it is irrelevant [to ask] whether there are contained in the Bible errors that do not concern what the Bible understands as the truthfulness of God and his word. . . . Thus, it is evident that neither the Greek vision of the problem of truth (*alêtheia*) nor the Scholastic and theological concept of truth (*adaequatio intellectus et rei*) is identical with the Semitic-biblical conception of truth. For the *biblical question* there arises, then, the essential realization that the

---

66 The work has already been cited above several times, but it will perhaps be useful to repeat it here: Oswald Loretz, *Das Ende der Inspirations-Theologie: Chancen eines Neubeginns*, vol. 1, *Untersuchungen zur Entwicklung der traditionellen theologischen Lehre über die Inspiration der Heiligen Schrift* (Stuttgart: Verlag Katholisches Bibelwerk, 1974). The work provides a very helpful history of the whole problem of biblical inspiration, beginning with a brief sketch of the early Christian and patristic landscape, but focusing primarily on the period after the Councils of Florence and Trent, encompassing also the fruitful tensions between theology and the natural sciences in this regard in the wake of the "Copernican Revolution" and the writings of Galileo Galilei and Johannes Kepler. Loretz's historical survey is more condensed and coherent even than Burtchaell's English-language study, also cited previously, *Catholic Theories of Biblical Inspiration since 1810*. The second volume of Loretz's work is comprised of a collection of documentation on biblical inspiration including papal and conciliar statements as well as their background drafts and progressive emendations. A review of the work is given by Francis Schussler Fiorenza in *The Catholic Biblical Quarterly* 42 (1980): 126–28.

problem *truth[fulness] of God / absolute inerrancy of Holy Scripture* ulti-mately constitutes a pseudo-problem that can arise only when the biblical question of truth is distorted by being cast into categories taken from the non-biblical and non-Semitic culture of late antiquity and of Europe.[67]

Wherever such a line of reasoning might eventually lead in terms of a theology of biblical inspiration and truth, Loretz's contribution—over and above his comprehensive historical survey of various attempts to clarify the theology of inspiration—illustrates that even before any attempt can be made to respond to the various questions that arise concerning these concepts, the underlying terms themselves can and must be examined. Yet the PBC clearly has not undertaken—let alone succeeded in—any such project. By limiting its field of inquiry to the biblical texts themselves and proceeding on the basis of their occasional assertions regarding own divine origin—a survey that com-prises roughly half of the entire document—the Commission sidesteps nearly two thousand years of ecclesial reflection on biblical inspiration and truth, beginning with the patristic era. Ironically, while seeking primarily to protect Catholic biblical studies from a fundamentalist reading, the Commission seems to adopt (at least methodologically) the very presupposition underlying Fun-damentalism itself: namely, that the Bible stands alone to vouch for its own authenticity and divine origin.

The testimony of Tradition and of recent theology is omitted from the PBC's attempt to address the task before it. The Commission states outright that it has no intention of entering into debates with academic theories of inspi-ration found in theological manuals, but it refrains altogether from any serious analysis of the theological dimension. It does not treat of past or existing the-ories of inspiration except to reject a notion of outright dictation in keeping with *Dei verbum*, §11. Its methodology is thoroughly untheological even while attempting to clarify one of the most important doctrines of fundamental the-ology. In fairness, the PBC was perhaps the wrong body to undertake such a project by itself, but that cannot be considered the fault of the members who simply set about to do what they were asked.

The Commission does examine at length the real contributions of the human authors and the engagement of their own creativity which was not sup-pressed by their enlistment in the composition of God's own word to human beings. Even so, a strong preoccupation with the human subjectivity of these authors turns out to be the real Achilles' heel of the document and a hindrance

---

67. Loretz, *Das Ende der Inspirations-Theologie*, 164–65 (the translation is by the present writer).

A *Critical Appraisal of the Pontifical Biblical Commission's Document*

to its effectiveness in clarifying the doctrine of inspiration. As Farkasfalvy had pointed out, the document's treatment is so heavily focused on the subjective *process* of biblical inspiration—approaching even this by a very flawed methodology incorporating as data only the Bible's own assertions—that it lacks much reflection on the objective existence throughout all ages of an *inspired text* in which God's Spirit continues to speak directly even now to devout readers. The importance of scientific methods of exegesis is underscored effectively by the document's emphasis on the importance of the human authors' contribution in its finite, time-bound context. But a rather humanistic articulation of the notion seems insufficient here for explaining why the inspired text must always be read not just with the aid of these methods, but "in the same spirit in which it is written" (*Dei verbum*, §12). In fairness, the document does cite this admonition of the Council in its conclusion of Part One (§53), admitting that "modern exegetical methods cannot take the place of faith" in biblical interpretation.

Such a treatment of inspiration has its effect also on what the document has to say about the "truth" of the Bible. Resting as heavily as it does upon subjectivity of the human authors, the document's attempted clarification of biblical truth is predisposed thereby to exhaust itself, in its Third Part (§§104–36), in the enumeration and handling of problematic passages exemplifying flawed and limited perspectives that must be sifted away like chaff in order to highlight the essential divine message. Some attention to the Fathers' understanding of Sacred Scripture, entailing an application of the analogy of the Incarnate Word to the *biblical text itself* rather than simply to the process of writing, might have been very helpful in bringing about a document that could escape such a deficit. But a relative lack of attention to the patristic heritage seems to have dogged the Commission at other times even despite the regular thorough renewal of its entire membership. For example, Farkasfalvy had criticized the Commission's earlier document on "Jews and Christians and their Scriptures" for the same reason.[68]

If the document had focused more effectively on the reality of the inspired text as such, which the Holy Spirit continues to inhabit and through which he continues to speak, it might have been able to probe more deeply the way in

---

68. Farkasfalvy, *A Theology of the Christian Bible*, 66n9. He relates that in his article "The Pontifical Biblical Commission's Document on Jews and Christians and Their Scriptures: Evaluation," *Communio* 29, no. 4 (2002): 716–37, "I pointed out how, in a collective document, distinguished Catholic biblical scholars remained inflexible in expressing a wholesale rejection of Origen's spiritual exegesis, as if the patristic renewal and its early alliance with the biblical renewal had never existed."

MICHAEL K. MAGEE

which God has uttered and still utters his truth not only in those isolated parts found to be unmarred by the time-bound and flawed human perspectives of its writers, but through every part including these, even as the fragility and wounds of the Word Incarnate were no less expressive of the Savior's interiority than were his eyes and lips that only ever spoke the unalloyed truth.

3. The Divine Voice of Sinai in Emended Scripture

Matthew C. Genung

In *The Inspiration and Truth of Sacred Scripture,* the Pontifical Biblical Commission recommends considering Exodus 19 to be at the head of the pericope which is "the basis for understanding the Bible as the word of God."[1] This chapter is the beginning of the pivotal pericope in which YHWH offers to enter into a covenant with Israel, a covenant which is solemnly ratified at Mount Sinai in Exodus 24. The result of the pericope is that Israel is constituted as God's people, with a written Torah and an institution of mediation between God and Israel within which to live this covenant. This foundational event is recounted in a particular way in Exodus 19 as God's self-revelation to and election of Israel as his own people, with Moses as the mediator of the divine word.

Coinciding with the account of Israel's constitution is the account of the origin of Israel's Scriptures. At one crucial point during the theophany, the divine speech is characterized as speaking "with a voice" (Exod 19:19).[2] The PBC document asserts that God's speaking to Moses "with a voice" underpins the notion of divine condescension, by which the transcendent God reveals himself in ways that are able to be received and appropriated by man in his historical and contingent condition.[3] The Bible has its origin in God, and is at the same

---

1. Pontifical Biblical Commission, *The Inspiration and Truth of Sacred Scripture: The Word That Comes from God and Speaks of God for the Salvation of the World,* trans. Thomas Esposito and Stephen Gregg (Collegeville, MN: Liturgical Press, 2014), §11. The PBC document makes reference to Exod 19–Num 10 and Deut 5ff. This paper will focus on Exod 19–24 because in this pericope what was revealed from the beginning takes a written form in Exod 24.

2. Biblical translations are my own, unless otherwise noted. My translations are based on Karl Elliger, Wilhelm Rudolph, eds., *Biblia Hebraica Stuttgartensia,* 4th ed. (Stuttgart: Deutsche Bibelgesellschaft, 1997).

3. *The Inspiration and Truth of Sacred Scripture,* §11. On *synkatabasis,* the Fathers of the Second Vatican Council draw on St. John Chrysostom's homily that comments on a principle

MATTHEW C. GENUNG

time written in a human form. At the conclusion of the pericope, during the covenant ratification ceremony, we are told that Moses wrote down "all the words of YHWH" (Exod 24:4), a writing called "the book of the covenant" (סֵפֶר הַבְּרִית, sēper habbĕrît) (v. 7). According to the narrative, the book of the covenant is a record of all the words spoken by God (cf. 19:8) and then written down by Moses at Sinai.[4]

The text that we read in our Bibles, or at least the legal portions of it,[5] is traditionally considered to be the *sēper* referred to in the text itself, the book of the covenant, depicted as having been written by Moses.[6] In contrast to this tradition, historical-critical scholarship has shown that the text before us is composite, having arisen from a much more complicated compositional history than the narrative portrays. This historical-critical position raises the hermeneutical question about the meaning of a redacted text claiming to originate in the context of theophanic divine revelation (Exod 19:19) and the immediate scripturalization of the entirety of its contents (Exod 24:4).

Taking the cue of the PBC document, this paper attempts to show that the narrative itself, illuminated by the historical-critical method, supplies the clues

needed to properly interpret Gen 3:8, specifically the attribution of legs to God who walks in the Garden of Eden during the heat of the day. According to St. John, the anthropomorphic portrayal of the divinity is not to be taken literally, but is rather a symbolic form of writing in which God reveals something about himself and his plan for creation in such fashion that the hearers of this passage are able to receive. The biblical text in question, which for St. John is divinely inspired and does participate in God's self-revelation, shows that God stoops to the level of the limited creature in order to communicate with him. This must be so, because God is omnipresent, and not confined to a garden. See Second Vatican Council, *Dei verbum* (November 18, 1965), pp. 817–35 in *Acta Apostolicae Sedis* 58 (1966), §13.

4. God is also a writer of some biblical texts: Exod 24:12; 31:18; 32:16; 34:1, 28; Deut 4:13; 9:10; 10:3. These texts indicate that God is the writer of the Torah (or teaching) and commandments in general (Exod 24:12), or the Decalogue in particular (Exod 34:28; Deut 4:13; 10:4). The PBC considers this the first of two ways the Pentateuch witnesses to its divine origin. The second way is Mosaic mediation. See *The Inspiration and Truth of Sacred Scripture*, §12.

5. Specifically, the so-called Covenant Code of Exod 20:22–23:33. This legal corpus gets its name from Exod 24:7. The only instance of the word 'covenant' (*bĕrît*) in Exod 20:22–23:33 is in 23:32, a prohibition against covenant making with foreign gods.

6. On the tradition of Mosaic authorship of the Pentateuch, see C. Houtman, *Der Pentateuch: Die Geschichte seiner Erforschung neben einer Auswertung*, CBET 9 (Kampen: Kok Pharos, 1994), 7–27; Christoph Dohmen, "'Mose schrieb diese Tora auf' (Dtn 31,9): Auf der Suche nach dem biblischen Ursprung der Vorstellung der mosaischen Verfasserschaft des Pentateuch," 256–65 in *"Gerechtigkeit und Recht zu üben" (Gen 18,19): Studien zur altorientalischen und biblischen Rechtsgeschichte, zur Religionsgeschichte Israels und zur Religionssoziologie. Festschrift für Eckart Otto zum 65. Geburtstag*, eds. Reinhard Achenbach and Eckart Otto, BZAR 13 (Wiesbaden: Harrassowitz, 2009).

The Divine Voice of Sinai in Emended Scripture

to understand its character as the word of God communicated and received over a different history than the story seems to indicate. This will be done by briefly surveying the aspects of the text that betray its redactional nature and identifying some important redactional additions, specifically the communicative symbolism within the theophany of Exodus 19. Next, the liturgical and religious features of the text will be discussed, showing that the mountain and the theophany which prefigure the Jerusalem temple, its cult, and its authority, prefigure the locus for Israel's continual hearing of and responding to divine revelation. This is manifested in the writing and revising of these sacred texts. While the writing of these texts is referred to at the close of the pericope in Exodus 24, the symbols in the narrative of the theophany in Exodus 19 point to the authority of their revision. These religious and cultic symbols indicate the theology of revelation and the institutional framework which both motivated and authorized its various redactional stages throughout its compositional history. Important hermeneutical conclusions should inform Catholic exegesis. The PBC's statement that "the concept of 'scripture' . . . is connected in a special way to the mediator of revelation, Moses" should be expanded to include the subsequent redactors of the canonical text.[7] The nature of Scripture as the word of God mediated in human form should be understood not only in relation to the linguistic form of Scripture, as human discourse, but also to its scriptural form as redactionally shaped over the course of Israel's history and in the context of its religious development.

1. The Compositional Character of Exodus 19

The first task is to briefly demonstrate the redactional character of Exodus 19. Even though most modern commentators agree that the text is composite, the details of its compositional history are not agreed upon.[8] Emblematic of the

---

7. *The Inspiration and Truth of Sacred Scripture*, §12.

8. The bibliography is vast. The classic text frequently referred to is Walter Beyerlin, *Origins and History of the Oldest Sinaitic Traditions* (Oxford: Basil Blackwell, 1965). See also Julius Wellhausen, *Die Composition des Hexateuchs und der historischen Bücher des Alten Testaments*, 3rd ed. (Berlin: Georg Reimer, 1899), 334; Martin Noth, *Exodus: A Commentary*, OTL (Philadelphia: Westminster, 1962), 153–55; Brevard S. Childs, *The Book of Exodus: A Critical, Theological Commentary*, OTL (Philadelphia: Westminster, 1974), 344–47; Thomas B. Dozeman, *God on the Mountain: A Study of Redaction, Theology, and Canon in Exodus 19–24*, SBLMS 37 (Atlanta: Scholars Press, 1989); Erhard Blum, *Studien zur Komposition des Pentateuch*, BZAW 189 (Berlin: Walter de Gruyter, 1990), 45–47; Bernard Renaud, *La théophanie du Sinaï: Exod 19–24: Exégèse et théologie*, CRB 30 (Paris: J. Gabalda, 1991); Cornelis Houtman, *Exodus*, vol. 2, *Chapters 7:14–19:25*, HCOT (Leuven: Peeters, 1993), 426–28; Erich Zenger, "Wie und wozu die

situation is this statement from Propp: "The Horeb-Sinai narrative will always frustrate our attempts to understand its composition history."[9] Nevertheless, some of the later additions can be identified with a high degree of probability.

The main elements within the text that specialists refer to regarding its disunity are what are sometimes considered doublets, as well as tensions in the logical coherence of the narrative.[10]

1.1 Doublets in Exodus 19

The following elements of the passage are often considered doublets. There are two itinerary notices, one in v. 1 and a second in v. 2. The passage uses two different names for God, YHWH (vv. 3, 7–11, 18, 20–24) and Elohim (vv. 3, 17, 19), without a clear reason for the variation in usage. The people either fear approaching the mountain (20:18), or need to be commanded not to approach the mountain under threat of death (19:12–13, 21). The theophany takes place with storm imagery (19:16–17, 19), and with volcanic imagery (v. 18). Moses already acts as mediator throughout chapter 19, but in 20:18–20, as a result of the theophany, the people request that he become a mediator. These doublets seem to indicate textual disunity.

Tora zum Sinai kam: Literarische und theologische Beobachtungen zu Exodus 19–34," 265–88 in *Studies in the Book of Exodus: Redaction – Reception – Interpretation*, ed. Marc Vervenne, BETL 126 (Leuven: Peeters, 1996); Joseph Blenkinsopp, "What Happened at Sinai? Structure and Meaning in the Sinai-Horeb Narrative (Exodus 19–34)," 155–74 in *Treasures Old and New: Essays in the Theology of the Pentateuch* (Grand Rapids: Eerdmans, 2004); Georg Fischer and Dominik Markl, *Das Buch Exodus*, NSK.AT 2 (Stuttgart: Verlag Katholisches Bibelwerk, 2009); Christoph Dohmen, *Exodus 19–40*, 2nd ed., HThKAT (Freiburg: Herder, 2012).

9. William H. Propp, *Exodus 19–40: A New Translation with Introduction and Commentary*, AncB 2A (New York: Doubleday, 2006), 141.

10. For arguments based on external evidence that support late redactional activity of the pentateuchal texts, see for example, on textual criticism, Emanuel Tov, "The Development of the Text of the Torah in Two Major Text Blocks," *Textus* 26 (2016): 1–27. On scribalism in ancient Israel, see André Lemaire, *Les écoles et la formation de la Bible dans l'ancien Israël*, OBO 39 (Fribourg: Vandenhoeck & Ruprecht, 1981); David W. Jamieson-Drake, *Scribes and Schools in Monarchic Judah: A Socio-Archeological Approach*, JSOTSup 109 (Sheffield: Almond Press, 1991); David M. Carr, *Writing on the Tablet of the Heart: Origins of Scripture and Literature* (New York: Oxford University Press, 2005); Karel van der Toorn, *Scribal Culture and the Making of the Hebrew Bible* (Cambridge, MA: Harvard University Press, 2007); Christopher A. Rollston, *Writing and Literacy in the World of Ancient Israel: Epigraphic Evidence from the Iron Age*, ABSt (Leiden: Brill, 2010); Christopher A. Rollston, "Inscriptional Evidence for the Writing of the Earliest Texts of the Bible," 15–45 in *The Formation of the Pentateuch: Bridging the Academic Cultures of Europe, Israel, and North America*, eds. Jan C. Gertz, Bernard M. Levinson, Dalit Rom-Shiloni, and Konrad Schmid, FAT 111 (Tübingen: Mohr Siebeck, 2016).

The Divine Voice of Sinai in Emended Scripture

1.2 Inconsistencies in Moses' Location and Movement in Exodus 19

There are tensions in the location and movement of both God and Moses. In vv. 3 and 18, God is already present on the mountain, but later in v. 20 he descends onto the mountain. According to many commentators, Moses' ascending and descending causes confusion. He ascends in v. 3a, but in v. 3b God calls to him from the mountain as though he were below. When Moses relates the divine message to the people in v. 7, he "came to them" (בוא, bw'). This verb never indicates descending motion in the Bible. Moses again ascends and descends the mountain to deliver messages in vv. 14, 20, and 25, but in vv. 7, 8, and 9 Moses relays messages back and forth between God and the people without ascending or descending. A similar difficulty of location is seen at the extremities of the revelation of the Covenant Code (Exod 20:22–23:33). In Exodus 20:21 we read that "Moses approached the dark cloud where God was." It is not stated that Moses ascended the mountain, but the location of the cloud on the mountain would imply this (cf. Exod 19:9, 11). After the conclusion of God's communication of the Covenant Code to Moses, Moses is told to ascend to the Lord (Exod 24:1), which assumes he was not already there. These tensions in Moses' location and movements also seem to indicate disunity.

1.3 Literary Tensions in Exodus 19

There are also literary tensions in Exodus 19. For example, vv. 8–9 and vv. 20–24 each present repeated narrative notices or discourses that lack coherence with their contexts, v. 13b narrates a divine command in tension with its context, and 19:25–20:1 contains an anacoluthon.

1.3.1 Repetition of the Narrative Report in Exodus 19:8–9

First, Exodus 19:8–9 contains a repetition, in that v. 9b repeats v. 8b without following the logic of the intervening action.

> ⁸And the entire people answered together and said, "Everything that YHWH said we shall do." *And Moses brought the words of the people back to YHWH.* ⁹And YHWH said to Moses, "Now, I am about to come to you in the dense cloud so that the people will hear my speaking with you and will really trust you forever." *And Moses announced the words of the people to YHWH.* ¹⁰And YHWH said to Moses, "Go to the people and sanctify them today and tomorrow, and they shall wash their clothes . . ."

The second notice that Moses related the people's response to YHWH does not logically cohere with what precedes or with what follows. There is nothing new for Moses to report; rather, intervening between the two identical notices is divine discourse. However, without v. 9b the context is coherent.

MATTHEW C. GENUNG

1.3.2 *Exodus 19:13b*
Similarly, a tension arises when reading v. 13b in its context:

> [11]They shall be ready for the third day, because on the third day YHWH will descend before the eyes of all the people upon Mount Sinai. [12]And bound the people all around, saying, "Be on guard going up to the mountain and touching its edge. All who touch the mountain will be put to death. [13]No hand shall strike him, but he shall be stoned or shot, whether beast or man; he shall not live. *When the horn (yôbel) sounds, they will go up the mountain."* [14]And Moses descended from the mountain to the people and sanctified the people and they washed their clothes. [15]And he said to the people, "Be ready for three days. Do not approach a woman."

The main problems with v. 13b are three. First, the text seems to contradict what was just stated. According to vv. 12–13a, no one is to approach the mountain under penalty of death. This is the message Moses is commanded to convey, and it is dutifully executed. Secondly, no *yôbel* ever sounds, but a shofar sounds. Why is the shofar not called a *yôbel*? When the shofar does sound, no group ascends the mountain. Rather, v. 17 states that they take their stand at the base of the mountain as commanded. This is not what is commanded in v. 13b, even though the temptation is to read it as such. Thirdly, who is referred to by "they"? From what has preceded, there is no logical answer. The only plausible solution is to look to contexts from the narrative as it proceeds, in which case it could refer to the priests mentioned in Exodus 19:22, or Aaron, Nadab, Abihu, and the seventy elders. This group does ascend the mountain with Moses, but not until after the completion of the theophany and YHWH's further communication of the Covenant Code to Moses (Exod 24:1, 9–11). This seems what the text most likely has in mind, but within the current context it is difficult to comprehend.

1.3.3. *Divine Command and Execution in Exodus 19:20–24*
There is also a difficulty in understanding the repetition of a divine command that had already been fulfilled. In Exodus 19:20–24, God calls Moses up the mountain only to tell him to descend to repeat a command which had already been given to Moses, communicated to the people, and even fulfilled by them.

> [20]And YHWH descended on Mount Sinai, to the peak of the mountain, and YHWH called to Moses to the peak of the mountain; and Moses ascended. [21]And YHWH said to Moses, "Descend, warn the people lest they break through to YHWH to see and many of them fall. [22]And even the priests approaching YHWH must keep themselves sanctified, lest YHWH break out against them. [23]And Moses said to YHWH, "The people is not able to

The Divine Voice of Sinai in Emended Scripture

ascend to Mount Sinai since you warned us, saying 'bound the mountain and sanctify it.'" [24]And YHWH said to him, "Go, descend, and ascend you and Aaron with you, and the priests and the people must not break through to ascend to YHWH lest he break out against them."

There are significant variations in the command, but in v. 23 Moses responds to the effect that the command has already been given and followed. This problem will be taken up below.

1.3.4 Anacoluthon of Exodus 19:25–20:1

The transition from Exodus 19:25 to 20:1 is incoherent. The text of Exodus 19:25–20:1 reads:

> [25]Moses descended to the people and he said to them. [1]And God spoke all of these words.

The Decalogue follows (Exod 20:1–17). According to the rules of Hebrew grammar, one would expect the content of Moses' discourse to be reported after what is read in v. 25, but instead the text reports that God spoke. When read in light of Deuteronomy 5:4–5, the reaction of the people in Exodus 20:18–21 is to the Decalogue which was spoken directly to the people without the mediation of Moses.

These are some of the main tensions in the passage which have given rise to a variety of theories on the compositional history of the text. Not all of these so-called tensions indicate disunity for all commentators.[11] It is, however, widely agreed upon that the text does not arise from a single author. What has not been reached is a consensus on the strata and the literary-historical relationship among them. According to some, the text is a composition from once independent, complete versions of the same story, later redacted together.[12] The main difficulty with this Documentary Hypothesis is the impossibility of reconstructing the strata into coherent versions. According to others, we are dealing with a narrative that has been reworked one or more times with textual insertions of greater or lesser extent, a theory generally referred to as _Fortschreibung_, or _redactional expansion_.

---

11. For synchronic approaches to the text, see Gregory C. Chirichigno, "The Narrative Structure of Exod 19–24," _Biblica_ 68 (1987): 457–79; André Wénin, "La théophanie du Sinaï (Ex 19,9–20,21): Une approche narrative," 57–77 in _Voir les dieux, voir Dieu_, eds. Françoise Dunand and François Boespflug (Strasbourg: Presses Universitaires de Strasbourg, 2002).

12. See note 8 for bibliography.

MATTHEW C. GENUNG

1.4 Redactional Expansions in Exodus 19

1.4.1 Wiederaufnahme *of Exodus 19:9*
One of the clearer examples of redactional expansion is Exodus 19:9, which was inserted using the common scribal technique known as *Wiederaufnahme,* or resumptive repetition.[13] The expansion literally reads:

> And YHWH said to Moses, "Now, I am about to come to you in the dense cloud so that the people will hear me speaking with you and will really trust you *forever*."[14]

This verse provides a strong link between the revelatory events of Sinai and the *lasting* recognition of Mosaic authority, as well as the place of the cloud in this Mosaic institution. The cloud will be discussed below.

1.4.2 *Exodus 19:20–25, an Example of* Fortschreibung
Also rather clear is Exodus 19:20–25, which expands the similar command in vv. 12–13, but includes priests in the list of those who must be sanctified. A specific class of priests is not defined until after the Golden Calf incident, in Exodus 32:26–29. Instead, according to Exodus 19:6, the entire people are conceived of as priests.[15] The command is anachronistic. This expansion also makes it clear that the mountain itself is the holy place, since in these verses Moses incorrectly repeats the previous divine command, recounted in vv. 10–12. In those earlier verses, God commands that *the people* be sanctified and then cordoned off, lest they approach the mountain and be killed, whereas in v. 23 Moses claims to the Lord that he had commanded that *the mountain* itself be cordoned off and sanctified. The terminology is the same, but the objects are different. Furthermore, the command of vv. 10–12 is fulfilled in v. 14, but the command as worded in vv. 20–24 is not reported as fulfilled. It seems likely

---

13. The *resumptive repetition,* or *Wiederaufnahme,* consists in the repetition of a previous phrase after an inserted text in order to facilitate the insertion of something new and to resume the flow of the original context. On this technique, see Jean-Louis Ska, *Introduction to Reading the Pentateuch* (Winona Lake, IN: Eisenbrauns, 2006), 77–82, with bibliography. For a brief survey of more conservative solutions, see Childs, *The Book of Exodus,* 374–75.

14. It is unfortunate that the NABRE does not translate לְעוֹלָם, lĕ'ôlām, which means "forever." Other modern translations do.

15. On the interpretation of this phrase, see Jean-Louis Ska, "Exodus 19:3–6 and the Identity of Post-Exilic Israel," 147–53 in *The Exegesis of the Pentateuch: Exegetical Studies and Basic Questions,* FAT 66 (Tübingen: Mohr Siebeck, 2009), with extensive bibliography. A classic study to be consulted is William L. Moran, "'A Kingdom of Priests,'" 7–20 in *The Bible in Current Catholic Thought,* ed. John L. McKenzie, Saint Mary's Theology Studies 1 (New York: Herder, 1962).

that Exodus 19:20–25 was inserted into a previous narrative in order to create a clear link between the priesthood as it functioned in the postexilic period and the sacred space where it functions with the Sinai revelation.[16]

1.4.3 The Decalogue

A third expansion to consider here is the Decalogue itself, Exodus 20:1–17.[17] The tension between Exodus 19:25 and 20:1 was noted above. The following verses, Exodus 20:18–21, recount the reaction of the people, which rather than a reaction to the Decalogue is a reaction to the elements of the theophany which preceded it. Exodus 20:18 recounts that the people witnessed the thunder, lightning, the shofar blast, and the mountain smoking. These are the details of the theophany according to Exodus 19:16–19. The people reacted by trembling, similar to the trembling mountain in Exodus 19:18. There is no clear reaction to the contents of the Decalogue which intervenes. The response of the people is loosely tied to the Decalogue because of the narrative sequence, but explicitly tied to the theophanic phenomena.

This brief survey of some recent scholarly positions presents some arguments only to demonstrate the redactional character of these texts. Recent scholarship shows that these texts were composed in the postexilic period, with the latest redactions dating well into the Hellenistic Period.[18]

2. Cultic Symbols on the Mountain in Exodus 19

The book of Exodus begins with Israel enslaved and oppressed in Egypt, *serving* Pharaoh and living among a pantheon of false gods.[19] The entire exodus

16. Childs, *The Book of Exodus*, 361–64; Renaud, *La théophanie du Sinaï*, 169–73.

17. Childs, *The Book of Exodus*, 391–401; Renaud, *La théophanie du Sinaï*, 75–77; Dominik Markl, "The Ten Words Revealed and Revised: The Origins of Law and Legal Hermeneutics in the Pentateuch," 13–27 in *The Decalogue and Its Cultural Influence*, ed. Dominik Markl, HBM 58 (Sheffield: Sheffield Phoenix, 2013).

18. See Jean-Louis Ska, "From History Writing to Library Building: The End of History and the Birth of the Book," 145–69 in *The Pentateuch as Torah: New Models for Understanding Its Promulgation and Acceptance*, ed. Gary N. Knoppers and Bernard M. Levinson (Winona Lake, IN: Eisenbrauns, 2007). On the dating of biblical texts, see Konrad Schmid, *The Old Testament: A Literary History* (Minneapolis: Fortress, 2012); Thomas Römer, "How to Date Pentateuchal Texts: Some Case Studies," 357–70 in *The Formation of the Pentateuch: Bridging the Academic Cultures of Europe, Israel, and North America*, eds. Jan C. Gertz, Bernard M. Levinson, Dalit Rom-Shiloni, and Konrad Schmid, FAT 111 (Tübingen: Mohr Siebeck, 2016).

19. The key word עבד,'bd in Exodus is translated variously as to serve, to be a slave, and to worship. At the beginning of the book, Israel serves Pharaoh. From the middle of the book, Israel begins to serve YHWH.

MATTHEW C. GENUNG

event is motivated toward the goal of Israel knowing and serving the one true and mighty God. The symbolic function of the mountain is nowhere clearer than in Exodus 3:12. In response to Moses' query about him leading Israel out of Egypt, God replies:

> "Because I will be with you, and this will be the sign to you that it is I who sent you. When I make you bring the people out of Egypt, you all will worship (*serve*) God at this mountain."

The first purpose of the mountain is said to be a sign of God's active presence in and through Moses and the people.

In Exodus 19–24, Mount Sinai becomes the primordial place of divine revelation and liturgical communion between God and Israel. But Sinai is not the definitive locus of such religion. The book of Exodus concludes with YHWH taking up his dwelling in the tabernacle (Exod 40:34–35). Some of the main phenomena pertaining to the theophany on Mount Sinai are present in and fulfill similar roles later in the story, specifically in the tabernacle and the temple. Not only does this indicate continuity from Sinai to the tent and then the temple as the loci of divine revelation, but it also creates continuity between the content and authority of the word revealed in these respective places.[20] Three of these phenomena illustrate this continuity, namely the cloud, the shofar, and the preparation of the people for the theophany.

2.1 The Cloud

The dense cloud in Exodus 19:9 functions as a sign of the divine presence.[21] In this verse, YHWH tells Moses that he is about to come to him in *a dense cloud*, a syntagma which is a *hapax legomenon*, and is not easy to translate.[22] The LXX considers this to be the same cloud pillar which had already accompanied Israel beginning with its departure from Egypt.[23] The divine manifestation in the pillar of cloud and fire serves to guide Israel from Egypt toward the Promised

---

20. On the relationship between the tabernacle and the temples in Jerusalem, see Dominik Markl, "The Wilderness Sanctuary as the Archetype of Continuity Between the Pre- and Postexilic Temples of Jerusalem," 227–51 in *The Fall of Jerusalem and the Rise of the Torah*, ed. Peter Dubovský, Dominik Markl, and Jean-Pierre Sonnet, FAT 107 (Tübingen: Mohr Siebeck, 2016).

21. For the cloud as a common symbol of divine presence in Canaanite religion and the Old Testament, see Richard J. Clifford, *The Cosmic Mountain in Canaan and the Old Testament* (Cambridge, MA: Harvard University Press, 1972), 112.

22. The MT reads בְּעַב הֶעָנָן (*bĕ'ab he'ānān*).

23. The LXX translates the unique MT syntagma as στύλῳ νεφέλης (*stylō nephelēs*). The pillar of cloud, עַמּוּד עָנָן (*'ammûd 'ānān*), is found together with the pillar of fire, עַמּוּד אֵשׁ (*'ammûd 'ēš*), in Exod 13:21, 22; 14:19, 24; Num 14:14; and Neh 9:12, 19. See also Ps 99:7.

60

The Divine Voice of Sinai in Emended Scripture

Land and to protect Israel on the way. In other texts, this cloud pillar indicates the divine presence at the tent of meeting when YHWH speaks to Moses (Exod 33:9–10), when he confirms Moses' prophetic authority as superior to Aaron and Miriam (Num 12:5), and when YHWH commissions Joshua as Moses' successor (Deut 31:15). In Exodus 19:9, the divine announcement that YHWH will come in a dense cloud is fulfilled during the theophany, along with the thunder, lightning, fire, smoke, and shofar (Exod 19:16).

The glory of YHWH had settled (שכן, škn) on Mount Sinai in this dense cloud which covered it (כסה, ksh). It is from this cloud that he called (קרא, qrʼ) to Moses. Beginning in Exodus 40:34 the cloud now covers (כסה, ksh) the tabernacle, and the glory of YHWH fills the dwelling within it (שכן, škn). From this tabernacle YHWH now calls (קרא, qrʼ) to Moses (Lev 1:1). From the end of the book of Exodus until the end of the Pentateuch, Moses and the people no longer interact with God on the mountain, but rather at/in the tabernacle.[24]

So already within the book of Exodus the mountain gives way to the tabernacle, of which it is a model (cf. Exod 26:30). The tabernacle is eventually replaced by the temple in Jerusalem (1 Kgs 8:6–11).[25]

> [6]Then the priests brought the ark of the covenant of the Lord to its place, in the inner sanctuary of the house, in the most holy place . . . [10]And when the priests came out of the holy place, a cloud filled the house of the Lord, [11]so that the priests could not stand to minister because of the cloud; for the glory of the Lord filled the house of the Lord.

The presence and function of the dense cloud on Sinai first prefigures the tabernacle, then the temple.[26] The temple becomes the great symbol of God's active presence among his people.

---

24. When YHWH takes up his dwelling in the tabernacle in Exodus, Moses is not yet able to enter (Exod 40:35). In Lev 1:1, YHWH speaks to Moses *from* the tabernacle. It is not until Num 1.1 that YHWH speaks to Moses *in* the tabernacle.

25. *The Holy Bible: New Revised Standard Version, Catholic Edition* (Washington, DC: National Council of Churches of Christ, 1993). For texts that link theophany with Zion and the temple, see Judg 5:4–5; 2 Sam 22:8–20; Pss 2; 18:8–20; 29; 50:1–3; 68:8–9; Hab 3:3–15. On this in the Psalms, see Sigmund Mowinckel, *The Psalms in Israel's Worship*, vol. 1 (Oxford: Basil Blackwell, 1962), 156–58.

26. See Richard J. Clifford, "The Temple and the Holy Mountain," 107–24 in *The Temple in Antiquity*, ed. Truman G. Madsen, RSMS 9 (Provo, UT: Brigham Young University, 1984); Jon D. Levenson, *Sinai and Zion: An Entry into the Hebrew Bible* (New York: Harper One, 1985), 89–184; L. Michael Morales, *The Tabernacle Pre-Figured: Cosmic Mountain Ideology in Genesis and Exodus*, BToSt 15 (Leuven: Peeters, 2012), 253–57.

2.2 The Voice of the Shofar

The theophanic images recounted in Exodus 19:16–19 include the blast of the shofar. This shofar sound accompanies the thunder, lightning, cloud, fire, smoke, and trembling mountain. It is the only non-natural theophanic image. The other images are of a thunderstorm, and perhaps a volcano. The shofar blast is linguistically linked with the natural phenomena. The sound of thunder and the sound of the shofar are of the same Hebrew root, קוֹל, qôl, so while it is unclear who is sounding the shofar, it is clear that the shofar belongs to the other theophanic phenomena. The voice of YHWH is heard in the "voice" of the storm in many biblical texts;[27] here it is heard also in the voice of the shofar.[28] Something similar is seen in Isaiah 58:1 (NRSVCE): "Shout out and do not hold back. Lift up your voice like a shofar and announce to my people their rebellion, to the house of Jacob their sins." In several other texts, the sound of the shofar accompanies the cultic epiphany of YHWH. For example, in 2 Samuel 6:2, 14–15, the Ark of YHWH was brought up to Jerusalem with the blast of the shofar.[29]

2.3 Preparations of the People for the Theophany

The symbols of the preparation of the people at Sinai are similar to other contexts which take place in the tabernacle and the Jerusalem temple. In Exodus 19:10–13, Moses is commanded to prepare the people for the theophany. All of the people are to be purified, and therefore consecrated and set apart for the event. This may also be the reason that here they are cordoned off: they are set apart. The Levites will be set apart as priests later. The preparations are that they be sanctified, wash their garments, and be cordoned off, lest they touch the mountain and be put to death. Moses relates the command, and includes a further detail: not to touch a woman.[30] The preparation is for an encounter with God. Similarly, the prophet Isaiah deems himself unprepared to be in the presence of God in his temple, and so liable to death, since he is unclean (Isa 6).[31] When Aaron and his sons are consecrated as high priests, and so authorized to enter into the sanctuary, they are given new garments.[32]

---

27. For example, 1 Sam 7:10; Amos 1:2; Isa 29:6; 30:30–31; Jer 10:13; Joel 4:16; Pss 18:14; 29:3–5.

28. See Beyerlin, *Origins and History of the Oldest Sinaitic Traditions*, 135–36.

29. Cf. 1 Chr 13:8; 15:28.

30. On sexual impurity as impediment for a divine encounter, see Lev 15; 18.

31. See Houtman, *Exodus*, 2:450. There are other texts which illustrate this: Num 11:18; Josh 3:5; 7:13; 1 Sam 21:5–6.

32. On the necessity for proper garments for a divine encounter, see Gen 35:2; 2 Sam 12:20; 2 Kgs 10:22.

The cloud, the sound of the shofar, and the way in which the people must prepare themselves for the theophany at Mount Sinai are typical of texts dealing with other epiphanies and liturgical rites in the tabernacle and the Jerusalem temple. The presence of these symbols at Sinai makes them paradigmatic of Israel's encounter with YHWH.

3. Sinai Revelation, Fixed or Revisable?

As already noted, Exodus 19–24 is often referred to as the constitution of Israel. The establishment of the covenant offered at Sinai in Exodus 19:3b–8 is clearly the main event, and at the conclusion of the pericope, in Exodus 24:3–8, the covenant is indeed established.[33] Furthermore, the covenant is established based upon divine revelation and its positive reception by Israel. Even though the pericope has a certain closure in terms of the content of revelation at Mount Sinai, there are also indications within the passage that the communicative or revelatory act remains open to revision and expansion. First, we will examine some aspects of the passage that communicate closure, then some that indicate openness to future modification.

3.1 The Words That YHWH Spoke Recorded in the Book

I would like draw attention to two characteristics of the revelation which imply its nature as definitive and permanently authoritative. The first is the nature of the covenant content which is specified by two corresponding formulas that indicate its connection with the words of YHWH. The second is the solemn liturgical act of covenant ratification which is framed by the thrice repeated acceptance by Israel, in the middle of which Moses writes and then recounts the book of the covenant.[34]

Exodus 19:3b–4:

[3]YHWH called to him from the mountain, saying *"Thus you shall say to the house of Jacob; thus you shall tell the sons of Israel:* [4]You have seen what I did to Egypt and that I carried you on eagles' wings and brought you to me.

---

33. On the nature of the covenant formula in Exod 19–24, especially on the end of the Sinai pericope, see Dennis J. McCarthy, *Treaty and Covenant: A Study in Form in the Ancient Oriental Documents and in the Old Testament*, 2nd ed. (Rome: Biblical Institute Press, 1978), 243–76; E.W. Nicholson, "The Covenant Ritual in Exodus 24:3–8," *Vetus Testamentum* 32 (1982): 74–86; Ska, "History," 160–64. See also Levenson, *Sinai and Zion*, 23–36.

34. The word "covenant," Hebrew בְּרִית, *běrît*, occurs only in these verses of our passage: 19:5; 23:32; 24:7.8. In 23:32, it is a prohibition from entering into a covenant with foreign gods.

MATTHEW C. GENUNG

[5]Now, if you truly listen to my voice and observe my covenant, you, of all peoples, will be my possession, for all the earth is mine. [6]And you will be to me a priestly kingdom and a holy nation. *These are the words which you are to speak to the sons of Israel.*" [7]And Moses came and called the elders of the people and placed before them all the words which YHWH commanded him. [8]And the entire people answered together and said, *"Everything that YHWH said we shall do."* And Moses brought the words of the people back to YHWH.

In the italicized text above, one may see the formulaic definition of the content of what God directs Moses to convey. YHWH declares to Moses exactly what he is to communicate to Israel. Once Moses conveys these divine words to the people, they all reply with complete acceptance. The vocabulary underscores that Israel is accepting the entirety of exactly what YHWH has communicated.

To this point, YHWH has not yet said much by way of details. The covenant develops through progressive stages. The first stage is the divine covenantal offer to Israel through Moses (Exod 19:5–6a). The offer contains a general stipulation and a general promise. The stipulation is contained in v. 5b: אִם־שָׁמוֹעַ תִּשְׁמְעוּ בְּקֹלִי (ʾim-šāmôaʿ tišmēʿû bĕqōlî), "if you truly listen to my voice." This phrase is imprecisely translated in the NAB as "if you obey me completely." Although obedience is the basic condition of the covenant, the terminology used is that of listening to the divine voice.

In a second stage this basic condition begins to be fleshed out. This takes place in the direct revelation of the Decalogue (Exod 20:1–17) and the mediated revelation of the laws and ordinances of the Covenant Code (Exod 20:22–23:33). In a third stage, in which the covenant is ratified, the tradition received by Moses is recounted (pi. ספר, spr) by him to Israel (Exod 24:3a), which responds (Exod 24:3b) with virtually the same formula as in Exodus 19:8.

19:8 וַיַּעֲנוּ כָל הָעָם יַחְדָּו וַיֹּאמְרוּ כֹּל אֲשֶׁר דִּבֶּר יְהוָה נַעֲשֶׂה
wayyaʿănû kol-hāʿām yaḥdāw wayyōʾmĕrû kōl ʾăšer-dibber yĕhwâ naʿăśe
And all the people answered together and said, "Everything *that YHWH said* we will do."

24:3b וַיַּעַן כָּל הָעָם קוֹל אֶחָד וַיֹּאמְרוּ כָּל הַדְּבָרִים אֲשֶׁר דִּבֶּר יְהוָה נַעֲשֶׂה
wayyaʿan kol-hāʿām qôl ʾeḥād wayyōʾmĕrû kol-haddĕbārîm ʾăšer-dibber yĕhwâ naʿăśe
And all the people answered with one voice and said, "All the words *that YHWH said* we will do."

These divine words just accepted were communicated to the people orally, just as in Exodus 9:8.

64

The Divine Voice of Sinai in Emended Scripture

Something different happens next. Instead of reporting back to YHWH, "*Moses wrote all the words of YHWH*" (Exod 24:4a), prepared and initiated the ritual of covenant ratification, and then proceeded to take "*the book of the covenant and read it in the ears of the people*" (Exod 24:7). The people respond a third time:

24:7b וַיֹּאמְרוּ כֹּל אֲשֶׁר דִּבֶּר יְהוָה נַעֲשֶׂה וְנִשְׁמָע

wayyō'mĕrû kōl 'ăšer-dibber yĕhwâ na'ăśe wĕnišmā'

And they said, "*Everything YHWH said* we will do and we will listen to."

The liturgy is completed when the remaining blood is poured on the people with the words "behold the blood of the covenant which YHWH cut with you *on these words*." The covenant that founds Israel is sealed based upon the revelation and acceptance of the divine will that is first related by Moses to Israel as an offer, which is gradually enfleshed in the Decalogue and subsequent laws. This elaborated revelation is once again related by Moses orally and accepted as such before it is fixed in writing. What Moses wrote was once again related orally, and once again accepted as the identical divine speech.[35]

The account drives home the point that what was written corresponds to what was communicated orally on each occasion. According to the narrative, the text written by Moses conforms perfectly to the words spoken by YHWH. This gives the reader the impression that the writing is of divine origin and therefore authoritative, and is also in a fixed form. However, the text itself shows a history of elaboration and development. This means that the basic structure of a communicative event which is self-contained and closed was not seen as completely fixed by the community to whom the writing of Moses was entrusted.

3.2 The Redacted Book, Forever the Words YHWH Spoke

3.2.1 Exodus 19:9

The basic condition for the covenant is given in Exodus 19:5: Israel must listen to the voice of YHWH in order to receive and remain in the special status promised by him. As was shown above, according to the narrative, the voice of YHWH did not cease at the cutting of the covenant at the foot of the mountain once Moses wrote the book of the covenant. Neither did it cease at the death of Moses. Exodus 19:9, which was shown to be a later addition to a preexisting text, seeks to ground the "eternal" nature of the Mosaic authority: "Now, I am about to come to you in the dense cloud so that the people will hear in my

35. Ska, "History," 165–69.

65

speaking with you and will really trust you *forever*." This text foresees Mosaic mediation beyond the confines of the event and identifies the authority of continued divine revelation.

3.2.2 *Exodus 19:19*

In Exodus 19:19, during the theophany, the "voice" of the shofar participates in the divine communication. "And the sound of the shofar went on getting much stronger. Moses would speak and the divinity would respond with a voice." There are two notable features of this text, as it pertains to an allusion to the lasting Mosaic authority. First, in this verse the initiative is with Moses. Moses speaks, and God responds to him with a voice. This is inverted as compared to the other instances of mediation, where instead it is God who calls to Moses, who reports to the people. This operation is also manifest when YHWH begins to dwell in Solomon's temple, in 1 Kings 8. Solomon entreats the Lord who then responds to him. Many of the other texts referenced above manifest this same mode of intercession to determine the divine will and request favor.

Second, as the shofar blast intensifies, the duplicate command in vv. 20–24 specifies something particular about the priests: they too must keep themselves sanctified when approaching YHWH. In v. 24, there is a different specification of who may ascend the mountain: Aaron is summoned to return with Moses, but the people and priests are forbidden once again from approaching YHWH. I propose that one may recognize in the intensification of the blast of the shofar a hint at the authoritative origin of the modification of the ordinances regarding the parties granted access to YHWH, and authority in the transmission of the Scriptures. The statements pertaining to authority in Exodus 19, whether of Moses in v. 19, the priests in v. 22, or Aaron in v. 24, each occur in texts identified as redactional insertions. This development in the text is emblematic of the mode of the development of the reception and scripturalization of divine revelation and the specification of the authority to participate in its transmission, both oral and written. When one considers the relatively later date of Exodus 24:1, 9–8, 11, which deal with the admission of Aaron, Nadab, Abihu, and the seventy elders into the divine presence on Mount Sinai, a logical link with these redactional insertions in Exodus 19 comes into view, indicating the sanction of the institutions established to enact the perpetual mediation of Moses promised in Exodus 19.[36]

---

36. On the exegesis of this text, with extensive bibliography, see Jean-Louis Ska, "Vision and Meal in Exodus 24:11," 163–83 in *The Exegesis of the Pentateuch: Exegetical Studies and Basic Questions*, FAT 66 (Tübingen: Mohr Siebeck, 2009).

Other texts support the locus of this mediation. Isaiah 2:2–4 and Micah 4:1–3 link the Jerusalem temple and the mountain of YHWH with the Law and judgment. Mount Zion is the highest mountain to which the nation and peoples will go for divine teaching and judgment, which will result in international peace.[37] In these texts, the law given at Sinai is renewed in the Jerusalem "tent." The symbols of the theophany, the cloud-smoke, fire-lightning, thunder-horn-quaking, and the location (Mountain of God) foreshadow the enduring mode of divine presence and communion between YHWH and Israel.

A final point to underline the openness in the text is seen in the third reply of the people regarding their assent to conform to the words of YHWH. The context of their third response is hearing the divine word in Moses' reading of the Book of the Covenant. Their third reply contains a promise in addition to that recounted in the previous two formulas of assent: the people promise not only to do, but also *to listen to* everything said by YHWH. The promise is given in the future tense.

> Exodus 24:7b וַיֹּאמְרוּ כֹּל אֲשֶׁר דִּבֶּר יְהֹוָה נַעֲשֶׂה וְנִשְׁמָע
> wayyō'mĕrû kōl 'ăšer-dibber yĕhwâ na'ăśe *wĕnišmā'*
> And they said, "Everything YHWH said we will do and *we will listen [to]."*

The verbal correspondence is identical to the condition stipulated by YHWH in Exodus 19:5, namely "if you *listen to* my voice." Hearing the Book of the Covenant is equivalent to hearing the voice of YHWH. Not only does this assent recognize the divine authority of the Scripture, it also recognizes the divine authority of its future textual developments (from the standpoint of the story), or the authority of its tradents and the emended form which became canonical.

4. Conclusion

The first communicative instance of divine revelation in Exodus 19 relates to the establishment of the covenant between God and Israel. Exodus 19:4 refers backward to the exodus event: "You have seen how I treated the Egyptians and how I bore you up on eagles' wings." The purpose of this text, which functions as a prologue to the covenant, is to motivate Israel's future acceptance of God's present offer to enter into covenant with him. So, while the beginning of the divine offer refers to the past, the unfolding of the covenant itself is presented

---

37. Cf. Ps 18:8–20; 2 Sam 22:8–20; Ps 29; Hab 3:3–15; Ps 68:8–9, 16–18; Judg 5:4–5; Ps 50:1–3, which particularly links the theophany at Sinai with the Jerusalem cult; Isa 4:5. On Ps 68, see Michael A. Fishbane, *Biblical Interpretation in Ancient Israel* (Oxford: Clarendon, 1985), 371.

biblically in such a way that this spectacular event does not remain under the dark cloud of history, but is to remain present to Israel in its cultic, prophetic, and political institutions, which with the Mosaic authority continue to mediate the divine will first expressed on Sinai.

This notoriously complex passage is imbued with liturgical symbolism evocative of the postexilic institutions in Jerusalem including the temple, the priesthood, the elders, and the scribes, with the effect that what is recounted in this text is not only the beginning of Israel, but also the basis by which Israel may continue to hear the voice of YHWH and live in accordance with it, and thus in communion with him. In this way, to borrow the historiographical terminology of Paul Ricœur, the text does not belong to the genre of documentary history, but is rather an instance of poetic history, in that it is primarily concerned with grounding the future of the community from the standpoint of a present situation, which is seemingly distant from the foundational encounter at the Holy Mountain, but in reality present and vital to Israel after having already inhabited (and re-inhabited) the Land.[38]

The nature and purpose of the redactional insertions shown in this text are analogous to the work of the Catholic exegete, which does not stop at discovering the meaning of the text intended by the author, but seeks to understand it spiritually, from the perspective of the paschal mystery and the life of the Church in the new age in order to continue to draw life from them. Brevard Childs, a great pioneer of canonical exegesis, holds that it is the final, canonical form of Scripture that must be interpreted. And, in order to achieve this goal, he holds that the study of the earlier stages and forms of its development clarify the meaning of the final form of the text.[39] If the role of the exegete in the Church is to seek out the meaning God wanted to communicate, it is to be done through investigating what meaning the sacred writers really intended, and what God wanted to manifest by means of their words.[40] In many texts, including the Sinai pericope, the sacred writers are anonymous and are likely many, but traces of the method of their composition and redaction of the biblical texts enable the interpreter to enter in and to encounter the divine voice, to hear it, and to have the opportunity to add their assent to that of Moses and Israel at the Mountain.

---

38. Paul Ricœur, *La critique et la conviction* (Paris: Calmann-Lévy, 1995). On this, see also Ska, "History," 145–69.

39. Childs, *The Book of Exodus*, 393.

40. *Dei verbum*, §12.

4. Inspiration and Truth When Prophecy Fails: Ezekiel's Temple Vision

Anthony Pagliarini

The final chapters of the Book of Ezekiel present a vision of restored Israel. The specific form of what they announce does not come about. In this respect, the prophecy fails. All the same, it is held to be a true and inspired text. In this, there is no contradiction. If we discern the function of the prophet's language and his theology of history, we can receive the Temple Vision as what it was always intended to be, namely an announcement of Israel's future spoken in the idiom of its past—not a prescription or blueprint but an adumbration of God's renewed presence among his people.

I. The Structure of the Book of Ezekiel and the Temple Vision

On thematic grounds, most commentators divide the book of Ezekiel into three principal units: Punishment against Israel and Jerusalem (1–24); Punishment against the nations (25–32); and Restoration of Israel and Jerusalem (33–48).[1] This is not without some difficulties created by the various date formulae and prophetic word announcements. It is perhaps best, following Terrence Collins, to note that prophetic books such as Ezekiel have "much in common with the modern art form of collage, in which juxtaposition of varied, even dissimilar items, is cultivated as a matter of style."[2] The "confusion" of overlapping

---

1. Cf. the "Majority Report" in Tyler D. Mayfield, *Literary Structure and Setting in Ezekiel*, FAT.2 43 (Tübingen: Mohr Siebeck, 2010), 24–28.

2. Terence Collins, *The Mantle of Elijah: The Redaction Criticism of the Prophetic Books*, BiSe 20 (Sheffield: JSOT Press, 1993), 29. Cited in Edgar Conrad, *Reading the Latter Prophets: Toward a New Canonical Criticism*, JSOTSup 376 (Sheffield: Continuum, 2004), 26.

ANTHONY PAGLIARINI

systems of textual organization may just form an invitation to a particular style of reading and thinking. It is a textual petition for the audience to fruitfully configure the material in various ways. Much like the habit of "resumptive exposition" we see in Ezekiel, the whole of its arrangement is fluid and overlapping.[3]

Within this loose thematic framework, the placement of the Temple Vision at the end of the work follows a trajectory of "resurrection, restoration, and resettlement."[4] As Jacob Milgrom explains:

> Ezekiel's sanctuary is not a chance appendix to his book; it is a logical and fitting climax to all that has preceded it. First comes the reunification, restoration, and purification of Israel, ending with the promise of a Davidic ruler and a new sanctuary (chaps. 36–37). Then follows the purification of the land after the slaughter and burial of Israel's enemies (chaps. 38–39, esp. 39:12–16). Once the people and the land have been purged, the new, divinely built sanctuary can be dedicated as operational (chaps. 40–46).[5]

The Temple Vision is itself a clearly demarcated textual unit. It is introduced by a date formula (Ezek 40:1) as well as the announcement of a visionary experience (Ezek 40:2; cf. 1:1; 8:3). Its ending in 48:35 closes the book. This coherence is moreover visible in the chapters' unique concern for the temple and its surrounding area, the whole of which is "the antithesis of what [Ezekiel] saw before."[6] The reader is presented with an inversion of the cultic and moral abuses for which Israel was thrust into exile and on account of which God's name was profaned. However one might delineate the rest of Ezekiel, the vision's boundaries and placement are clear.

II. The "Failure" of the Temple Vision

The placement of chapters 40–48 within the trajectory of the book informs our judgment about the role of the Temple Vision and allows us to comment on its success or failure. The Book of Ezekiel is an instance of "inscribed prophecy."[7] It is not, as in the case of other books, a collection of spoken oracles but rather a work of literature created for the exilic community in Babylon. In that context,

3. Moshe Greenberg, *Ezekiel 1–20: A New Translation with Introduction and Commentary*, AncB 22 (New York: Doubleday, 1983), 25–27, 137–38.

4. Jacob Milgrom and Daniel I. Block, *Ezekiel's Hope: A Commentary on Ezekiel 40–48* (Eugene, OR: Cascade, 2012), 3.

5. Milgrom and Block, *Ezekiel's Hope*, 43.

6. Robert W. Jenson, *Ezekiel*, BTCB (Grand Rapids: Brazos, 2009), 301.

7. Stephen L. Cook, *Ezekiel 38–48: A New Translation with Introduction and Commentary*, AYB 22B (New Haven: Yale University Press, 2018), 3.

Inspiration and Truth When Prophecy Fails: Ezekiel's Temple Vision

the Temple Vision possessed both "an indicative . . . [and] also an imperative aspect."[8] What is described by the prophet is not a simple blueprint for a complex that Israel is commanded to build, but it is an indication of what will come to pass when God acts to vindicate his name. As such, the temple tour is a "proclamation of salvation encoded in [an] architectural plan."[9]

This proclamation culminates in the return of the divine *kabod* (Ezek 43:1–5). At issue in this announcement is, however, not simply the return of God but so also the return of Israel. It is in the repair of his people that God's sovereignty is made manifest, such that the nations will know that Yahweh is Lord (cf. Ezek 48:35). Israel is itself the image by which God is made known. Before the return of the *kabod*, the very announcement of its return in Ezekiel's vision already begins to effect the restoration of Israel. The proclamation of the temple measurements is tasked with producing shame among the exiles (Ezek 43:10). And if they indeed become ashamed (cf. Ezek 43:11), the prophet is to show them more such that, somehow even in the period of exile (cf. Ezek 11:16), "they may observe and perform all its laws and all its ordinances" (Ezek 43:11 RSV2CE). In this we pass from the indicative to the imperative, from the simple announcement of God's plan of restoration to the demands made as the correlate of that restoration.

Several features of the text lead to the judgment that the prophecy of these chapters awaited immediate fulfillment. To be sure, the text speaks in an apocalyptic or utopian register about an endpoint of history, but it does not necessarily do so with reference to a distant future. To speak of a text as eschatological is to make an epochal and not a strictly temporal designation; it signals what is new and not necessarily what is far removed from the present.[10] The "latter days" (Ezek 38:16) spoken of in the Gog oracle may, perhaps, be read in

---

8. Walther Zimmerli, *Ezekiel: A Commentary on the Book of the Prophet Ezekiel, Chapters 1–24*, trans. Ronald E. Clements, Hermeneia (Philadelphia: Fortress, 1979), 361.

9. Walther Zimmerli, *Ezekiel: A Commentary on the Book of the Prophet Ezekiel, Chapters 25–48*, trans. James D. Martin (Philadelphia: Fortress, 1983), 419.

10. Even if we place the final redaction of Ezekiel some centuries later and judge that the Temple Vision has settled into a familiar schema of theophany, war against enemies, and refoundation of the cult, nothing of the text's impending character is lost. As seen in chapter 20, the course of Israel's history is driven by the free and sovereign divine will. The restoration about which the Temple Vision speaks remains a possibility to be realized at any moment. "The Lord whom you seek will come suddenly to his Temple" (Mic 3:1). On this schema as present within Ezekiel's final redaction, cf. Marco Nobile, "Ez 38–39 ed Ez 40–48: I due aspetti complementari del culmine di uno schema culturale di fondazione," *Antonianum* 62 (1987): 141–71.

reference to Nebuchadnezzar.[11] So too, Israel's reestablishment in 34–36 and her ingathering in 37 can be understood as reversals expected to come about not in some distant future but within the lifetime of the prophet. Read sequentially, the ingathering would then precede the downfall of Babylon, and both would anticipate the renewed temple in the land.

Details of the vision lend support to this idea. Chapters 40–42 concern themselves with the particulars of the sanctuary's dimensions. They refer only sparingly to the activity that will later take place in the temple. We do, however, hear of the washing and slaughter of offerings, the instruments involved (Ezek 40:38–43), and of the priests (Ezek 40:45–46). In the following chapter the prophet himself is the one tasked with the consecration of the altar (Ezek 43:18–27). In both instances, the level of specificity implies that the text communicates a reality expected to come about in the near future.

This is not to argue that the author speaks of Israel's restoration in a way that is plainly referential. There is no one-to-one correspondence between what is seen and what will come to pass. These chapters are a vision, an "appearance" (מַרְאָה), of what is genuinely historical—of what is really the case—but cast in a manner of speech that disallows any simple correspondence with the events of history as we experience them. Prophetic vision "is always a seeing of what exceeds the prospects of vision and . . . the symbols deployed are inadequate to what they aim to disclose."[12] To speak of the vision as history, flatly understood, would be to overdetermine the scope of its referentiality. To speak of the vision as purely symbolic, however, would be to lose hold of its relation to real events in the life of Israel. Blenkinsopp is right in his judgment that what is seen in the Temple Vision is "the real city, the longing for which is intensified by exile, but it is also a symbol, an ideal location, a projection of a future reality that exists only as aspiration and desire."[13] The vision operates at the "intersection of myth and history."[14] It is not reducible to either, but it includes both. The

11. Julie Galambush, "Necessary Enemies: Nebuchadnezzar, Yhwh, and God in Ezekiel 38–39," 254–67 in *Israel's Prophets and Israel's Past*, ed. Brad E. Kelle and Megan Bishop Moore, LHB 446 (London: T&T Clark, 2006).

12. Cyril O'Regan, *The Anatomy of Misremembering: Von Balthasar's Response to Philosophical Modernity*, vol. 1, *Hegel* (Chestnut Ridge, NY: Herder & Herder, 2014), 377.

13. Joseph Blenkinsopp, *Ezekiel*, Int. (Louisville: John Knox, 1990), 198.

14. Margaret Odell, *Ezekiel*, SHBC (Macon, GA: Smyth & Helwys, 2005), 497. Cf. Jon D. Levenson, *Theology of the Program of Restoration of Ezekiel 40–48* (Atlanta: Scholars Press, 1986), 1–53. In contrast, Milgrom and Block, *Ezekiel's Hope: A Commentary on Ezekiel 40–48*, 52, write that "There is no point in seeking the origins of Ezekiel's sanctuary in the myths of Mt. Sinai, the Garden of Eden, and Mount Zion. There is nothing miraculous about the structure."

Inspiration and Truth When Prophecy Fails: Ezekiel's Temple Vision

specificity mentioned above and the placement of those details within the sweep of the book as a whole argue in favor of understanding these chapters as vision of something that awaited realization both soon and in a manner closely prescribed by the details given.

As further evidence we might add the sense of immediacy created by the similarity of Ezekiel to Moses. In addition to their role in providing a law code for Israel, both prophets attend to Israel on the cusp of their entry into the Land. As Moses on Mount Nebo (Deut 32:29, 52), Ezekiel surveys the Land from a "very high mountain" (Ezek 40:2). As God spoke to Moses from the Tent of the Meeting, he speaks directly to Ezekiel from the Temple (Ezek 43:6). And as Moses sacrifices at the initiation of the Tabernacle altar (Exod 29:36–37), so Ezekiel, as just mentioned, is tasked in the Temple Vision to purify and make atonement for the newly erected altar in the Temple (Ezek 43:18–27).[15] Both prophets inaugurate the cult and set in motion the events that culminate in Israel's (re)entry into the Land.

Problematically, none of what is spoken of in the Temple Vision comes to pass. "Wherever Ezekiel's program can be checked against subsequent events," writes Moshe Greenberg, "it proves to have had no effect."[16] The imminent historical realization of the text does not come to pass, and by this measure we must characterize the whole of it as a failure.

This, we should note, is true whether the Temple Vision is an original, unified composition from the period of the exile or if it is a much redacted, composite text produced in the early postexilic period.[17] In either case, we are asked to read the text as prophecy. Specifically, we are asked to understand the vision from the standpoint of the exiles in Babylon and with the expectation of imminent fulfillment. And from this vantage we cannot help but be confronted with the text's failure to speak concerning the life of Israel in the years following the exile.

> In everything relating to the Temple personnel and rituals the laws of Moses superseded those of Ezekiel. His program remains of interest chiefly as a practical extension of his prophecy, as additional evidence of his graphic

15. Milgrom and Block, *Ezekiel's Hope,* 217.

16. Moshe Greenberg, "The Design and Themes of Ezekiel's Program of Restoration," *Interpretation* 38, no. 2 (1984): 181–208, at 208.

17. Beginning with Greenberg's "The Design and Themes of Ezekiel's Program of Restoration," more commentators have accepted that the Temple Vision was composed in a relatively short period of time in the exile. Thomas Renz, *The Rhetorical Function of the Book of Ezekiel,* VT.S 76 (Leiden: Brill, 2002), 122, is correct in his judgment that "None of the material needs to be later than the late-exilic period."

mentality, his love of system and detail; and above all, for his lofty conception of a prophet's responsibility in an age of ruin.[18]

More simply, according to Greenberg, the Temple Vision is a "dead letter."[19]

III. Reading with *Dei verbum*

This judgment, which is largely correct, puts us at something of an impasse. "All Scripture is inspired by God" (2 Tim 3:16). It is inspired and true. What then would it mean in this instance to regard the text as a failure in one respect and nevertheless hold that it is true and that it is something which, as Jesus says, "cannot be nullified" (John 10:35)?

To work past this difficulty, we should take note of an implicit judgment that has shaped our reading thus far. In *Dei verbum,* the Council Fathers ask us to consider the historical circumstances in which the texts of Scripture were authored. "But," it says, "since Holy Scripture must be read and interpreted in the same spirit in which it was written, no less serious attention must be given to the content and unity of the whole of Scripture if the meaning of the sacred texts is to be correctly worked out."[20] This second instruction does not function as a trump card on the first. The canonical or ecclesial reading may not run roughshod over what historical considerations reveal. Rather, *Dei verbum* invites us to regard the historical particulars of the text not as closed in on themselves but as moments in the unified and ongoing work of divine providence.

Said differently, the teaching of *Dei verbum,* in keeping with the example of the New Testament itself, offers us a mechanism to escape the historicism that can, at times, hobble what we might, broadly speaking, identify as modern and postmodern readings of Scripture. In the first instance, the meaning of Scripture is limited at a particular moment in the past. The Book of Ezekiel was not written for you but for an exilic and postexilic audience in Israel. The meaning of the text is limited to that historical moment. And as in our reading above, its success or failure is limited to a consideration of that historical moment. Conversely, in postmodern readings, we can speak of the autonomy of the text.[21] Works are unmoored from any concrete circumstance, and their

18. Greenberg, "The Design and Themes of Ezekiel's Program of Restoration," 208.

19. Greenberg, "The Design and Themes of Ezekiel's Program of Restoration," 208.

20. Second Vatican Council, *Dei verbum* (November 18, 1965) (Boston: Pauline Books & Media, 1965), §12.

21. Cf. Paul Ricœur, "The Hermeneutical Function of Distanciation," 93–106 in *Hermeneutics and the Human Sciences: Essays on Language, Action and Interpretation,* CPhC

Inspiration and Truth When Prophecy Fails: Ezekiel's Temple Vision

meaning is determined uniquely by the readership. The Book of Ezekiel was not written for you, but that is irrelevant. The meaning of the text, unhinged from its origin, is what you, the reader, determine it to be. As Roger Lundlin summarizes, "texts demand nothing but yield everything under the proper caresses."[22]

While they appear very different, these approaches are in one respect identical. Both of them understand the meaning of Scripture as something that is generated uniquely by a human subject, be it the author or the audience.[23] As such, meaning is constrained by the finitude of the author or the reader. The first cannot intend a universal audience and so cannot speak directly to future readerships; the second only realizes meaning within his or her own person and nowhere else. Unexpectedly, therefore, both approaches show themselves as cognate forms of historicism, specifically as this emerges from modernity's disavowal of the transcendent. Said differently, the common thread of what, with broad strokes, I have painted as the modern and postmodern poles of exegesis, is a kind of immanentism—that is to say, the collapse into a non-transcendent view of history.[24]

This is precisely what *Dei verbum* inveighs against. The Council Fathers remind us that history itself and those sacred texts which speak of that history are steeped in the work of divine providence. The great Dominican scholar Roland de Vaux captures this idea well: "Revelation is communicated simultaneously by the actions and the word of God, which are inseparably bound

(Cambridge: Cambridge University Press, 2016). "Writing renders the text autonomous with respect to the intention of the author. What the text signifies no longer coincides with what the author meant; henceforth, textual meaning and psychological meaning have different destinies" (101).

22. Roger Lundlin, Anthony C. Thiselton, and Clarence Walhout, *The Promise of Hermeneutics* (Grand Rapids: Eerdmans, 1999), 41.

23. Cf. Leo G. Perdue, *The Collapse of History: Restructuring Old Testament Theology*, OBT (Minneapolis: Fortress, 1994).

24. I have in mind principally the secularization theses of Voegelin and of Löwith upon whom he draws. Cf. Eric Voegelin, *New Science of Politics* (Chicago: University of Chicago Press, 1952); Karl Löwith, *Meaning in History: The Theological Implications of the Philosophy of History* (Chicago: University of Chicago Press, 1949). Henrik Syse, "Karl Löwith and Eric Voegelin on Christianity and History," *Modern Age* 42, no. 3 (2000): 253–62, at 254, notes that for both of these authors "the essence of modernity is immanentism." This stands in sharp contrast with "St. Augustine's model for a Christian view of history, which accorded real meaning only to transcendent history . . . the *civitas Dei*. . . . This is a history that is certainly also reflected in life on earth; in the sacred history of the Old Testament, in the appearance of Christ, and in the earthly pilgrimage of the Church. But, it is not a history which foresees any immanent this-worldly resolution."

together. . . . God is at once master of the events of history, which he controls, and master of their interpretation."[25]

This understanding permeates the Book of Ezekiel itself. It possesses a robust notion of divine authorship. "It is striking," says Zimmerli, "how, throughout the entire book of Ezekiel, the activity is set almost exclusively in the words and actions of Yahweh."[26] As we hear concerning the prophecy that Ezekiel is to deliver, "I will speak the word and perform it, says the Lord God" (Ezek 12:25; cf. 26–28). The book also understands its audience as not limited to the community in exile and its early aftermath. Ezekiel speaks to "the whole house of Israel" (e.g., Ezek 37:11), an impossible collection inclusive of even those northern tribes largely lost to history. And most importantly for our purposes, Ezekiel grasps the providential shape of history in which the events of the past establish the contours of God's future action. As we will see below, the Temple Vision in chapters 40–48 is best understood as a reading forward of Israel's past. To use a beautiful phrase from Cyril O'Regan, the Temple Vision is a "memory of the future."[27] It presents the restoration of Israel in the language and imagery of its idolatrous past. In so doing, it gives a reading of the future cast in specific imagery but not bound to those particulars as a condition of its truthfulness. A "dead letter" in one respect, the text is nevertheless inspired and true.

IV. The Success of the Temple Vision

It would be helpful at this juncture to speak of the "illocution" of the text. This, as Vanhoozer explains, is "what speakers and authors have *done* in tending to their words as they have."[28] The words of the Temple Vision—the locution—speaks

---

25. Roland de Vaux, "Is It Possible to Write a 'Theology of the Old Testament'?," 49–62 in *The Bible and the Ancient Near East*, trans. Damian McHugh (London: Darton, Longman & Todd, 1972), 58.

26. Zimmerli, *Ezekiel, Chapters 1–24*, 24.

27. O'Regan, *The Anatomy of Misremembering*, 1:375. In his remarks on Christianity, we might hear something of the impulse behind the Temple Vision in it refiguration of a past reality: "Christianity is not the classist dream of the contained past and its limited forms. For Christianity never affirms the old as the old, but only the old as the new, the ever new, as Augustine intimated with such unsurpassed eloquence in the *Confessions* (Bk 10)" (1:10). Further, concerning the Apocalypse, whose substance and form borrow much from Ezekiel, O'Regan remarks that "Revelation is a text of panoramic vision that provides a view of the whole of history from creation to eschaton that manages to be both retrospective and anticipatory as once" (1:383).

28. Kevin J. Vanhoozer, "From Speech Acts to Scripture Acts," 159–203 in *First Theology: God, Scripture, and Hermeneutics* (Downers Grove, IL: InterVarsity, 2002), 173; italics in original.

Inspiration and Truth When Prophecy Fails: Ezekiel's Temple Vision

of a specific form of law, temple architecture, and apportionment of land. The illocution of the text is nevertheless not characterized most fully by the desire to institute this specific reality. Rather, the intention of the text includes this realization as a proximate goal—that point must be kept in view—but it has as its real end the creation of a situation in Israel where, contrary to that past in comparison to which the vision is cast, the holiness of God is made manifest in Israel and to the world. Said differently, the language of the passage is not vague or limited to the realm of ideas. It is specific, but this does not thereby signal that the text is concerned most deeply and uniquely with the concrete realization of a specific form of worship as an end in itself.

If we bind the meaning of the Temple Vision to its ostensive referents, much as Greenberg has done in his pronouncement of the passage as a "dead letter," the prophecy is in fact a failure without remainder. This, though, is not correct. It mistakes two levels of function in language. That to which the text refers is distinct from what speakers and authors have done in tending their words. This can be seen already for the first generation of the model audience in Babylon, an audience for whom there still existed the possibility of a future in precisely the terms given by the vision. Even in that time, when the "failure" of the text is not yet come about, we see that the work the text wishes to do is related but not bound to the referents of its language. By reading forward Israel's idolatrous past toward a situation in which the holiness of God is made manifest in all respects, the text is designed to generate shame in those who hear it (43:10–11). The first burden of the text is to prepare Israel to acknowledge God's holiness, both in a moment to come and already now as God dwells among them in the exile "in small measure" (cf. Ezek 11:16 [author's translation]). That, in addition, this should find its full realization in exactly the terms given is one possibility, but it is not a necessary one. It might well have happened just so. That it did not injures nothing.

Lest this seem like a strained reappropriation of an otherwise "dead" text, we should take note of two features of the vision already mentioned but not sufficiently emphasized: the relation of Ezekiel to Moses and the exilic community's performance of what is commanded.

These final chapters of Ezekiel are a vision of the future cast in terms of a past reality, a future spoken in the register of and grounded in the past. The Book of Ezekiel means to predict a future in the terms given, but as in the Tabernacle and the temple of Solomon, the specifics of the construction and of the ritual are not ends in themselves. If this were so, Ezekiel would have no grounds on which to reform the Law and its traditions to which is he is identifiably an heir. This, however, is precisely what he does, and that he proceeds not

ANTHONY PAGLIARINI

in ignorance or defiance of Mosaic authority but in the form of a second Moses reveals a deep understanding of the nature of what was commanded from Sinai onwards. It is not the precept as such but that which, at heart, it commands that is the substance of law, be it Moses' or his own. Reading with the Holiness school, to whom Ezekiel shows such dependence,[29] we may take this unifying center as the command "You shall be holy, for I the LORD your God am holy" (Lev 19:2). Or, as said in reference to the temple precincts in 43:12, "This is the law of the temple. The whole territory round about upon the top of the mountain shall be most holy. Behold, this is the law of the temple."

Implicit in Ezekiel's reconfiguration of the Mosaic Torah is an awareness that his own torah stands open in principle to the same process of reconfiguration. Also, implicit in the allusion to Moses is the understanding that a modified law is not competitive but actually contributes to the same one unchanging center of the law itself. The torah presented in the Temple Vision, and its correlative in the temple structure and apportionment of the land, does not now aim at a new goal, distinct from that of what came before. Were this so, the historical recitals that Ezekiel offers earlier in the book would make no sense, and inveighing against temple practices in Jerusalem would be irrelevant to future worship. Rather, it is the same one end approached with analogous but modified means. The successive law codes, or portions of law codes, might in this way be taken on analogy with the stories of the beloved sons in Genesis, each of which, incomplete in itself, adds depth to the understanding of what it means for Israel to be "my first-born son" (Exod 4:22). Were the precepts ends in themselves and not expressive and nourishing of a more basic condition to be generated in Israel, any change would constitute a total break. As it is, like the beloved sons, the new torah of Ezekiel in the Temple Vision highlights that for the sake of which the Law is actually given, namely, the belonging of Israel to God, a relationship in and through which the glory of God's name is made manifest.

For as much, then, as the vision of chapters 40–48 looks forward to a renewed Israel in the terms given in those chapters, it is nevertheless not bound to those terms as an all-or-nothing condition of the prophecy's success. Rather, as the text itself shows in its relation to Moses and earlier elements of the Torah, there is a distinction in the proclamation of law between the principle itself and the concrete form of a principle's manifestation.[30] Indeed, the latter always

---

29. Cf. Michael Lyons, *From Law to Prophecy: Ezekiel's Use of the Holiness Code*, LHB (New York: T&T Clark, 2009).

30. It is worthwhile to note the rabbinic discussion over the identity / non-identity of the Mosaic Torah and the Heavenly Torah, with the latter position implying the possibility of new

Inspiration and Truth When Prophecy Fails: Ezekiel's Temple Vision

already bears only a contingent relation to the principle, namely, as an exemplar within a given context.[31] To insist otherwise—to insist that the precepts themselves must never be altered in any respect—is, on the one hand, to deny the validity of Ezekiel's own prophetic activity (and by extension that of Moses in the Deuteronomy) and on the other hand, to lose any ground for maintaining this "failed" text in the canon. That Ezekiel is, of course, a prophetic book of Scripture is evidence enough of a more generous understanding of law and prophecy than a restrictive historicism would allow.[32]

None of this is to suggest that the precepts are merely veiled presentations of underlying principles, riddles to be decoded and dismissed. Rather, they are the means of actualizing an underlying principle. As such, they are necessary, for there is no keeping of the heart of the law without the keeping of some one set of precepts that embody that center. What it does suggest is that the precepts as such are only derivatively authoritative, only binding in virtue of their being expressive of an underlying principle.

Viewed in this way, the sharp disjunction between the more visionary elements of 40:1–43:13; 47:1–48:35 and the precise legislation in 43:13–46:24 begins to soften. As seen already, the measurement of the temple provides

and definitive revelation. Cf. Abraham Heschel, *Heavenly Torah: As Refracted Through the Generations* (New York: Continuum, 2005), 271–72.

31. Aquinas, *Summa Theologica*, I-II, q. 104, a. 1, distinguishes between the essence of the law and its various applications in differentiating moral, ceremonial, and juridical precepts: "In every law, some precepts derive their binding force from the dictate of reason itself, because natural reason dictates that something ought to be done or to be avoided. These are called *moral* precepts: since human morals are based on reason. At the same time there are other precepts which derive their binding force, not from the very dictate of reason (because, considered in themselves, they do not imply an obligation of something due or undue); but from some institution, Divine or human: and such are certain determinations of the moral precepts. When therefore the moral precepts are fixed by Divine institution in matters relating to man's subordination to God, they are called *ceremonial* precepts: but when they refer to man's relations to other men, they are called *judicial* precepts." *Summa Theologica: Complete English Edition in 1 Volume*, trans. Fathers of the English Dominican Province (Notre Dame, IN: Christian Classics, 1981), 4:1088.

32. The fact of canonicity is itself a hermeneutical guide which must govern our reading of certain works. Making this point in reference to the "failed" prophecy of Haggai, Brevard S. Childs, *Introduction to the Old Testament as Scripture* (Philadelphia: Fortress, 1979), 470–71, writes: "The attempt of critical scholarship to bring a biblical passage into sharper historical focus by means of historical reconstruction runs the acute danger of destroying the particular theological witness which the passage carries in its final canonical shape. Particularly in the case of Haggai . . . the hermeneutical axiom that meaning is acquired only through ostensive reference . . . renders the exegete incapable of hearing the canonical witness because it is often quite different from the original historical level."

ANTHONY PAGLIARINI

an instance—and not the only instance (cf. Exod 25–31; 35–40)—of a sanctuary complex that befits the dignity of God. At issue in Ezekiel is not the exact appearance of this temple but of the reality to which this temple and its measurements give witness. So too in the case of the precepts, to which the measurements are in fact held in parallel. There is, for instance, nothing absolute about six lambs for the celebration of the Sabbath (Ezek 46:4–7) as opposed to two (Num 28:9–15). It may represent a corrective in the direction of more clearly announcing God's holiness and its power to effect blessing in Israel. Though the legislation resists a simply transcendent reading, this in truth cannot be absent. All legal precepts have a transcendent function in that they instantiate and so make visible the principle that subtends the law and that serves as its summation. In this way, the visionary context of this set of precepts is highly appropriate, for it makes evident the dynamic that is present in all law, not least the covenant precepts. That is, as an *imitatio Dei*, the law shows forth the pattern of divine life to which Israel, as God's image, is ordered. The Law is God's wisdom (Deut 4:5–8; Sir 24; Wis 7:22–30), "a reflection of eternal light, a spotless mirror of the working of God, and an image of his goodness" (Wis 7:26).[33] The correlative of the dwelling of the *kabod* is a place and a practice that image that holiness and so announce it as well. We see in the vision a physical and practical form of the command: "You shall be holy; for I the LORD your God am holy" (Lev 19:2) and so also a physical and practical form of the announcement of Yahweh's lordship to which the whole of the work, and the whole of history, tends. With this in mind, we should take both the measurements and the precepts as proclamations of the divine holiness and, precisely as such, realities to be brought about in Israel. But as seen above in the relationship between Ezekiel and Moses, neither the measurement nor the precepts are necessary forms of achieving this end. All remain, necessarily, an analogy of divine life and so, in principle, open to modification.

Before a readership which cannot make good on the actual practice of the law in exactly the form described, the legislation functions as an announcement of that in imitation of which the law commands, namely, the holiness

---

33. Cf. Jon D. Levenson, "The Theologies of Commandment in Biblical Israel," *Harvard Theological Review* 71, no. 1/2 (1980): 17–33, at 25, who writes: "In Sirach, Wisdom, although as universal as creation itself and ruler of all peoples (Sir 24:3–6), yet sets up her tent in Israel alone (Sir 24:8). There, Wisdom is actually identified with the 'Book of the Covenant' and the Mosaic law (Sir 24:23). Wisdom and covenant become one, or, to be more precise, are revealed as having been one all along. In other words, the norms of Israel's covenant are here simply the intensification of a universal *bonum*, *Heilsgeschichte* being merely the self-expression within the medium of history of a cosmic, protological constant."

of God. As such, the vision aims to produce shame and hope among those in the exile, and it enlivens in them a certain way of being. The latter of these, which begins a renewed liturgical practice in the form described, has as its primary and unifying referent the command to imitate the holiness of God present in the temple. This can be seen in the two-fold action of casting the prophet in the figure of Moses, the center of whose law, with which Ezekiel is certainly familiar, is the command: "You shall be holy; for I the LORD your God am holy" (Lev 19:2) and, secondly, in Ezekiel's deliberate reformulation of the Mosaic precepts to better realize that goal. To the model readership, namely, all of Israel in exile—even "the Israel of God" (Gal 6:16) in this vale of tears—the Temple Vision, in its measurements and apportionment as also in its legislation, remains not as a "dead letter" or an "evidence of [Ezekiel's] graphic mentality"[34] but as an abiding command to acknowledge the holiness of God and as an adumbration of the way in which the holiness will take shape among his people in time to come.[35] A passage from the midrash makes this point beautifully. When Ezekiel heard the command to relate the whole of this vision to the exiles, he responded:

> "Until now, we are put into exile in the land of our enemies; and You say to me to go and inform Israel about the form of the Temple, and 'write it in their eyes, and they should preserve its form and all of its statutes and do them.' And are they able to do them? Leave them until they emerge from the exile, and afterwards, I will go and tell them." So the Holy One, blessed be He, said to Ezekiel, "And because my children are in exile, the building of my Temple should be idle?" The Holy One, blessed be He, said to him, "Its reading in the Torah is as great as its building. Go and say it to them, and they will occupy themselves to read the form of the Temple in the Torah. And in reward for its reading, that they occupy themselves to read about it, I count it for them as if they were occupied with the building of the Temple."[36]

V. Concluding Detour

In trying to summarize this approach to the text, allow me to turn briefly to Psalm 137 and the commentary of Saint Augustine. The Psalmist, writing from the perspective of the exile, invokes a blessing on those who take vengeance on

---

34. Greenberg, "The Design and Themes of Ezekiel's Program of Restoration," 208.

35. Cf. Gary Anderson, "Mary in the Old Testament," *Pro Ecclesia* 16, no. 1 (2007): 33–55.

36. *Midrash Tanhuma, Tzav* 14. Accessed September 1, 2021 and cited with modification from https://www.sefaria.org/Midrash_Tanchuma%2C_Tzav.14.1?lang=bi&with=all&lang2=en.

ANTHONY PAGLIARINI

Israel's captors. "O daughter of Babylon, you devastator! Happy shall he be who repays you with what you have done to us! Happy shall he be who takes your little ones and dashes them against the rock!" (Ps 137:8–9). Commenting on these verses, Augustine understands that Babylon and the plight of the exiles are the referent of the text. That much is plain. Even so, the text is received and interpreted with reference to Christ and to his Body, the Church. This is not misappropriation—not necessarily—but an acknowledgement of history's providential character. It is a narrative in which, as Auerbach explains, "an occurrence signifies not only itself but at the same time another, which it predicts or confirms, without prejudice to the power of its concrete reality here and now."[37] The psalm speaks of Nebuchadnezzar's Babylon and of all the other Babylons which that nation prefigures (cf. Rev 17:5). The psalm speaks of the exile and of that larger ontological exile in which humanity has found itself since Eden. As the *Midrash Tehillim* says, "Everything which David said in his book was said of himself, of all Israel, and of the past and future of Israel."[38] Augustine is free, therefore, to interrogate the particulars of the text and to find in them a meaning which the Psalmist never knew. Said differently, he is free to read the Psalm "in the same spirit in which it was written."[39]

In Augustine's reading, Babylon is this world,[40] particularly the devil and his angels.[41] "'The waters of Babylon' are all things which here are loved, and pass away,"[42] and the Children of Babylon are "evil desires at their birth."[43] When, therefore, "lust is born, before evil habit gives it strength against you, when lust is little, by no means let it gain the strength of evil habit; when it is little, dash it. But you fear, lest though dashed it die not; 'Dash it against the Rock; and that Rock is Christ.'"[44]

A similar process is at work in the Temple Vision, likewise set by the waters of Babylon (Ezek 1:1). The specific features of these chapters are never abandoned. They are, however, discerned differently within a canonical and ecclesial setting, which is to say, within a setting that acknowledges God's

37. Erich Auerbach, *Mimesis: The Presentation of Reality in Western Literature,* trans. William R. Trask (Princeton: Princeton University Press, 1953), 555.

38. *Midrash Tehillim* 17.1.

39. *Dei verbum,* §12.

40. Augustine, *Enarrationes in Psalmos,* 137.12.

41. Augustine, *Enarrationes in Psalmos,* 137.6.

42. Augustine, *Enarrationes in Psalmos,* 137.2 (NPNF 1/8:630).

43. Augustine, *Enarrationes in Psalmos,* 137.12 (NPNF 1/8:632).

44. Augustine, *Enarrationes in Psalmos,* 137.12 (NPNF 1/8:632, slightly altered); cf. 1 Cor 10:4.

Inspiration and Truth When Prophecy Fails: Ezekiel's Temple Vision

authorship of history and of its interpretation. The failure of the text to be realized in all of its original specificity is incidental. The illocution of these chapters was always to convey the radical holiness of God and to move the exilic audience to acknowledge and respond to that holiness. It is so still, not least as we encounter it woven throughout the Book of Revelation. And just as the specific features of Babylon in Psalm 137 are allowed to function now in reference to the life of the Church, so also the details of the Law and Temple in Ezekiel's vision present us with an understanding of God's holiness as it has "pitched its tent" (cf. John 1:14) among us and as it will yet do so.

In one respect, the prophecy of the Temple Vision fails. All the same it is a true and inspired text. There is no contradiction in this. If we discern the function of the prophet's language and his theology of history, we can receive the Temple Vision as what it was always intended to be, namely an announcement of Israel's future spoken in the idiom of its past—not a prescription or blueprint but an adumbration of God's renewed presence among his people.

5. Ratzinger on the Historicity of the Gospels: A Case Study of the Last Supper Narrative

Aaron Pidel, SJ

"Well, if it's a symbol, to Hell with it!" These words, once spoken by Flannery O'Connor on the subject of the Eucharist,[1] could also well describe one side of Joseph Ratzinger's attitude toward the Gospels. In the introduction to the first volume of *Jesus of Nazareth*, he writes, "The *factum historicum* . . . is not an interchangeable symbolic cipher for biblical faith, but the foundation on which it stands. *Et incarnatus est*—when we say these words, we acknowledge God's actual entry into real history."[2] Any denial of Christianity's basic historicity, he again observes in "Exegesis and the Magisterium of the Church," "disincarnates the faith" and ends in "Gnosticism."[3] Indeed, it is precisely because it is the "very essence of biblical faith to be about real historical events" that the historical-critical method constitutes an "indispensable dimension of exegetical work."[4] Ratzinger, in short, seems to have little use for any approach that would reduce the Gospels to *merely* edifying symbols.

---

1. See the letter of December 16, 1955 addressed "To A.," in Flannery O'Connor, *The Habit of Being*, ed. and introduced by Sally Fitzgerald (New York: Vintage Books, 1980), 125.

2. Joseph Ratzinger, *Jesus of Nazareth: From the Baptism in the Jordan to the Transfiguration*, trans. Adrian J. Walker (San Francisco: Ignatius, 2007), xv. Hereafter JN 1:xv.

3. Joseph Ratzinger, "Exegesis and the Magisterium of the Church," 126–36 in *Opening up the Scriptures: Joseph Ratzinger and the Foundations of Biblical Interpretation*, ed. José Granados, Carlos Granados, and Luis Sánchez-Navarro (Grand Rapids: Eerdmans, 2008), 134. The essay was originally published in 2003.

4. JN 1:xv. In an early essay, and in the same spirit, Ratzinger opines that exegetical investigation of Scripture's "literal sense preserves the connection with the *sarx* of the Logos against every kind of Gnosis." "The Question of the Concept of Tradition," 41–89 in *God's Word: Scripture—Tradition—Office*, ed. Peter Hünermann and Thomas Söding, trans. Henry Taylor (San Francisco: Ignatius, 2008), 66.

Ratzinger on the Historicity of the Gospels

That being said, Ratzinger hardly denies that the Gospels symbolically embellish their basically factual account. He sees in the genealogies of Matthew and Luke a "symbolic structuring of historical time."[5] He admits that what Jesus' post-Resurrection "table fellowship with the disciples really looked like is beyond our powers of imagination."[6] He cites approvingly the following, rather qualified, affirmation of the Gospels' historicity by the German exegete Rudolf Schnackenburg: "The historical ground is presupposed but is superseded in the faith-view of the evangelists."[7] The question, Ratzinger suggests, is not whether the Gospels reshape the historical ground from a faith perspective, but "how far the 'historical ground' actually extends."[8] Ratzinger thus admits in principle some distance between the empirical Jesus and the narrated Jesus, even if he also hints at his dissatisfaction with how much distance mainstream biblical criticism presumes.

In affirming both the substantial historicity of the Gospels and some degree of theological elaboration, Ratzinger arguably does little more than restate the teaching of the Second Vatican Council's Dogmatic Constitution on Divine Revelation. On the one hand, *Dei verbum* observes that Scripture in general must be acknowledged as teaching "solidly, faithfully, and without error that truth which God wanted put into sacred writings for the sake of our salvation."[9] It goes on to affirm that God wanted the Gospels to have a "historical character" (*historicitatem*), such that they "faithfully hand on what Jesus Christ, while living among men, really did and taught for their eternal salvation until the day he was taken up into heaven."[10] One the other hand, *Dei verbum* also acknowledges that the Gospels may have reshaped their source materials in ways that do not conform to our historical conventions. The Council grants that the Evangelists taught

> with that clearer understanding which they enjoyed after they had been instructed by the glorious events of Christ's life and taught by the light of the Spirit of truth. The sacred authors wrote the four Gospels, selecting some

---

5. See Joseph Ratzinger, *Jesus of Nazareth: The Infancy Narratives*, trans. Philip J. Whitmore (New York: Image, 2012), 9. Hereafter JN 3:9.

6. Joseph Ratzinger, *Jesus of Nazareth: Holy Week: From the Entrance into Jerusalem to the Resurrection*, trans. Philip J. Whitmore (San Francisco: Ignatius, 2011), 272. Hereafter JN 2:272.

7. Rudolf Schnackenburg, *Jesus in the Gospels: A Biblical Christology*, trans. O. C. Dean, Jr. (Louisville: Westminster John Knox, 1995), 321; cited in JN 1:xiii.

8. JN 1:xiii.

9. Second Vatican Council, *Dei verbum* (November 18, 1965) (Boston: Pauline Books & Media, 1965), §11.

10. *Dei verbum*, §19.

things from the many which had been handed on by word of mouth or in writing, reducing some of them to a synthesis, explaining some things in view of the situation of their churches, and preserving the form of proclamation, but always in such fashion that they told us the honest truth about Jesus.[11]

Whereas contemporary historians aim at a kind of photorealism in their representation of the past, and would thus see selection, synthesis, and composition with a view to contemporary concerns as declensions from this ideal, *Dei verbum* presents these techniques as compatible with conveying the "honest truth about Jesus." Indeed, as a wave of recent research has confirmed, ancient biographers felt that good history required a creative fidelity to their sources not unlike that described by *Dei verbum*.[12]

But just how much "theological symbol"[13] can the Gospel narratives admit before ceasing to portray what Ratzinger claims they portray, namely, "the real, 'historical' Jesus in the strict sense of the word"? The Pontifical Biblical Commission's 2014 statement, *Inspirazione et Verità della Sacra Scrittura*, gives little general guidance on this question. Preferring case studies to hermeneutical principles, it concludes, for instance, that the historical discrepancies between the Matthean and Lucan Infancy Narratives "concern secondary aspects vis-à-vis the central figure of Jesus."[14] But how does one determine what aspects are primary or secondary to the Gospels? Ratzinger's own answer to that question would, I believe, depend on the narrative under consideration. He would admit that the Gospels intend to affirm the "historical ground" to varying degrees, but he would also offer a rather consistent set of criteria for assessing that intention, or at least for estimating the lower bounds of historicity.

With a view to showing how this is so, this reflection will proceed in stages.

---

11. *Dei verbum*, §19.

12. For the pioneering work in this field, see Richard A. Burridge, *What Are the Gospels?: A Comparison with Greco-Roman Biography*, 2nd ed. (Grand Rapids: Eerdmans, 2004). According to Craig Keener, Burridge's book "swiftly and successfully shifted the consensus of scholarship about the Gospels." Craig Keener, *Christobiography: Memory, History, and the Reliability of the Gospels* (Grand Rapids: Eerdmans, 2019), 13.

13. JN 1:xxii. I owe the language of "theological symbol" to Richard H. Bell, "The Transfiguration: A Case Study in the Relationship between 'History' and 'Theological Symbol' in the Light of Pope Benedict's Book," 159–75 in *The Pope and Jesus of Nazareth: Christ, Scripture and the Church*, ed. Adrian Pabst and Angus Paddison (London: SCM, 2009).

14. Pontifical Biblical Commission, *Inspirazione et Verità della Sacra Scrittura* (February 22, 2014), https://www.vatican.va/roman_curia/congregations/cfaith/pcb_documents/rc_con_cfaith_doc_ 20140222_ispirazione-verita-sacra-scrittura_it.html, §124. My translation from the Italian.

First, it will review Ratzinger's four criteria for identifying Scripture's central affirmations in any domain. Then it will show how Ratzinger applies these criteria analogously to the Gospels narrative, taking as a case study Ratzinger's treatment of the dating of the Last Supper, especially his conclusion that the Synoptic chronology is theologically structured. Some consideration will also be given to the relevance of a historical solution unconsidered by Ratzinger: Brant Pitre's "Passover Hypothesis."

I. Distinguishing Scripture's Intention

Though the limited scope of this essay prevents a full-scale treatment of Ratzinger on inspiration and inerrancy, a few brief remarks are in order.[15] These remarks concern Ratzinger's understanding of biblical authorship and his criteria for distinguishing Scripture's true intentions from the ideas merely accompanying those intentions.

With respect to the question of authorship, Ratzinger understands Scripture to be the product of three interacting subjects. More specifically, Scripture bears the intentions of (1) God, (2) the individual literary authors and redactors employed by God, and (3) a transhistorical corporate personality—the "People of God." Because the People of God represents an even "deeper 'author'" of Scripture than any literary author,[16] discerning what Scripture intends to affirm with respect to any given question requires discerning a corporate intentionality. Perhaps for this reason, Ratzinger prefers already in 1962 to speak not of the intentions of plural authors but of the intention of Scripture itself. Criticizing what he considered the wooden model of inerrancy contained in *De fontibus revelationis*, the Second Vatican Council's first draft schema on Divine Revelation, Ratzinger observed, "Scripture is and remains inerrant and beyond doubt in everything that it properly intends to affirm, but this is not necessarily so in that which accompanies the affirmation and is not part of it."[17] Ratzinger subtly breaks with the neo-Scholastic model of inspiration by making Scripture as a whole, not its individual literary authors, the grammatical subject of the intention to affirm.

Given the fact that a corporate subject "bears" Scripture, Ratzinger concludes that one must consult the People of God when distinguishing Scripture's

15. For a fuller treatment, see my "Joseph Ratzinger on Biblical Inerrancy," *Nova et Vetera* 12, no. 1 (2014): 307–33.

16. For this threefold authorship, see JN 1:xx–xxi.

17. Jared Wicks, SJ, "Six Texts by Prof. Joseph Ratzinger as Peritus before and during Vatican Council II," *Gregorianum* 89, no. 2 (2008): 233–311, at 280.

AARON PIDEL, SJ

intended (and thus revealed) contents from its accompanying (and thus potentially culture-bound) ideas. In an early essay on Bultmann's project of demythologization, "Zum Problem der Entmythologisierung des Neuen Testaments," Ratzinger writes,

> What is revelation and what is rind [*Schale*] can never be ascertained by the individual theologian—from his own perspective—on the basis of scholarly presuppositions [*wissenschaftlicher Vorgegebenheiten*]; this, in the end, only the living community of faith can decide, which—as the Body of Christ—is the abiding presence of Christ, who does not let his disposal over his work slip from his grasp.[18]

In other words, only the whole Church, a hermeneutical community guided by Christ's spirit, enjoys the transcendent perspective from which to distinguish the central and peripheral elements of the biblical worldview.[19] And it is ultimately from this same perspective that one best determines just "how far the historical ground actually extends." In discerning just how far the Gospels affirm the historical value of a given narrative, one must consult not only archeological records and Synoptic parallels but the faith of the Church.

But this raises a further question. How can a criterion as unwieldy and undifferentiated as the faith of a transhistorical community serve to sift Scripture's revealed center from its accompanying periphery? Ratzinger gives perhaps his most succinct and concrete answer in his essay "Farewell to the Devil?" (1973), which, admittedly, treats not so much a question of historicity as a question of worldview. "Farewell to the Devil?" responds to Tübingen *Alttestamentler* Herbert Haag's proposal to demythologize the Devil once and for all. As Haag saw things, the whole biblical realm of the demonic represented nothing more than a culturally conditioned way of expressing what we would nowadays call structural sin.[20] One need not believe in the existence of

---

18. Joseph Ratzinger, "Zum Problem der Entmythologisierung des Neuen Testaments," *Religionsunterricht an höheren Schulen* 3 (1960): 2–11, at 11 (author's translation).

19. Ratzinger elsewhere observes that it is legitimate to redraw the boundaries between what belongs to faith and what belongs to worldview, provided one "does not forget the insight that faith can be put into practice only by believing with the Church and that it is not subject to private decisions about what is or is not to be regarded as defensible." "Abschied vom Teufel?," 225–34 in *Dogma und Verkündigung* (München, Erich Wewel, 1973), 199; English version: "Farewell to the Devil?," 199–206 in *Dogma and Preaching*, trans. Michael J. Miller and Matthew J. O'Connell (San Francisco: Ignatius, 2011), 227–28. Henceforth I will distinguish German and English pagination by a virgule, e.g., *Dogma*, 227–28/199. Citations without a virgule refer to the English pagination.

20. Ratzinger refers to Herbert Haag, *Abschied vom Teufel* (Einsiedeln: Benziger, 1969).

Ratzinger on the Historicity of the Gospels

demons or the Devil, Haag implied, provided one retains the notion of structural evil.

Ratzinger responds to Haag's proposed demythologization by noting that biblical ideas cannot be relegated to the "mythological" periphery simply because they were more readily accepted by premodern cultures. More discerning criteria must be applied. "Although there is no standard that automatically indicates in all particular cases where faith ends and world view begins," he explains, "there is still a series of aids to judgment [*Urteilshilfe*] that show the way as we look for clarifications."[21] He enumerates four such rules of thumb: (1) the "relationship between the two Testaments,"[22] (2) the connection to Christ's mission as portrayed in the New Testament,[23] (3) the degree of reception into the "faith of the Church,"[24] and (4) "compatibility with scholarly [*wissenschaftlicher*] knowledge."[25] Together these four tests, representing both faith and reason, help the exegete discern the Bible's intention in disputed questions.

Applying these criteria to the case at hand, Ratzinger demonstrates that the Devil occupies a very different place in the architecture of Scripture than other premodern ideas like geocentrism. Turning to the relation between the Old and New Testaments, for example, Ratzinger attends to the intertestamental trajectory of each notion. The demonic plays a rather marginal role in the Old Testament but then explodes in the New, appearing in the Pauline, Johannine, and Synoptic traditions. It thus shows a trajectory of expansion. Cosmological speculation, by contrast, tapers off from Old Testament to New, showing a trajectory of contraction. On the first test, then, the Devil tests positive for abiding normativity while geocentrism tests negative.[26]

The second and third tests, which Ratzinger describes as "closely connected,"[27] yield a similar result. Examining first the broader New Testament portrayal of Jesus' religious experience, Ratzinger finds that combat with demons forms an "inseparable part of Jesus' spiritual way," whereas the relative motions of sun and earth in no way alter the "figure of Jesus, his spiritual physiognomy."[28] Ratzinger next considers how far respective beliefs in the demonic and in geocentrism have entered into the Church's "authentic interior act of

---

21. *Dogma*, 228/199.

22. *Dogma*, 228/199.

23. *Dogma*, 231/202.

24. *Dogma*, 231/202.

25. *Dogma*, 232/203.

26. *Dogma*, 229/200.

27. *Dogma*, 231/202.

28. *Dogma*, 230–31/201–2.

AARON PIDEL, SJ

faith, into the fundamental form of prayer and life, above and beyond the variations of tradition."[29] By way of response, he appeals to the fact that exorcism and renunciation of Satan belong to the core event of putting on Christ, namely, baptism. And those who live out their baptism best, the canonized saints, often continue to have a very realistic sense of combat with the demonic. Demythologizing the Devil would, therefore, inevitably change both the meaning of baptism and the basic "conduct of Christian life."[30] Ratzinger considers it obvious that geocentrism has never entered into the Church's faith to the same extent.

The last of the tests, the relation to "scientific knowledge," remains the hardest to apply. With respect to demonology, Ratzinger concedes that a kind of technocratic "functionalist perspective" has become increasingly ascendant in contemporary Western culture, rendering the existence of the Devil increasingly implausible to the average person. But any exegete identifying the functionalist perspective with rationality as such, he counters, will ultimately rule out much more than just the Devil. "There is no room in a functionalistic perspective for God, either," he writes, "and no room for man as man, but only for man as function."[31] Only a rational standard that leaves the central elements of biblical worldview intact can plausibly claim to guide "demythologization." Whereas geocentrism proves incompatible with specific findings of astronomy, belief in the Devil contradicts only a vague functionalist sensibility, which itself amounts to a totalizing worldview. According to each of the four "aids to judgment," then, belief in the Devil passes the normativity test, whereas geocentrism fails.

Though Ratzinger's enumeration of these "tests" in "Farewell to the Devil?" remains somewhat *ad hoc*, doubtlessly adapted to the particular cases of demonology and astronomy, they are not without parallels elsewhere. The three criteria of faith map closely onto the historical strata of tradition that Ratzinger identifies in his seminal 1965 essay, "The Question of the Concept of Tradition."[32] A comparable set of "standards" appears as guides for preaching

---

29. *Dogma*, 231/202.

30. *Dogma*, 232/203.

31. *Dogma*, 232–33/203.

32. Ratzinger, "The Question of the Concept of Tradition," 60–61. Ratzinger speaks there of four relectures internal to Scripture: the "Old Testament theology of the Old Testament," the "New Testament Theology of the Old Testament," the "New Testament Theology of the New Testament," and the "ecclesial theology of the New Testament." The first two correspond roughly to the relationship between Old and New Testament, the third to the holistic New Testament portrait of Christ, and the fourth to ecclesial reception.

90

in *Dogma and Preaching*.[33] And the same criteria, somewhat differently enumerated, resurface in *In the Beginning*, now as aids to discerning "form and content" in the creation narratives.[34] The tests of "Farewell to the Devil?" represent merely the fullest and most methodologically transparent exposition of Ratzinger's recurrent strategy for distinguishing Scripture's central concerns from the vehicles of their expression.

I would argue, moreover, that Ratzinger uses a version of these tests to navigate apparent conflicts not only between Scripture and scientific reason but between Scripture and historical reason as well.[35] Indeed, in "Exegesis and the Magisterium of the Church," after laying out the basic principles governing the relationship between biblical revelation and the natural sciences, he notes that "something analogous can be said with respect to history."[36] It is to such an analogous historical application of these criteria that we now turn, examining Ratzinger's appraisal of the historicity of the Last Supper narrative's chronology.

II. Historicity of Last Supper Chronology

As a case study, I have chosen Ratzinger's treatment of Last Supper chronology in *Holy Week*, the second volume of his *Jesus of Nazareth* trilogy. There are several reasons for this decision. First, the Last Supper is a topic that Ratzinger has revisited several times and reflected on at length.[37] Second, Ratzinger is

33. *Dogma*, 26–27. Here Ratzinger mentions four "standards": "the interrelated unity of Old and New Testament," "Creeds," the "living magisterium," and the "concrete faith of the Church in her communities." The first standard effectively condenses the first two "aids to judgment" of "Farewell to the Devil?," namely, the relationship of Old to New Testament and coherence within the New Testament itself. The last three "standards" simply subdivide the last "aid to judgment" of "Farewell to the Devil?," namely, ecclesial reception.

34. Joseph Ratzinger, *'In the Beginning...': A Catholic Understanding of the Story of Creation and the Fall*, trans. Boniface Ramsey (Grand Rapids: Eerdmans, 1995), 4. Ratzinger appeals to "the unity of the Bible as a criterion for its interpretation" and "Christology as a criterion" (8, 15). The exposition includes considerations of patristic interpretations, and thus of ecclesial reception; as well as of evolutionary theory, and thus of scientific reason (16, 50–58).

35. To see how Ratzinger uses these same tests to negotiate the apparent conflict between biblical monogenism and evolutionary polygenism, see my essay, "How True is the Bible? Ratzinger on Faith, Reason, and Scripture," *Review for Religious: New Series* 1, no. 2 (Fall 2021): 143–58.

36. Ratzinger, "Exegesis and the Magisterium of the Church," 134.

37. For earlier treatments, see Ratzinger's exploration of the "Idea of the Covenant in the Texts of the Last Supper" (German original: 1995), 57–66 in *Many Religions—One Covenant: Israel, the Church, and the World*, trans. Graham Harrison (San Francisco: Ignatius, 1999); as

91

AARON PIDEL, SJ

highly attentive to method here. The preface to *Holy Week* describes its project as "finally putting into practice the methodological principles formulated for exegesis by the Second Vatican Council (in *Dei Verbum* 12), a task that unfortunately has scarcely been attempted thus far."[38] The same preface goes on to suggest that an adequate method requires being "guided by the hermeneutic of faith, but at the same time adopting a responsible attitude toward historical reason, which is a necessary component of that faith."[39] Careful attention to how Ratzinger applies this faith-and-reason method, however, reveals that he means something like the four "tests" studied above, the first three of which represent the criteria of faith, the last of which represents scholarly reason. In drawing attention to the background influence of these criteria, I hope to strengthen and nuance Matthew Ramage's claim that *Holy Week's* treatment of the Last Supper illustrates Ratzinger's "Method C" approach to biblical interpretation.[40] Finally, since new proposals for reconciling the Last Supper chronology have appeared even since the publication of *Holy Week*, the book offers a model for serenely navigating historical *Unstimmigkeiten* on the basis of even imperfect historical data.

With a view to showing how Ratzinger forms his judgment, I reorganize Ratzinger's arguments as a kind of back-and-forth negotiation between reason and faith. I will begin with the challenge posed by historical reason to the historicity of the Last Supper narratives, then show how Ratzinger uses the tests of faith, the test of scholarly reason, and then the tests of faith again to narrow the field of historical proposals. Criteria analogous to those in "Farewell to the Devil?" lead him to conclude both that the Johannine and Synoptic chronologies of the Last Supper cannot be reconciled and that the Synoptic chronology is more likely to be symbolically structured.

---

well as his treatment of "Form and Content in the Eucharistic Celebration," 33–60 in *Feast of Faith*, trans. Graham Harrison (San Francisco: Ignatius, 1986). This chapter represents a translation and expansion (through appendices) of: "Gestalt and Gehalt der eucharistischen Feier," *Internationale Katholische Zeitschrift—Communio* 6 (1977): 385–96.

38. JN 2:xv.

39. JN 2:xv.

40. Matthew J. Ramage, *Jesus Interpreted: Benedict XVI, Bart Ehrman, and the Historical Truth of the Gospels* (Washington, DC: Catholic University of American Press, 2017), 156–64. "Method C" refers to Ratzinger's proposal, made after his 1988 Erasmus Lecture, that exegetes develop a new method combining the strengths of both patristic-medieval (Method A) and historical-critical (Method B) approaches (58).

II / Test of Scholarly Reason: Difficulties Raised by Historical Reason

Among the impediments to taking the Gospels as unvarnished transcripts of the Last Supper's happenings stands an ostensible calendrical discrepancy. Put simply, the Synoptics and John seem to differ on whether the Last Supper happened on the Jewish Passover, the 15th of Nisan. The Synoptic Gospels follow Mark's rather precise dating: "On the first day of Unleavened Bread, when they sacrificed the Passover Lamb, his disciples said to him, 'Where will you have us go and prepare for you to eat the Passover?'" (Mark 14:12 NAB). Since the first day of Unleavened Bread is 14 Nisan, the Synoptic chronology has Jesus celebrating his Passover meal at the beginning of 15 Nisan (Thursday evening), suffering death toward the end of the 15 Nisan (Friday afternoon), resting in the tomb on the Sabbath (Friday evening through Saturday evening), and rising on the "first day of the week" (Sunday).

John's Gospel, however, appears to tell a different story. It reports that the Jewish authorities, after hauling Jesus before Pilate, avoided entering the Praetorium "so that they might not be defiled, but might eat the Passover" (John 18:28). The fact that the Passover was still to be eaten suggests that the supper Jesus held with his disciples (John 13–17) took place the evening before Passover, at the commencement of 14 Nisan. John also places Pilate's condemnation of Jesus at the sixth hour of the "Preparation of the Passover" (Παρασκευὴ τοῦ πάσχα) (John 19:14), which Ratzinger, following many exegetes, takes to be the Day of Preparation for Passover and an implicit reference to the hour when paschal lambs were slaughtered.[41] At several points, then, John's Gospel seems to date both Jesus' Last Supper and his death to 14 Nisan, the day before the ritually prescribed Jewish Passover.

Until recently, when exegetes were deciding which way of relating Jewish Passover and Last Supper enjoyed greater historical probability, they typically favored one of three positions. The German Protestant exegete Joachim Jeremias made an influential case for the historical plausibility of the Synoptic calendar, highlighting perceived references to the Jewish Passover ritual in all accounts of the Last Supper.[42] The American Catholic exegete John Meier favors the Johannine chronology, according to which Jesus' meal occurred before the calendrical Passover: "Both the pre-Synoptic and Johannine traditions

---

41. JN 2:108–9. Brant Pitre notes that the Παρασκευὴ τοῦ πάσχα can be taken as a subjective rather than objective genitive, meaning not the "day of preparation *for* the Passover" but the "day of preparation *of* Passover [week]" or, simply, Friday of Passover. Brant Pitre, *Jesus and the Last Supper* (Grand Rapids: Eerdmans, 2015), 357–60.

42. Joachim Jeremias, *Die Abendmahlsworte Jesu,* 4th ed. (Göttingen: Vandenhoeck & Ruprecht, 1967).

are much better explained by a special farewell meal, planned and executed by Jesus according to his own desires and peculiar circumstances."[43] The French Catholic exegete Annie Jaubert, for her part, argued that both John and the Synoptics can be correct, since there are actually two different Passovers in play. She noted that some Jews, especially Essenes associated with Qumran, calculated Passover in such a way that the meal fell on Tuesday evening. Jesus could thus have celebrated Passover on Tuesday according to the Qumran calendar and died on Friday afternoon, just before Passover began on the Temple calendar.[44]

The initial evidence that the test of scholarly reason is operative in *Holy Week* is that Ratzinger feels obliged to admit the irreconcilability of the narratives at the historical level and choose among the proposed solutions. As we will see, this eventually leads him to judge John's "off-Passover" dating of the Last Supper as more historically plausible and to construe the Synoptic dating theologically. It is worth noting, however, that in 2015 Brant Pitre's *Jesus and the Last Supper* added a fourth, highly compelling, option, which argues that the calendrical discrepancies between John and the Synoptics are only apparent. Since the position appeared too late for Ratzinger's consideration in the second volume of *Jesus of Nazareth*, I will consider it only after showing how Ratzinger uses his "tests" to assess the three earlier proposals.

II.2 Applying the Three Tests of Faith

Turning to the first of the three faith-based tests, that of the relationship between Old and New Testaments, we do well to recall how Ratzinger reckons a trajectory of surprising intensification to be a mark of authenticity. "Farewell to the Devil?" ascribed the existence of the Devil to Scripture's core affirmations because, even though the demonic appears in both Testaments, it asserts itself with a surprising vehemence in the New. Ratzinger finds in Meier's option for a Johannine chronology a similar pattern of surprising intensification.[45] For if the Johannine chronology is more historically accurate, then Jesus did not celebrate the Passover meal as legally prescribed. Here lies surprise, or

---

43. John Meier, *A Marginal Jew: Rethinking the Historical Jesus*, vol. 1, *The Roots of the Problem and the Person* (New York: Doubleday, 1991), 399.

44. There exist numerous variations on this argument. Colin J. Humphreys proposes that the Synoptics make use of Israel's preexilic way of reckoning the Passover, according to which Passover would fall on Wednesday evening. See Colin J. Humphreys, *The Mystery of the Last Supper: Reconstructing the Final Days of Jesus* (Cambridge: Cambridge University Press, 2011), 193–94.

45. For Ratzinger's debt to Meier, see JN 2:113–14; Meier, *Marginal Jew*, 1:429–30.

discontinuity.[46] At the same time, Jesus would have organized a solemn meal in the atmosphere of the Passover festival, suffered, and experienced divine rescue. Here lies the typological continuity. The whole conjunction of events suggests that Jesus intended to celebrate a "new" and definitive Passover: "Even though the meal that Jesus shared with the Twelve was not a Passover meal according to the ritual prescriptions of Judaism," writes Ratzinger, "nevertheless, in retrospect, the inner connection of the whole event with Jesus' death and Resurrection stood out clearly. It was Jesus' Passover. . . . The old was not abolished; it was simply brought to its full meaning."[47] If the Johannine narrative were historical, in other words, it would not lack this note of analogical intensification between the Testaments.[48]

A similar case could be made, of course, for the alternative chronologies. Both Jaubert's and Jeremias's hypotheses presume that Jesus innovated on the Passover ritual at least by adding his own meaning to it. The first test is not yet conclusive.

The second test, that of compatibility with the broader New Testament portrait of Christ, proves a bit more discriminating. It at least counts against Jaubert's hypothesis, which Ratzinger seems to have favored as recently as 2007.[49] For Jaubert supposes Jesus to have followed a calendar linked principally to the Qumran and Essene communities, who, because they rejected the Herodian Temple, also shunned the calendar of the Temple aristocracy.[50] Yet elsewhere in the Gospels, Ratzinger notes, Jesus "still followed the Jewish festal calendar, as is evident from John's Gospel in particular."[51] This dissonance with

---

46. Rabbi Walter Homolka argues that Jesus behaves at the Last Supper just like a pious Jew celebrating a Seder. Walter Homolka, "Jesu Letztes Abendmahl," 195–99 in *Der Jesus Buch des Papstes: Passion, Tod, und Auferstehung im Disput*, ed. Herman Häring (Berlin: LIT, 2011), 199. As Josef Wohlmuth notes, however, the Seder seems to postdate the Last Supper, making its celebration an unlikely intention for Jesus. Josef Wohlmuth, "Die Sicht auf Judentum im zweiten Band des Jesusbuches," 179–93 in *Der Jesus des Papstes: Passion, Tod, Auferstehung im Disput*, ed. Herman Häring (Berlin: LIT, 2011), 187.

47. JN 2:113–14.

48. Treating the relationship between the Last Supper and the Passover, Ratzinger observes, "There is nothing fortuitous in this interplay of old and new. It is the exact and necessary expression of the new existing situation in salvation history. Jesus prays his new prayer within the Jewish liturgy." "Form and Content in the Eucharistic Celebration," 41.

49. As Benedict XVI, Ratzinger still presented Jesus' celebration of the Passover according to the Qumran calendar as a "plausible hypothesis." See Homily at the Mass of the Lord's Supper (April 5, 2007), English trans. in *L'Osservatore Romano* 40, no. 15 (April 11, 2007): 3.

50. JN 2:33.

51. JN 2:111.

AARON PIDEL, SJ

Jesus' customary respect for the Temple and its ceremonies, evident in many strands of the Gospel tradition, strains credibility.

The same criterion might seem to favor the Synoptic chronology over the Johannine, since the Johannine chronology would have Jesus celebrating the Passover "off" the Temple calendar that he elsewhere respected. But Ratzinger argues that this need not weigh decisively against the Johannine chronology. Two other features of the New Testament Christology merit consideration: evidence of Jesus' habitual freedom with regard to ritual prescriptions; evidence of an early Passover theology possibly motivating the Synoptics to move the meal back "on" calendar.

In certain respects, Ratzinger's treatment of the Last Supper hearkens back to his treatment of Jesus' attitude toward the Law, found in the first volume of *Jesus of Nazareth*. There Ratzinger dwells at length on both Jesus' seemingly cavalier attitude toward Sabbath observance and his justification for it, namely, that the "Son of Man is Lord of the Sabbath" (Mark 2:28; cf. Matt 12:8, Luke 6:5). Ratzinger cites Rabbi Jacob Neusner's impression of what Jesus' Jewish contemporaries would have gathered from his words and deeds: "Jesus was not just another reforming rabbi, out to make life 'easier' for people.... Jesus' claim to authority is at issue."[52] Similar language appears in Ratzinger's treatment of the originality of Jesus' words and deeds at the Last Supper. "Something so utterly extraordinary was scarcely compatible with the picture of the friendly rabbi that many exegetes draw of Jesus."[53] Just as Jesus' sovereignty vis-à-vis the Sabbath implies more than a "liberal rabbi," so does his originality at the Last Supper imply more than a "friendly rabbi." The parallel subtly implies that the one who acted as Lord of the Sabbath could also plausibly act as Lord of the Passover.[54] The broader New Testament portrait of Jesus thus supports the idea that he might have handled the Passover creatively, even to the point of holding *his* Passover a day earlier.

But if Jesus moved his Passover-like meal "off calendar," why would Mark move it back "on calendar"? Mark does after all take pains to specify that the preparations for the Last Supper took place on the "first day of the Feast of

52. Jacob Neusner, *A Rabbi Talks with Jesus* (Montreal: McGill-Queen's University Press, 2000), 85; cited in JN 1:110.

53. JN 2:117–18.

54. This is also the solution of Romano Guardini, who was much admired by Ratzinger: "The last time [celebrating the Passover, Jesus] did not strictly adhere to the ritual. The very day was changed from Friday to Thursday, for was not he who called himself Lord of the Sabbath also Lord of the Passover?" *The Lord*, trans. Elinor Castendyk Briefs (Chicago: Henry Regnery, 1954), 369.

96

Unleavened Bread, when they sacrificed the Passover lamb" (Mark 14:12a; cf. Mark 14:1). Here Ratzinger can point to a kind of Passover lamb Christology, featuring a Christological interpretation of this same succession of feasts, evident in the earliest strata of the New Testament tradition. Already in First Corinthians, for instance, Paul expects to be readily understood when he exhorts the community in the following terms: "Cleanse out the old leaven that you may be new dough, as you really are unleavened. For Christ, our Paschal Lamb, has been sacrificed" (1 Cor 5:7). Extending the work of John Meier, Ratzinger explains its significance as follows: "The first day of Unleavened Bread and the Passover follow in rapid succession, but the older ritual understanding is transformed into a Christological and existential interpretation. Unleavened bread must now refer to Christians themselves, who are freed from sin by the addition of yeast. But the sacrificial lamb is Christ."[55] If Christ actually died when the paschal lambs were being sacrificed, as some think John implies,[56] it would be easy to explain how such a theology of Christ as Passover lamb came to pervade every strand of the New Testament (1 Pet 1:19; Rev 5:6, John 1:29). Mark's placement of the Last Supper on the Passover would then be a way of emphasizing the paschal character not only of Jesus' death but of his Last Supper as well.

Though more will be said on this topic below, these considerations suffice to show how the test of compatibility with the New Testament portrait of Christ continues to guide Ratzinger's judgment even on the Gospels' historical intentions. Positively, it begins to tip the scales against Jaubert's hypothesis. Negatively, it prevents him, by identifying a plausible theological rationale for redating the Last Supper to Passover, from excluding the historicity of the "off-Passover" dating out of hand. But it is not conclusive. Ratzinger is also aware that the same Paschal-lamb Christology could have motivated John to move the Passover to Friday (to underscore the paschal character of Christ's death), just as easily as it could have motivated the Synoptics to move it to

---

55. JN 2:114–15. Referring to 1 Cor 5:7, Meier remarks, "[Paul] apparently can presuppose that his Gentile converts understand the metaphor without any explanation. This implies that as early as the mid-fifties of the 1st century the idea of Christ's death as a Passover sacrifice was common Christian tradition." *Marginal Jew*, 1:429n108.

56. Raymond Brown, for instance, notes that Jesus was condemned at noon, "the very hour at which the priests began to slaughter the paschal lambs in the temple area." Raymond E. Brown, *The Gospel According to John*, vol. 2, *XIII–XXI*, AncB 29A (New York: Doubleday, 1970), 556. Pitre counters, however, that both Second-Temple and rabbinic sources place the sacrifice of the lambs between 3 p.m. and 5 p.m. Pitre, *Jesus and the Last Supper*, 327.

AARON PIDEL, SJ

Thursday (to underscore the paschal character of his Last Supper).[57] Additional criteria must be deployed.

The third "test," that of reception into the faith of the Church, proves still more discriminating. For Ratzinger, it tells rather decisively against Jaubert's harmonizing hypothesis. Jaubert's thesis, as we saw above, places the Last Supper on a Tuesday evening. Knowing that this represents something of a novel position, she attempts to show that the third-century *Didascalia Apostolorum* preserves an authentic memory of this chronology.[58] But Ratzinger counters that a less ambiguous and more enduring tradition, starting in the second century, places the Last Supper on Thursday.[59] Though Ratzinger does not himself provide references, he doubtlessly has in mind the passages that Jaubert herself cites in the course of anticipating objections. According to a fragment of Clement of Alexandria known as Περὶ τοῦ πάσχα, to name just one such example, Jesus taught his disciples that he was the true Passover Lamb by washing his disciples' feet on the day of "the consecration of the unleavened bread and the preparation of the feast" (ὁ ἁγιασμὸς τῶν ἀζύμων καὶ ἡ προετοιμασία τῆς ἑορτῆς), and suffering "the next [day]" (τῇ ἐπιούσῃ).[60] Irenaeus of Lyons corroborates the one-day interval between meal and death.[61] Since the early Church universally considered Friday the day of Christ's death, one might say the fourth-century Church "received" this one-day interval by choosing a Thursday for the annual commemoration of the Lord's Supper.[62]

---

57. Ratzinger observes that the exegetical field has tended to find in the Synoptics a historical chronology and in John a kind of "theological chronology," one that allowed Jesus' death to coincide with the symbolically significant slaughter of the Passover lambs. JN 2:108.

58. Jaubert provides French translations of the relevant excerpts of the *Didascalia Apostolorum*, cap. 21, x–xx in "La date de la dernière Cène," *Revue de l'histoire des religions* 146 (1954): 140–73, at 142–44. Joachim Jeremias counters that Jaubert's citations placing the Last Supper earlier in the week derive from the weekly Wednesday and Friday fast, which Christians began to associate retrospectively with Jesus' arrest and execution. Jeremias, *Abendmahlsworte Jesu*, 19.

59. JN 2:111. Ratzinger mentions sources starting in the second century but does not provide references. Jaubert, however, provides a list of such references in the course of denying their probative force ("Date de la dernière Cène," 149).

60. Clement of Alexandria, *Stromata Buch VII und VIII, Excerpta ex Theodoto, Eclogae Propheticae, Quis Dives Salvetur, Fragmente*, 2nd ed., ed. Otto Stählin and Ludwig Früchtel, GCS 17 (Berlin: Akademie Verlag, 1970), 216. My translation.

61. Irenaeus of Lyons reports that Jesus went up from Bethany to Jerusalem, "eating the Pasch and suffering the following day" (*manducans pascha et sequenti die passus*). In *Against Heresies* 2.22.3; cited in Jaubert, "Date de la dernière Cène," 150.

62. The annual celebration of the *coena domini* is already mentioned by the Third Council of Carthage (397 AD), which dispenses celebrating priests from fasting in view of the fasting

Ratzinger on the Historicity of the Gospels

In Ratzinger's mind, the test of ecclesial reception mainly tells against Jaubert's hypothesis, which requires several days of trials between Last Supper and Crucifixion. He wisely refrains from inferring too much from Clement's rather Johannine placement of the footwashing and its accompanying meal on the "preparation of the feast." That Clement describes the Passion as occurring on the day "following" the footwashing indicates that he was not reckoning days as most Jews did, that is, from evening to evening. At all events, it is worth noting that Ratzinger, though he ends up agreeing with Meier in discounting Jaubert's hypothesis, arrives at this conclusion by a slightly different route. Meier finds Jaubert's hypothesis wanting principally because it fails the test of multiple attestation. It discards the one calendrical fact about which Mark and John agree: "the Last Supper was on Thursday evening and Jesus died on the next day, Friday."[63] Ratzinger, by contrast, finds Jaubert's proposal lacking principally because it fails to explain the Last Supper's patristic and liturgical trajectory. Ratzinger's tendency to reason from the text's effective history back to proportionate historical cause represents one of the distinctives of his exegetical style.

II.3 Back to the Test of Scholarly Reason

Though the tests of faith suffice to discriminate against Jaubert's proposal, it is the test of scholarly reason that in Ratzinger's eyes seems to tell more decisively against Jeremias's Synoptic solution, tipping the balance in favor of Meier's Johannine proposal. But here it is worth noting that Ratzinger adopts the same discerning attitude toward historical reason that he adopted toward scientific reasoning in "Farewell to the Devil?" There, it will be remembered, Ratzinger insisted on compatibility with the solid findings of scientific investigation but not with the global sensibilities of the scientific worldview, which he dubbed the "functionalist perspective." In his treatment of the chronology of the Last Supper, Ratzinger works with a similar operative distinction between historical reason as such and the unexamined worldview of critical historiography.

---

required on Friday and Saturday. Third Council of Carthage (397), pp. 880–94 in *Sacrorum Conciliorum nova et amplissima collectio*, vol. 3, *Ab anno CCCXLVII ad annum CCCCIX*, ed. J.-D. Mansi (Florence: Antonii Zatta Veneti, 1749), cap. xxix.

63. Meier, *Marginal Jew*, 1:429n109. Meier also draws a "rough analogy from textual criticism." Just as textual criticism sees accepting a "hypothetical reconstruction that is witnessed in none of the manuscripts or versions" as a last resort, so also "creating a scenario for the date of Jesus' death that is supported by none of the Gospel traditions and to prefer it over Gospel traditions that are by no means impossible brings us close once again to writing a novel" (1:429n109).

AARON PIDEL, SJ

Ratzinger analyses the elements of this historiographical worldview most fully in his 1988 essay, "Biblical Interpretation in Conflict." There he notes that biblical criticism, in a misguided attempt to ape the rigor of the natural sciences, has often uncritically accepted the "simple transfer of the evolutionary model from natural science to the history of the mind."[64] Influenced unconsciously by this evolutionary paradigm, exegetes often perceive discrepancies within the canon as differences between simple and complex theological species, whose emergence they can plot along a developmental timeline.[65] Relying on highly subjective impressions of what counts as theologically complex, generations of exegetes identified Jesus' eschatological pronouncements as the historically authentic kernel, to which an inventive community allegedly added everything narrative, cultic, legal, and Hellenistic.[66] When weighing historical evidence, Ratzinger always seeks to correct for uncritically examined evolutionary thought schemas.

Meier's success in persuading Ratzinger of the Johannine chronology owes much to the fact that he makes certain arguments free from such evolutionary influence. Ratzinger seems to be particularly impressed by Meier's observation that the Temple authorities could hardly have chosen the Passover itself as the day for undertaking the whole series of actions culminating in Jesus' execution.[67] Far from marginalizing the cultic, this argument seems to take the liturgical reverence of Jesus' Jewish contemporaries very seriously.[68] Critics have chided Ratzinger for relying too much here on reconstructed Jewish psychology, and thus "making too much of *a priori* reasoning in the study of history."[69] Pitre's recent "Passover hypothesis," to be considered below, lends extra

64. Joseph Ratzinger, "Biblical Interpretation in Conflict," 91–126 in *God's Word: Scripture, Tradition, Office*, ed. Peter Hünermann and Thomas Söding, trans. Henry Taylor (San Francisco: Ignatius, 2008), at 106.

65. "Biblical Interpretation in Conflict," 104.

66. For Ratzinger's fuller exposition of this dialectic between the simple and complex, see "Biblical Interpretation in Conflict," 102–11.

67. JN 2:106–8.

68. For the importance of liturgy to Ratzinger, see Christopher Ruddy, "*Deus adorans, Homo adorans*: Joseph Ratzinger's Liturgical Christology and Anthropology," 173–88 in *The Center Is Jesus Christ Himself: Essays on Revelation, Salvation & Evangelization in Honor of Robert P. Imbelli*, ed. Andrew Meszaros (Washington, DC: Catholic University of America Press, 2021).

69. John P. Joy, "Ratzinger and Aquinas on the Dating of the Last Supper: In Defense of the Synoptic Chronology," *New Blackfriars* 94 (2012): 224–339, at 330. Joy points to the fact, recounted by Ratzinger himself, that Jewish Zealots slaughtered pilgrims in the Temple on 14 Nisan 70 AD. The fact that Jews were willing to defile the Temple for political reasons suggests

Ratzinger on the Historicity of the Gospels

weight to this criticism.[70] Ratzinger, however, is too reflective an interpreter to imagine that any historian can bracket all *a priori* reasoning. One can only hope to reason from the right *a priori*. In this case, whether rightly or wrongly, he finds Meier's *a priori* fitting.

It is instructive to note how differently Ratzinger treats Meier's corroborating argument that Mark's Passover references (14:1a, 12–16) are later redactional additions. Ratzinger discounts this effort as "artificial."[71] But since he does not give reasons for this dismissal, one is left to speculate based on his broader interpretive sensibility. To judge from his remarks in "Biblical Interpretation in Conflict," cited above, Ratzinger probably detects a subtle evolutionary *a priori* at work in Meier's account. Though Ratzinger has no principled objection to characterizing certain texts as "redactional," he does oppose the tendency to substitute such genetic analyses for an explanation of the final text's meaning. And since Ratzinger has come to suspect that the Synoptics place the Last Supper on the Passover to identify it as the "New Passover," he may see this as a yet another instance of the tendency to postdate cultic themes.

Since the publication of the second volume of *Jesus of Nazareth*, a new case has emerged that the Synoptic and Johannine chronologies can be reconciled in such a way as to render both Meier's redactional explanation and Ratzinger's theological explanation superfluous. In 2015 Brant Pitre's *Jesus and the Last Supper* argued, rather convincingly, that the Johannine time references have long been misconstrued. The word Passover (πάσχα) has, in fact, four biblically attested meanings: (1) the Passover lamb, sacrificed on 14 Nisan in the afternoon; (2) the Passover meal, eaten on 15 Nisan in the evening; (3) the Passover Peace Offering, offered and eaten daily from 15–21 Nisan; and (4) Passover week, spanning 15–21 Nisan.[72] With the full semantic range of πάσχα taken into account, nothing in John's narrative proves incompatible with placing both the Last Supper and Passion on 15 Nisan, the same Passover Feast identified in the Synoptic accounts. For example, when Jewish leaders refuse to enter the Praetorium so that, by avoiding defilement, they "might eat the Passover" (φάγωσιν τὸ πάσχα) (John 18:28), "Passover" here likely bears the third meaning, the

---

that they may have been willing to disregard some of the finer points of Passover observance (330). To this point, however, it might be objected that Zealots are more plausible candidates for sacrilege against the Temple than the Temple authorities themselves.

70. Pitre argues that none of the happenings mentioned in the Synoptics is strictly prohibited on Passover, adding that later rabbinic sources even required certain criminals to be held until major feast days. Pitre, *Jesus and the Last Supper*, 295–304.

71. JN 2:112–13.

72. Pitre, *Jesus and the Last Supper*, 333.

AARON PIDEL, SJ

Passover Peace Offering performed daily during 16–21 Nisan.[73] Likewise, when John depicts Pilate condemning Jesus on the "Preparation of the Passover" (Παρασκευὴ τοῦ πάσχα) (John 19:14), "Passover" here likely bears the fourth meaning, Passover week. And since Παρασκευή often means simply Friday, the day before Sabbath, the day indicated may simply be "Friday of Passover week."[74] As it turns out, then, both John and the Synoptics may agree on the fact that Christ dined with his disciples at the beginning of the Jewish Passover and died toward the end of the same day, 15 Nisan.

Should Pitre's "Passover hypothesis" gain widespread acceptance, it would obviously render Ratzinger's particular conclusions obsolete. But it would at the same time vindicate Ratzinger's more general insistence that historical reason, being inescapably self-involving and probabilistic, cannot aspire to the rigor of the physical sciences. And even if Ratzinger's own application of historical reason turns out to be based on premature scholarly consensus, his way of reconciling historical reason and faith may still prove instructive. It is to this point that we turn or, rather, return.

II.4 Back to the Third Test of Faith: Compatibility with Dei verbum
After all that has been said, it might seem that historical reason alone proved decisive for Ratzinger, at least in leading him to favor the historical plausibility of John's putative pre-Passover dating of the Last Supper. But the reality is subtler. Ratzinger's final judgment reflects not only on the greater historical burden he perceives in the Synoptic solution, such as the improbability of Jesus' execution on the Passover, but also the discovery of a "theo-logic" for the Synoptic chronology with a metaphysical foundation. A closer examination of this theo-logic allows us to see another application of the third test of faith, that of ecclesial reception, and to concretize Ratzinger's understanding of the "historical character" affirmed by Dei verbum, §19.

In the last sentence of his treatment of the Last Supper chronology, Ratzinger hints at how he understands the significance of the Synoptics' allegedly theological dating of the Last Supper. He first recalls how Paul, John, and the whole primitive Church came to see Christ's Cross and Resurrection as the "Passover that endures." He then continues: "On this basis, one can understand how it was that very early on, Jesus' Last Supper—which includes not only a prophecy, but a real anticipation of the Cross and Resurrection in the

---

73. Pitre, *Jesus and the Last Supper*, 352–56.
74. Pitre, *Jesus and the Last Supper*, 357–60.

102

eucharistic gifts—was regarded as a Passover: as *his* Passover. And so it was."[75] They key phrase here is "real anticipation." In a similar passage, already cited, Ratzinger speaks of an "inner connection" between the Last Supper and the Cross and Resurrection. Both phrases imply that the events of Thursday evening were somehow one and the same with those that, on Ratzinger's hypothesis, would have formed an *inclusio* around the Passover, namely, the Cross and Resurrection. To use the language of the Council of Trent, Jesus' eucharistic action "represented" his sacrificial death-unto-resurrection, making its power already present in reality.[76] It was the Synoptics' inchoate grasp of this sacramental representation, Ratzinger speculates, that led them to treat the time signatures more flexibly.

This sacramental warrant introduces a kind of asymmetry in the respective arguments for taking either the Johannine or the Synoptic chronology as "theological symbol." On the supposition that John restructured the chronology, the connection between the historical date and the theological date would exist mostly in the mind of the author: John moves the crucifixion from Passover back to the Day of Preparation to make the theological point that Jesus is the true lamb. But on the supposition that the Synoptics restructured the chronology, the connection between historical date and theological date would enjoy a greater *fundamentum in re*: Mark moves the Last Supper from the Day of Preparation to Passover not simply to remind his readers that the Eucharist is the New Passover, but because he knows the Last Supper "really" anticipates the events spanning Passover: Jesus' passion-unto-resurrection. Meier's Johannine solution appeals to Ratzinger not only because the scenario of pre-Passover execution seems more plausible historically, but also because its corollary, the symbolic character of the Synoptic chronology, seems less "fictive" theologically. Though symbolic, the Passover dating would not be *just* a symbol.

In drawing attention to the *fundamentum in re* enjoyed by the Synoptic chronology, Ratzinger paints a picture of the redactional process that the authors of *Dei verbum*, §19 would have readily recognized. When Ratzinger conjectures that the apostles grasped the metaphysical connection between Last Supper and Passion "very early on," this implies that they taught with that "clearer understanding which they enjoyed after they had been instructed by

75. JN 2:115.

76. Trent teaches that Jesus offered his body and blood under the species of bread and wine at the Last Supper "in order to leave to his beloved Spouse the Church a visible sacrifice ... by which the bloody <sacrifice> [sic] that he was once for all to accomplish on the Cross would be represented [*repraesentaretur*]." Council of Trent, Session 22, *Canones de Missae sacrificio*, (September 17, 1562), c. 1 (DH 1740).

103

AARON PIDEL, SJ

the events of Christ's risen life and taught by the light of the Spirit of truth."
And when he conjectures that the Synoptic chronology reflects inchoate intu-
itions about sacramental representation, he acknowledges that the evangelists
were "reducing some of [the things handed down about Jesus] to a synthesis,"
and "explaining some things in view of the situation of their churches." The
Synoptics "synthesize" the Last Supper with Christ's death-unto-resurrection,
in other words, with a view to "explaining" to the churches how Jesus refounds
the Jewish Passover in the Eucharist. Ratzinger still allows for significant theological enhancement of the historical ground, but opts for the theological
enhancement that enjoys the strongest basis in reality.

Does Ratzinger thereby weaken the credibility of the Gospels, "whose
historical character the Church unhesitatingly asserts"? Or concede that the
Synoptics fail to tell us the "honest truth about Jesus"?[77] It cannot be denied
that Ratzinger here allows a higher ratio of theological elaboration to historical
fact than many exegetes of the premodern era,[78] and perhaps more than even
certain redactors of *Dei verbum*.[79] But Ratzinger was himself a redactor of *Dei
verbum*.[80] One could therefore view his study of the dating of the Last Supper
as an important indicator of how to think through Gospel historicity according
to the mind of the Council. Ratzinger accepts that the evangelists reshape historical ground with types and symbols, but shows a bias in favor of "realistic"
solutions, whether historically or metaphysically.

77. *Dei verbum*, §19.

78. When Thomas Aquinas learns that certain Greek theologians consider the passion
chronology of the Synoptic Gospels simply mistaken, he responds with the following hermeneutical principle: "But it is heresy to say that there is anything false not only in the Gospels but
anywhere in the canonical scriptures. Consequently, we have to say that all the Evangelists state
the same thing and do not disagree." *Super Ioannem*, cap. 13, lec. 1; cited and translated in Joy,
"Ratzinger and Aquinas on the Dating of the Last Supper," 332.

79. See the postconciliar reflections on biblical inerrancy by Augustin Bea, whom Paul
VI sent to the Theological Commission to advocate for a less ambiguous affirmation of Gospel
historicity: *The Word of God and Mankind*, trans. Dorothy White (London: Geoffrey Chapman,
1967), 184–93.

80. For Ratzinger's work during the Third Session of Vatican II on the subcommission for
revising the schema *De Divina Revelatione*, see Helmut Hoping, "Theologische Kommentar zur
Dogmatischen Konstitution über die göttliche Offenbarung," 697–819 in *Herders Theologischer
Kommentar zum Zweiten Vatikanischen Konzil*, vol. 3, ed. Peter Hünermann and Bernd Jochen
Hilberath (Freiburg: Herder, 2005), 730–31.

III. Conclusion

A wit once summarized the conclusion of the decades-long debate over the authorship of the Shakespearean canon in the following sentence: "No one could possibly have written all the works attributed to Shakespeare—unless, of course, he were a genius like Shakespeare." The tongue-in-cheek remark highlights how judgments regarding historical plausibility often depend on convictions impatient of historical verification. How far can a genius exceed the capacities of the average person? How unexampled can a historical event be? Historical judgment is simply too self-involving to admit of perfect scientific neutrality.

Keenly aware of these limitations, Ratzinger opts to exercise historical reason within an overarching hermeneutic of faith. This does not require, as we have seen, reconciling every narrative discrepancy on the historical plane, even where it may prove possible to do so. Nor does it require holding that the Gospel narratives remain free of theological restructuring. But it does oblige him to consult the faith of the People of God, represented in the first three tests, when gauging just how far the historical ground extends. It also obliges him to hold that the evangelists, as often as they have enriched the historical ground, do so only to convey better the true nature and significance of the events narrated, some dimensions of which necessarily escape the historical method. This seems to be what Ratzinger means when he said that the Gospels depict "the real, 'historical' Jesus in the strict sense of the word."[81] And if Ratzinger may be taken as a reliable guide to the intentions of *Dei verbum*, then this is also what the Dogmatic Constitution meant when it unhesitatingly affirmed the *historicitas* of the Gospels.

That being said, the subsequent publication of Pitre's *Jesus and the Last Supper* casts an interesting backward light on Ratzinger's analysis. Ratzinger's *Jesus of Nazareth* trilogy has typically been criticized for its "grudging and very uneven acknowledgment" of any distance between the so called "historical" Jesus and his narrative representations.[82] Should Pitre's argument stand the test of time, however, it will turn out that, at least in this case, Ratzinger accepted such a distance rather too uncritically. In this eventuality, we can continue to learn not so much from Ratzinger's particular conclusions as from his general approach. Ratzinger's tests of faith prevent him from settling on any solution

---

81. JN 1:xxii.

82. Richard Hays, "Ratzinger's Johannine Jesus: A Challenge to Enlightenment Historiography," 109–18 in *The Pope and Jesus of Nazareth: Christ, Scripture and the Church*, ed. Adrian Pabst and Angus Paddison (London: SCM, 2009), 115.

where the paschal character of the Last Supper, an idea so deeply pervasive of the New Testament and the early Church, would remain entirely fictive. Pitre's "Passover hypothesis," if accepted, would thus only confirm Ratzinger's basic interpretation of the event: the Last Supper is "Jesus' Passover." Ratzinger's faith-and-reason criteriology thus serves him as a kind of ballast in the choppy waters of historical-critical inquiry, allowing him to test the seaworthiness of his image of Jesus without risking capsize at every new wave of scholarly hypotheses.

6. Changing Gender Roles and the Unchanging Message of 1 Corinthians 11:2–16

Marcin Kowalski

The Pauline letters seem to be an intriguing case of biblical inspiration. The document of the Pontifical Biblical Commission, *The Inspiration and Truth of Sacred Scripture*, devotes a considerable amount of space to them. References to the letters of Paul appear in all three parts of the document, which talk about the origin of the Sacred Books from God (Part One), the truth revealed in them (Part Two), and finally the challenges connected with their interpretation (Part Three). Speaking about the origin of the Pauline letters from God, the document accentuates first of all the testimony of Galatians 1–2, where the apostle explicitly states that his Gospel was revealed to him directly by Christ.[1] Its inspired character is confirmed by the dedicated ministry of Paul and the testimony of other apostles (2 Cor 10–13; Gal 2:7–9).[2] Ultimately, the divine origin of the Pauline letters can be deduced from Paul's emphasis on accepting his teaching proclaimed in the authority of the Lord and in absolute fidelity to Christ's Gospel. The Pauline letters are inspired because they come from a credible disciple of the Lord and are an extension of the Gospel.[3]

In Part Two, the document ponders the inspired character of the Pauline Gospel, summarizing it in four points: a) Paul knows revelation from his own calling and from the Church's tradition; b) God reveals himself in the Crucified

---

1. Pontifical Biblical Commission, *The Inspiration and Truth of Sacred Scripture: The Word That Comes from God and Speaks of God for the Salvation of the World*, trans. Thomas Esposito and Stephen Gregg (Collegeville, MN: Liturgical Press, 2014), §40.

2. *The Inspiration and Truth of Sacred Scripture*, §41.

3. *The Inspiration and Truth of Sacred Scripture*, §42. See 1 Cor 7:12, 17, 25; 2 Cor 2:14–17; 3:1–6; 5:20; 6:1–2; 7:2–4; 10:7–8; 11:1–4; 13:1–10.

and Risen Christ; c) salvation is received and lived within the Church, the Body of Christ; d) the fullness of salvation consists in the resurrection of Christ.[4] Finally, in Part Three, highlighting the ethical and social problems generated by Sacred Scripture, numerous references to the texts of Paul are given.[5] They deal exclusively with the status and position of women. In Col 3:18, Eph 5:22–33, and Tit 2:5, Paul commands them to submit to men, in 1 Cor 14:34–38 he forbids them speaking in assemblies, and in 1 Tim 2:11–15 he justifies their lower status in social and ecclesial environments by the fact that they are responsible for original sin.

Pauline texts have shaped the Christian understanding of gender issues and related social roles for centuries, and for some this is a very problematic understanding, tinged with patriarchal culture which delegated women to the margins of society and church life.[6] Looking at 1 Cor 14:34–38 and other texts coming from his school, Paul might be regarded as responsible for stopping the revolution of women in early Christian communities. The apostle eventually subjugated them to men, thus perpetuating the patriarchal model for centuries, if not for millennia. Some scholars spot these unfortunate tendencies also in 1 Cor 11:2–16.[7] The Pontifical Biblical Commission refers only indirectly to this text, indicating that in 1 Cor 11:3 Paul demands respect for the social order which gives power to men.[8] At first glance, then, the phrase in which Paul calls a man the head of a woman (11:3) loses its significance for us, as well as the rest of the notoriously difficult 1 Cor 11:2–16. In the passage in question, the apostle forbids men to prophesy and pray with their heads covered, while women are not allowed to pray with their heads uncovered (1 Cor 11:4–6). Paul explains it further by saying that a man is the image and glory of God, while a woman is the glory of a man (1 Cor 11:7). The fragment reeks of patriarchal ideology which seems to reduce women to the role of men's appendix (1 Cor 11:8–9). Does Paul's teaching on sexuality and gender roles contained in 1 Cor 11:2–16

4. *The Inspiration and Truth of Sacred Scripture*, §§91–95.

5. *The Inspiration and Truth of Sacred Scripture*, §§132–34.

6. See, e.g., Antoinette C. Wire, *The Corinthian Women Prophets: A Reconstruction through Paul's Rhetoric* (Minneapolis: Fortress, 1990).

7. On the patriarchal rhetoric of Paul in 1 Cor 11:2–16, see Caroline Vander Stichele and Todd C. Penner, "Paul and the Rhetoric of Gender," 287–310 in *Her Master's Tools?: Feminist and Postcolonial Engagements of Historical-Critical Discourse,* ed. Caroline Vander Stichele and Todd C. Penner, GPBS 9 (Leiden, Boston: Brill, 2005), 309–10. Francis Watson, *Agape, Eros, Gender: Towards a Pauline Sexual Ethic* (Cambridge: Cambridge University Press, 2000), 53–54 believes that what Paul suggests in 1 Cor 11:2–16 negatively affects both the dignity of women and men and is unacceptable today.

8. *The Inspiration and Truth of Sacred Scripture*, §134.

remain relevant to a modern audience? To what extent is it inspired and inspiring for twenty-first century society?

The matter is further complicated by the fact that 1 Cor 11:2–16 seems to comply with the characteristics of biblical inspiration as articulated in the conciliar constitution *Dei verbum*. According to it, God, the author of Sacred Scripture, chose and employed men, called true authors, with their power and abilities, heritage of faith, knowledge and culture, though whom he "consigned to writing everything and only those things which he wanted."[9] The conciliar constitution itself does not allow us to look at biblical inspiration as a purely theological construct, divorced from history and socio-cultural institutions. The pericope 1 Cor 11:2–16 is clearly rooted in the Judeo-Hellenistic world of Paul. At the same time, the message we find here transcends Paul's times and culture, containing a universal core, applicable to every time and culture. We will try to demonstrate this particular combination of historicity and universality, as well as the ecclesial character of inspiration and truth in 1 Cor 11:2–16. The verdict on its inspiration is important because this fragment touches upon hotly-debated ethical issues regarding gender roles and the relationship between men and women. We shall first have a look at the Pauline thought in context and at the rhetorical structure of 1 Cor 11:2–16. Next, we shall analyze various layers of Pauline argumentation, trying to resolve, when necessary, some dilemmas of an exegetical nature. Finally, in the summary, the article will offer a comprehensive view of the inspiration of 1 Cor 11:2–16 in which theology, culture, and nature are interlocked together to establish the unchanging message on the relationship between man and woman in our changing human world.

1 Cor 11:2–16 in Context

The analyzed text of 1 Cor 11:2–16 is part of chapter 11 of 1 Corinthians. The first verse of that chapter, according to the majority of exegetes, belongs to the preceding rhetorical unit of 1 Cor 8:1–11:1. Paul describes there the question of εἰδωλόθυτα, meat sacrificed to pagan idols, and then proceeds to the matter of the appearance and dress of women and men taking part in prayer gatherings (11:2–16). This passage is linked to the next unit, 1 Cor 11:17–34, through the vocabulary related to tradition (11:2, 23) and the appraisal of the Corinthians (11:2, 17). In 1 Cor 11:2, the community is praised for following the teaching of the apostle (ἐπαινῶ), whereas in 1 Cor 11:17 Paul cannot applaud them any longer (οὐκ ἐπαινῶ) when it comes to their behavior during the Eucharist.

9. Second Vatican Council, *Dei verbum* (November 18, 1965) (Boston: Pauline Books & Media, 1965), §11.

The difference in style and emotive tone in Paul's teaching, which is discernible in sections 1 Cor 11:2–16 and 11:17–34, does not stop scholars from looking for the connections between them and from putting them together in the broader context of the apostle's discursive strategy. According to some, 1 Cor 11:2–34 constitutes a coherent block concerning the correction of the Corinthians' behavior during prayer gatherings.[10] Others extend the context of cult and prayer also to chapters 12–14, incorporating in this section practically the entirety of chapter 11.[11] Still others spot the thematic links between 1 Cor 11:2–16 and the principle of community building expressed in 1 Cor 8:1–11:1.[12] Finally, the fragment under examination is placed as one of the many themes of the section in which Paul responds to the problems of the Corinthians (7:1–14:40; 15:58; 16:4; 16:12)[13] or as a part linked with the main thesis of Paul's argumentation which concerns the threatened unity of the Church (1 Cor 1:10).[14]

No matter how 1 Cor 11:2–16 is positioned, it is clear that it is not as detached from the argumentative context of 1 Corinthians as postulated by some supporters of its non-Pauline origin.[15] Their arguments, stressing the dif-

---

10. Raymond F. Collins, *First Corinthians*, SaPaSe 7 (Collegeville, MN: Liturgical Press, 1999), 392; Anthony C. Thiselton, *The First Epistle to the Corinthians: A Commentary on the Greek Text,* NIGTC (Grand Rapids: Eerdmans, 2000), 800; John P. Heil, *The Rhetorical Role of Scripture in 1 Corinthians,* SBLMS 15 (Atlanta: Society of Biblical Literature, 2005), 12–13, 15; William F. Orr and James A. Walther, *I Corinthians: A New Translation,* AncB 32 (New Haven: Yale University Press, 2007), 258; Joseph A. Fitzmyer, *First Corinthians: A New Translation with Introduction and Commentary,* AYB 32 (New Haven: Yale University Press, 2008), 404–5.

11. Archibald Robertson and Alfred Plummer, *A Critical and Exegetical Commentary: The First Epistle of St Paul to the Corinthians,* 2nd ed., ICC (Edinburgh: Clark, 1975), 226; Hans Conzelmann, *1 Corinthians: A Commentary on the First Epistle to the Corinthians,* trans. James W. Leitch, Hermeneia (Philadelphia: Fortress, 1975), 181; Leon Morris, *1 Corinthians: An Introduction and Commentary,* TNTC 7 (Downers Grove, IL: InterVarsity, 1985), 148; Margaret M. Mitchell, *Paul and the Rhetoric of Reconciliation: An Exegetical Investigation of the Language and Composition of 1 Corinthians* (Louisville: Westminster John Knox, 1993), 185, 258–59; Wolfgang Schrage, *Der erste Brief an die Korinther,* vol. 2, *1 Kor 6,12–11,16,* EKKNT 7/2 (Dusseldorf: Benziger, 1995), 487; Richard B. Hays, *First Corinthians,* Int. 46 (Louisville: Westminster John Knox, 1997), 181–82; Thiselton, *The First Epistle to the Corinthians,* 798; Roy E. Ciampa and Brian S. Rosner, *The First Letter to the Corinthians,* PilNTC (Grand Rapids: Eerdmans, 2010), 499–503; Mark Taylor, *1 Corinthians,* NAC 28 (Nashville: Broadman & Holman, 2014), 251–52.

12. Thiselton, *The First Epistle to the Corinthians,* 799; Taylor, *1 Corinthians,* 252.

13. C. K. Barrett, *The First Epistle to the Corinthians* (London: Black, 1968), 153; Gordon D. Fee, *The First Epistle to the Corinthians,* NICNT (Grand Rapids: Eerdmans, 1987), 266; Hays, *First Corinthians,* 110; Fitzmyer, *First Corinthians,* 273.

14. Taylor, *1 Corinthians,* 252.

15. William O. Walker, Jr., "1 Corinthians 11:2–16 and Paul's Views Regarding Women," *Journal of Biblical Literature* 94, no. 1 (1975): 94–110; William O. Walker, Jr., "The 'Theology of

ference between 1 Cor 11:2-16 and the Pauline thought elsewhere, especially in Gal 3:28, were rejected by modern exegesis.[16] It would be a mistake, however, to exaggerate the links existing between the analyzed passage and the whole of 1 Corinthians. Paul is accustomed to arrange his argumentation in thematic blocks and 1 Cor 11:2-34 is such a separate block. It is linked with the preceding section of 1 Cor 8:1-11:1 by the topic of community building and by the cultic context.[17] This context also binds together 1 Cor 11:2-16 and 1 Cor 11:17-34. Chapters 12-14 have, in turn, their own argumentative and thematic structure, focusing on the gifts of the Spirit.[18] Thus, it can be concluded that 1 Cor 11:2-34 is a separate thematic block, focusing on the Corinthians' prayer gatherings.[19] In this block, there are two separate arguments on gender roles (vv. 2-16) and differences in economic status (vv. 17-34), which negatively affect the liturgical gatherings at Corinth.[20]

The Rhetorical *Dispositio* in 1 Cor 11:2-16

We shall start with the rhetorical structure of 1 Cor 11:2-16, which should allow us to understand the flow of Paul's thought and the logical connection between

---

Woman's Place' and the 'Paulinist' Tradition," *Semeia* 28 (1983): 101-12; William O. Walker, Jr., "The Vocabulary of 1 Corinthians 11:3-16: Pauline or Non-Pauline?," *Journal for the Study of the New Testament* 11, no. 35 (1989): 75-88; Lamar Cope, "1 Cor 11:2-16: One Step Further," *Journal of Biblical Literature* 97 (1978): 435-36; Garry W. Trompf, "On Attitudes toward Women in Paul and Paulinist Literature: 1 Corinthians 11:3-16 and Its Context," *Catholic Biblical Quarterly* 42, no. 2 (1980): 196-215; Christopher Mount, "1 Corinthians 11:3-16: Spirit Possession and Authority in a Non-Pauline Interpolation," *Journal of Biblical Literature* 124, no. 2 (2005): 313-40. See also Conzelmann, *1 Corinthians*, 182.

16. J. Murphy-O'Connor, "Non-Pauline Character of 1 Corinthians 11:2-16," *Journal of Biblical Literature* 95, no. 4 (1976): 615-21; J. Murphy-O'Connor, "1 Cor 11:2-16 Once Again," *Catholic Biblical Quarterly* 50 (1988): 265-74; Schrage, *Der erste Brief an die Korinther*, 2:496-97; Mitchell, *Paul and the Rhetoric of Reconciliation*, 261-630 [?] Collins, *First Corinthians*, 393-91.

17. Collins, *First Corinthians*, 404; Ciampa and Rosner, *The First Letter to the Corinthians*, 500-1.

18. Collins, *First Corinthians*, 392; Fitzmyer, *First Corinthians*, 406.

19. Barrett, *The First Epistle to the Corinthians*, 246-77; Collins, *First Corinthians*, 392; Bruce J. Malina and John J. Pilch, *Social-Science Commentary on the Letters of Paul* (Minneapolis: Fortress, 2006), 105; Orr and Walther, *I Corinthians*, 258; Fitzmyer, *First Corinthians*, 404.

20. Ben Witherington, *Conflict and Community in Corinth: A Socio-Rhetorical Commentary on 1 and 2 Corinthians* (Grand Rapids: Eerdmans, 1995), 231; David E. Garland, *1 Corinthians*, BECNT (Grand Rapids: Baker Academic, 2003), 505; Alan F. Johnson, *1 Corinthians*, The IVP New Testament Commentary Series 7 (Westmont, IL: IVP Academic, 2004), 177, reads 1 Cor 11:2-16 as a separate argument forming a new section of chapter 11.

MARCIN KOWALSKI

various arguments he uses in this section.[21] The rhetorical *dispositio* of 1 Cor 11:2–16 may be presented as follows:[22]

Introduction—ecclesial reference (11:2): Praise for the Corinthians who hold on to the Pauline tradition
> **Christologico-theological thesis (11:3):** Christ as the head of a man, a man as the head of a woman, God as the head of Christ
>> **Cultural argument (11:4–6):** A man is dishonored by praying with his head covered; a woman is dishonored praying with her head uncovered
>>> **The argument from the theology of creation and its evangelical qualification (11:7–10, 11–12):** A man is the image and glory of God, a woman is a man's glory; their divine descent and equality in the Lord
>> **The natural law argument (11:13–15):** Nature teaches about the proper covering of the head and differences between men and women
> **Closing—ecclesial reference (11:16):** The teaching of Paul in accordance with the custom of God's churches

In the above outline, v. 2 serves as an *exordium*, an introduction to the topic which Paul will discuss further.[23] The apostle begins by praising the Corinthians, who obey the tradition he has given them. In this statement, some commentators saw irony (patristic and medieval exegesis: Theodoret, Ambrosiaster, Peter Lombard, Thomas Aquinas), as they believed there were no reasons

---

21. Collins, *First Corinthians*, 392 describes 1 Cor 11:2–34 as the "fourth rhetorical demonstration" subordinated to the *prothesis* in 1 Cor 1:10 (see also 69). He qualifies the passage as a "piece of deliberative rhetoric that uses political language to appeal for the unity of the community (cf. 1:10)" (404). A similar view is presented by Heil, *The Rhetorical Role of Scripture in 1 Corinthians*, 12–13, 15. Mitchell, *Paul and the Rhetoric of Reconciliation*, 149–51, 184–85, 258–63 defines 1 Cor 11:2–16 as a sub-section of the unit 11:2–14:40 and gives it a title: "Third Section of Proof: Manifestations of Corinthian Factionalism when 'Coming Together.'"

22. A similar argumentative structure for 1 Cor 11:2–16 has been suggested by Keith A. Burton, "1 Corinthians 11 and 14: How Does a Woman Prophesy and Keep Silence at the Same Time?," *Journal of the Adventist Theological Society* 10, nos. 1–2 (1999): 268–84, at 272–73; Ciampa and Rosner, *The First Letter to the Corinthians*, 504–41. See also Fitzmyer, *First Corinthians*, 408.

23. Ciampa and Rosner, *The First Letter to the Corinthians*, 504–6. On the characteristic and function of *exordium* in ancient rhetoric, see Aristotle, *Rhet.* 3.14–15; Cicero, *Inv.*, 1.15.20–18.26; Quintilian, *Inst.* 4.1.

Changing Gender Roles and the Unchanging Message of 1 Corinthians 11:2–16

for praising the community.[24] Others have rightly noticed here the *captatio benevolentiae*, in which the speaker strives to ensure a kind reception of his words by listeners.[25] Paul can, indeed, praise the members of the community who hold on to the tradition transmitted to them, as John Chrysostom claimed, commenting on 1 Cor 11:2.[26] The tradition in question may signify both the transmission of faith and the practice of Christian life, more specifically the joint participation of Corinthian men and women in prayer and prophecy. Paul could have praised such a tradition without blurring the differences between men and women in the community.[27] The rhetorical figure of *derivatio/pleonasm* in καθὼς παρέδωκα ὑμῖν, τὰς παραδόσεις κατέχετε suggests an emphasis on the faithful preservation of the Pauline tradition. Collins rightly notes that the beginning of the argumentation bears very strong traces of the appeal to the ethos of the apostle who presents himself as a promoter of the unity of the Church.[28]

Next, Paul formulates the thought which will lead his argument in this section and which in the rhetorical nomenclature can be described as a *propositio*.[29] Its compact, parallel structure distinguishes it clearly from v. 2 and from

24. Thiselton, *The First Epistle to the Corinthians*, 810. Among the twentieth-century commentators, see, e.g., E.-B Allo, *Saint Paul premiere epitre aux Corinthiens* (Paris: Gabalda, 1934), 255; James Moffatt, *The First Epistle of Paul to the Corinthians*, MNTC 7 (New York: Harper and Brothers, 1938), 149. James B. Hurley, "Did Paul Require Veils or the Silence of Women: A Consideration of 1 Cor 11:2–16 and 14:33b-36," *Westminster Theological Journal* 35, no. 2 (1973): 190–220, at 191–93 is strongly against this view.

25. Robertson and Plummer, *A Critical and Exegetical Commentary*, 228: "With his usual tact and generosity, the apostle, before finding fault, mentions things which he can heartily and honestly praise." See also Conzelmann, *1 Corinthians*, 182; John P. Meier, "On the Veiling of Hermeneutics (1 Cor 11:2–16)," *Catholic Biblical Quarterly* 40, no. 2 (1978): 212–26, at 215; Fee, *The First Epistle to the Corinthians*, 500 (Chapters 11–14); Schrage, *Der erste Brief an die Korinther*, 2:490; Mitchell, *Paul and the Rhetoric of Reconciliation*, 260; Jason D. BeDuhn, "'Because of the Angels': Unveiling Paul's Anthropology in 1 Corinthians 11," *Journal of Biblical Literature* 118, no. 2 (1999): 295–320, at 315–16; Burton, "1 Corinthians 11 and 14," 273; Collins, *First Corinthians*, 394–95; Garland, *1 Corinthians*, 513.

26. John Chrysostom, *Hom. 1 Cor.* 26.2 (with reference to NPNF 1/12:148–57).

27. David G. Horrell, *The Social Ethos of the Corinthian Correspondence: Interests and Ideology from 1 Corinthians to 1 Clement*, SNTW (Edinburgh: T&T Clark, 1996), 169; Thiselton, *The First Epistle to the Corinthians*, 811.

28. Collins, *First Corinthians*, 394. On *ethos*, which the speaker frequently refers to in the *exordium*, see Aristotle, *Rhet.* 3.14.7; Cicero, *Rhet. Her.* 1.5.8 (LCL).

29. Murphy-O'Connor, "1 Cor 11:2–16 Once Again," 274 ("programmatic statement"); Mitchell, *Paul and the Rhetoric of Reconciliation*, 261 ("subargument"); Burton, "1 Corinthians 11 and 14," 273; Martina Böhm, "1 Kor 11,2–16: Beobachtungen zur paulinischen Schriftrezeption und Schriftargumentation im 1. Korintherbrief," *Die Zeitschrift für die Neutestamentliche*

MARCIN KOWALSKI

the following v. 4. The *propositio* separates from the *exordium* by the statement Θέλω δὲ ὑμᾶς εἰδέναι, in which the particle δέ can be qualified as adversative, suggesting a certain tension and opposition to the praise which resounds in the *exordium*. The community, although holding on to the Pauline παραδόσεις, needs to be instructed on how to apply it in its social and religious context.[30]

We are entering here the *stasis*, the rhetorical situation of the text which gives rise to the entire argument developed in 1 Cor 11:2–16.[31] A sharp difference between the severe admonition in v. 17 and the instructions in v. 3 suggests that the Corinthians' behavior was dictated by ignorance or lack of experience rather than a spirit of rebellion.[32] The *propositio* reminds them that the head of a man is Christ, while the head of a woman is a man and the head of Christ is God. Murphy-O'Connor rightly observes that v. 3 introduces an argument from the theology of creation ("the head of a woman is a man") and the motif of "new creation" ("the head of every man is Christ"), thus announcing respectively the themes of vv. 7–10 and 11–12.[33] Similarly, Collins spots in 1 Cor 11:3 a reference to the role of Christ in the work of creation, reappearing in 1 Cor 11:11.[34] Leaving aside for now the interpretation of the term κεφαλή, Paul introduces a clear Christological-theological thesis which should guide the community in understanding and experiencing their gender roles. The thesis is short and

---

Wissenschaft und die Kunde der älteren Kirche 97, no. 2 (2006): 207–34, at 214; Fitzmyer, *First Corinthians*, 408–9 ("programmatic statement"/"fundamental theological principle"); Ciampa and Rosner, *The First Letter to the Corinthians*, 506–11 ("statement of the basis for Christian practice").

30. Ciampa and Rosner, *The First Letter to the Corinthians*, 506. E. Schüssler Fiorenza takes an adverse view, stating that Paul does not react to the abuses but introduces regulations which have already functioned in other Christian communities. See Elisabeth Schüssler Fiorenza, *In Memory of Her: A Feminist Theological Reconstruction of Christian Origins* (New York: Crossroad, 1994), 226.

31. On rhetorical *stasis*, see Cicero, *Inv.* 1.8.10–11.16; 2.4.12–39; Cicero, *Rhet. Her.* 1.10.18–17.27; Quintilian, *Inst.* 3.6 (LCL).

32. Contra Benjamin A. Edsall, "Greco-Roman Costume and Paul's Fraught Argument in 1 Corinthians 11.2–16," *Journal of Greco-Roman Christianity and Judaism* 9 (2013): 132–46, at 145. The author believes that 1 Cor 11:2–16 is an example of *insinuatio*. According to Edsall, Paul carefully gains ground because his cause might not be popular among the listeners and he does not have a strong position among them.

33. J. Murphy-O'Connor, "Sex and Logic in 1 Corinthians 11:2–16," *Catholic Biblical Quarterly* 42, no. 4 (1980): 482–500, at 494–96. Similarly Böhm, "1 Kor 11,2–16," 219, 230.

34. Collins, *First Corinthians*, 412. Similarly J. Delobel, "1 Cor 11:2–16: Toward a Coherent Explanation," 369–89 in *L'Apôtre Paul: Personnalité, style et conception du ministère,* ed. Albert Vanhoye, BETL 73 (Leuven: Leuven University Press; Uitgeverij Peeters, 1986), at 384; Garland, *1 Corinthians*, 530.

Changing Gender Roles and the Unchanging Message of 1 Corinthians 11:2–16

concise, which belongs to its definition in antiquity, and its vocabulary will be reflected in every part of Paul's argumentation.[35] The fact that the term κεφαλή is repeated nine times in 1 Cor 11:2–16 suggests that it is crucial for this section. Paul will use it in various configurations (paranomasia/polyptoton) in the literal sense, speaking of the part of the body (vv. 4, 5, 7, 10), and in the metaphorical way (vv. 3, 4, 5).[36] What is important, in v. 3, κεφαλή carries a metaphorical meaning which suggests that the Pauline reflection in 1 Cor 11:2–16 exceeds the problem of head covering at Corinth, focusing further on gender roles and the understanding of the relationship between a man and a woman.

The thesis (*propositio*) formulated in v. 3 leads the apostle's thought which revolves around three basic arguments.[37] In this respect, the studies by Judith Gundry-Volf are invaluable for the deeper understanding of the Pauline discourse. The author identifies three levels of argumentation in 1 Cor 11:2–16: cultural, eschatological, and the level based on the theology of creation.[38] According to Gundry-Volf, Paul corrects behavior related to head covering and hairstyle at Corinth, which blurs the differences between women and men during common gatherings. The apostle refers to the socio-cultural code of his time, interpreting gender roles in terms of hierarchy. At the same time, the new

35. On *propositio* in ancient speeches, see Aristotle, *Rhet.* 1.3.7; Quintilian, *Inst.* 4.4.19 (LCL); Heinrich Lausberg, David E. Orton, and R. D. Anderson, *Handbook of Literary Rhetoric: A Foundation for Literary Study* (Leiden: Brill, 1998), §346. On the concise character of *propositio,* see Aristotle, *Rhet.* 3.13; Quintilian, *Inst.* 3.9.5; 4.2.7, 30. On the Pauline technique of argumentation and the character of *propositiones,* see Jean-Noël Aletti, "La dispositio rhétorique dans les épîtres pauliniennes: Propositions de méthode," *New Testament Studies* 38, no. 3 (1992): 385–401; Jean-Noël Aletti, "La rhétorique paulinienne: Construction et communication d'une pensée," 47–66 in *Paul, une théologie en construction,* ed. Jean-Noël Aletti et al., MoBi(G) 51 (Geneva: Labor et Fides, 2004).

36. Collins, *First Corinthians,* 405.

37. Murphy-O'Connor, "Sex and Logic in 1 Corinthians 11:2–16," 491 also distinguishes three levels: the order of creation (vv. 3, 7–11), nature (vv. 13–15), and the customs of churches (v. 16). See also Murphy-O'Connor, "1 Cor 11:2–16 Once Again," 274. Fitzmyer, *First Corinthians,* 407 identifies five levels of argumentation in 1 Cor 11:2–16: 1) biblical, based on the order of creation (vv. 7–12); 2) theological (v. 3); 3) social, based on nature (vv. 13–15); 4) ecclesial discipline (v. 16); 5) angelology (v. 10).

38. See Judith M. Gundry-Volf, "Gender and Creation in 1 Cor 11:2–16: A Study in Paul's Theological Method," 151–71 in *Evangelium, Schriftauslegung, Kirche: Festschrift für Peter Stuhlmacher,* ed. J. Adna, Scott J. Hafemann and O. Hofius (Göttingen: Vandenhoeck & Ruprecht, 1997); Judith M. Gundry-Volf, "Gender Distinctives, Discrimination, and the Gospel," *Evangelical Review of Theology* 21, no. 1 (1997): 41–50; Judith M. Gundry-Volf, "Putting the Moral Vision of the New Testament into Focus: A Review," *Bulletin for Biblical Research* 9 (1999): 277–87. Thiselton, *The First Epistle to the Corinthians,* 803; Johnson, *1 Corinthians,* 183 refer to the study of Gundry-Volf.

MARCIN KOWALSKI

creation and the work of Christ allows Paul to reinterpret the Book of Genesis in an eschatological manner, stressing the egalitarian dimension of the relationship between a man and a woman. In his argumentation, the apostle maintains the tension between the socio-cultural model of his time and the Gospel. The tension is necessary for the Church to realize her mission in the world. Paul does not intend to eliminate the differences between the sexes but relativizes them as not decisive for the coexistence between a man and a woman "in the Lord."

Undertaking the intuition of Gundry-Volf, though not necessarily agreeing with her in every detail, the apostle in 1 Cor 11:4–6 begins an argument based on socio-cultural premises.[39] A man, praying or prophesying with his head covered (a literal sense), disgraces it (a metaphorical sense) (v. 4). A woman, in turn, disgraces her head if she does not cover it (a literal and metaphorical sense) (v. 5). In the latter case, Paul compares the situation to cutting her hair and shaving her head, which in the ancient world was a punishment for adulteresses and bad mothers, a sign of loss of honor and ultimate degradation (v. 6). Regardless of the habits associated with head covering by men and women in antiquity, Paul refers here to the issue of honor and shame, which has serious socio-cultural implications. The behavior of the Corinthians, in which male and female roles are mixed up, is described by the apostle as a disgrace which threatens the social status of a man and a woman. It affects and shames their metaphorical heads, namely, Christ for a man and a man for a woman.

In the second argument, which is the heart of 1 Cor 11:2–16, the apostle refers to the theology of creation.[40] It is comprised of two parallel parts: vv. 7–10 and 11–12. In vv. 7–10, the apostle argues against covering the head by a man during prayer, because he is the "image" and "glory" of God (v. 7). Next, referring to Gen 2:18–25, Paul describes the creation of a woman from a man and for a man (vv. 8–9).[41] She is his glory (v. 7c) and for the sake of the angels

39. Fee, *The First Epistle to the Corinthians*, 498; Ciampa and Rosner, *The First Letter to the Corinthians*, 511–22.

40. Heil, *The Rhetorical Role of Scripture in 1 Corinthians*, 173–75, quotes a wide range of texts from the Old Testament which are associated with the theology of creation and linked with Paul's argumentation in 1 Cor 11:7–12: Gen 1:26–27, 31; 2:18, 20–23; 3:16; 5:1; 9:6; Sir 17:3; 36:1; Wis 2:23; Ps 7:6; 8:6; Amos 5:8; Isa 40:6–8; 45:7; Prov 11:16; 31:30–31; Eccl 3:11.

41. L. A. Jervis, "'But I Want You to Know . . .': Paul's Midrashic Intertextual Response to the Corinthian Worshipers (1 Cor 11:2–16)," *Journal of Biblical Literature* 112, no. 2 (1993): 231–46 suggests that in 1 Cor 11:7–12 Paul applies the technique of midrash, combining Gen 1:27–28 and Gen 2 to correct the wrong views of the Corinthians contesting sexual differences. Earlier on this, see Robin Scroggs, "Paul and the Eschatological Woman," *Journal of the American Academy of Religion* 40, no. 3 (1972): 283–303, at 298–302. On the allusions to Gen 1:27;

she should cover her head (v. 10). In order to avoid the impression that Paul simply subjugates women to men (this is not the purpose of his arguments), an important qualification is introduced in vv. 11–12.[42] A woman means nothing without a man and neither does a man without a woman, "in the Lord" (v. 11). Just as a woman originates from a man, a man is born of a woman and everything comes from God (v. 12). The role of the qualifiers "in the Lord" (v. 11) and "from God" (v. 12) is extremely important as they give this part a clear Christological and theological character. There is also an allusion to the Scriptures, the story of creation (Gen 1–2), which qualifies this section as the *ex auctoritate* argument (*atechnoi* proofs in Aristotle's nomenclature).[43] The importance and nature of the argumentation contained here makes 1 Cor 11:7–12 the core of Paul's discourse.[44] In accordance with v. 3, Christ and God determine the roles and behavior of men and women. The work of creation made them different and endowed them with different roles, while the work of redemption emphasized their equality in grace and calling. Paul does not abolish social differences but encourages the believers to regard them through the lens of the history of salvation. According to Murphy-O'Connor and Gundry-Volf, the apostle interprets the work of creation from the perspective of the new creation in Christ.[45]

In the third argument (vv. 13–15), Paul returns to the theme of honor and shame but adds an important dimension from which he argues for maintaining differences regarding head coverings. His argumentation is based on the observable law of nature (φύσις) (v. 14).[46] It instructs the Corinthians that it is not right for a woman to pray with her head uncovered (v. 13), whereas for a man it is shameful to cover his head (v. 14). The law of nature and analogy with hair, which has been given to a woman for natural covering (περιβόλαιλαιον), suggest that she should cover her head (v. 15). Verse 16, which ends Paul's

2:18, 21 24; 3:16 In 1 Cor 11:2 16, see Heil, *The Rhetorical Role of Scripture in 1 Corinthians*, 12 13, 15, 173–90.

42. Fitzmyer, *First Corinthians*, 408 ("qualifying counterargument in the Lord"). Murphy O'Connor, "1 Cor 11:2 16 Once Again," 274 describes vv. 11 12 as a "parenthesis."

43. On the non-artificial arguments (*atechnoi*) which the speaker has at his/her disposal (laws, testimonies, oaths), see Aristotle, *Rhet.* 1.2.2; Quintilian, *Inst.* 5.1 (LCL). On the arguments from the Scriptures in the rhetoric of the New Testament authors, see George A. Kennedy, *New Testament Interpretation through Rhetorical Criticism*, Studies in Religion (Chapel Hill: University of North Carolina Press, 1984), 14; Heil, *The Rhetorical Role of Scripture in 1 Corinthians*, 3–10.

44. Heil, *The Rhetorical Role of Scripture in 1 Corinthians*, 173.

45. Murphy-O'Connor, "Sex and Logic in 1 Corinthians 11:2–16," 494–95; Gundry-Volf, "Putting the Moral Vision of the New Testament into Focus," 283–84.

46. Murphy-O'Connor, "1 Cor 11:2–16 Once Again," 274.

MARCIN KOWALSKI

argumentation, should be set apart and qualified as *peroratio*.[47] It is marked by a reference to the tradition, which appeared in the *exordium*. The ecclesial context provides a framework for Paul's arguments in 1 Cor 11:2–16, suggesting that by following Paul's directions the unity of the Church community is built. The apostle once again refers to the speaker's ethos, encouraging the audience to follow him in his role of the promoter of the Church's peace and unity.[48]

After a general outline of the Pauline arguments in 1 Cor 11:2–16, we will now look closely at how the apostle, while resolving the current problems at Corinth, introduces his audience to the Christian understanding of the relationship between a man and a woman.

The Relationship between a Man and a Woman according to 1 Cor 11:2–16

Ecclesial Framework of Paul's Arguments (1 Cor 11:2, 16)

As has already been remarked, Paul begins by praising the Corinthians who adhere to the tradition/precepts (παράδοσις) which he passed on to them (11:2).[49] The term παράδοσις denotes the transmission of legends, doctrines, tradition, or what is passed down, namely, teaching.[50] In this sense it does not occur in the LXX, but it does appear in Josephus Flavius and Philo.[51] In the New Testament, παράδοσις generally signifies the content of transmission, norms, and regulations which the community should observe.[52] The term is used by the apostle in Gal 1:14, where he speaks of the traditions of his ancestors for which

47. On *peroratio*, see Aristotle, *Rhet.* 3.19; Cicero, *Part. or.* 15.52–60; Cicero, *Inv.* 1.51.98–56.109; Cicero, *De or.* 2.81.332; Cicero, *Rhet. Her.* 2.30.47–31.50; Quintilian, *Inst.* 6.1 (LCL). According to Murphy-O'Connor, "1 Cor 11:2–16 Once Again," 274 it is the last argument based on the Church tradition.

48. On thematic *inclusio* between 1 Cor 11:2 and 15, see Collins, *First Corinthians*, 395.

49. According to Fee, *The First Epistle to the Corinthians*, 491, it is an allusion to the letter from the Corinthians in which they claimed to hold on to the Pauline tradition. See a possible paraphrase of the letter from the community in: Hays, *First Corinthians*, 182–83; BeDuhn, "'Because of the Angels,'" 319; Ciampa and Rosner, *The First Letter to the Corinthians*, 501–2. E. E. Ellis, "Traditions in I Corinthians," *New Testament Studies* 32, no. 4 (1986): 481–502, at 491–94, reads here references to the household codes (Haustafeln) and rules on relationships between husbands and wives. Craig Blomberg, *1 Corinthians,* The NIV Application Commentary (Grand Rapids: Zondervan, 1994), 208 thinks of the tradition associated with the equality between women and men (Gal 3:28) and with the Eucharist (1 Cor 11:23). For more on the tradition in 1 Cor 11:2, see Collins, *First Corinthians*, 395–96.

50. On παράδοσις, see BDAG, "παράδοσις," 763; LSJ, "παράδοσις," 1309.

51. F. Büchsel, "παράδοσις," TDNT 2:172–73.

52. W. Popkes, "παράδοσις," EDNT 3:21.

118

he was extremely zealous. The noun assumes a similar meaning in Matt 15:2, 3, 6 and Mark 7:3, 5, 8, 9, 13. The apostle also uses παράδοσις in Col 2:8 with regard to human philosophies which threaten the primacy of Christ. Finally, the term appears in the Thessalonian correspondence, where Paul refers to the teaching, conveyed by his speech or by letter, by which the community is to abide (2 Thess 2:15). It is based on the example of the apostle's life and provides an antidote for the disorder which others cause (2 Thess 3:6–7).

In 1 Cor 11:2 the noun παράδοσις denotes Paul's teaching and the example of his life in Corinth. The term refers to both the Gospel and related moral rules, especially the rules of joint participation of women and men in prayer meetings, which, however, still require the apostle's correction. The parallel for παράδοσις in v. 2 is the term συνήθεια in v. 16. This word can signify a relationship of closeness, companionship, friendship, habit, routine, or a way of behaving.[53] In the first, relational sense, it appears in 4 Macc 2:13; 6:13 and 13:22, 27. In John 18:39, it denotes the Jewish custom of freeing a prisoner for the Passover feast. In one more passage, 1 Cor 8:7, it signifies customary sacrifices offered to pagan gods in Corinth. Although Engberg-Pedersen and Mitchell refer the term in 1 Cor 11:16 to the attitude of Paul, who did not typically prolong disputes, it is more likely that it alludes to everything that Paul spoke of in 1 Cor 11:2–16, namely, the practices of blurring gender roles at Corinth.[54]

The apostle states that he does not know the custom according to which men cover their heads and women uncover them during prayer. This use is also absent in other communities he founded. Paul's statement is not simply to take the wind out of the sails of those who still want to argue.[55] It is not the rhetoric of power with which he intends to make the female prophets at Corinth obey patriarchal authority.[56] It is the recognition that a properly understood and experienced sexuality has an ecclesial dimension which serves to build a community.[57] The ecclesial nature of Paul's argument integrates his thought in which respect for one's sexual identity determines the

---

53. BDAG, "συνήθεια," 971; LSJ, "συνήθεια," 1715; James H. Moulton and George Milligan, *The Vocabulary of the Greek Testament* (London: Hodder & Stoughton, 1930), 607.

54. Troels Engberg Pedersen, "1 Corinthians 11:16 and the Character of Pauline Exhortation," *Journal of Biblical Literature* 110 (1991): 679–89, at 684–86; Mitchell, *Paul and the Rhetoric of Reconciliation*, 262.

55. On φιλόνεικος in 1 Cor 11:16 and its reference to divisions in antiquity, see Mitchell, *Paul and the Rhetoric of Reconciliation*, 150–51, 262; Bruce W. Winter, *After Paul Left Corinth: The Influence of Secular Ethics and Social Change* (Grand Rapids: Eerdmans, 2001), 138–41.

56. Wire, *The Corinthian Women Prophets*, 33.

57. Ciampa and Rosner, *The First Letter to the Corinthians*, 540.

MARCIN KOWALSKI

functioning of the Church community. Without the experience of gender differences as a gift and part of the divine plan, the metaphor of the Church as a body, where everyone serves and complements each other, loses its significance. In such a case the images with which Paul describes Christ as the Bridegroom and the Church as his Bride also cease to be comprehensible (2 Cor 11:2–3; Eph 5:25–27).

Christological-Theological Thesis (1 Cor 11:3)

After the introduction, Paul puts forward a statement which can be characterized as a thesis (*propositio*) to the argumentation contained in 1 Cor 11:2–16. The apostle states that Christ is the head of every man, a man is the head of a woman, and God is the head of Christ. The main problem is to determine the meaning of the term "head" (κεφαλή) used by Paul. Taking into consideration the remarks of commentators on the polymorphous nature of the analyzed concept, the following interpretations are suggested:[58]

1) κεφαλή, *head in the sense of hierarchy, power, and leadership.* This interpretation, which can be labeled as "traditional," has been challenged by some modern commentators.[59] Joseph Fitzmyer, who is one of its contemporary advocates, relies on cases in which the term κεφαλή in the LXX translates the Hebrew ראש to support his claim that Hellenized Jews, like Paul, inferred from it reference to power, leadership, and being the first and the most important.[60] The author points at similar meanings which the noun assumes in Philo, Josephus Flavius, and Greek authors. The other proponent of κεφαλή conceived as a reference to authority is Wayne Grudem.[61] In over two thousand examples of

---

58. The most detailed presentation can be found in Thiselton, *The First Epistle to the Corinthians,* 812–22.

59. Among the earlier proponents of this interpretation, see Johannes Weiss, *Der erste Korintherbrief* (Göttingen: Vandenhoeck & Ruprecht, 1910), 269–70; Allo, *Saint Paul premiere epitre aux Corinthiens,* 256; Robertson and Plummer, *A Critical and Exegetical Commentary,* 229.

60. Joseph A. Fitzmyer, "Another Look at Kephalē in 1 Corinthians 11.3," *New Testament Studies* 35 (1989): 503–11; Joseph A. Fitzmyer, "Kephale in I Corinthians 11:3," *Interpretation* 47, no. 1 (1993): 52–59; Fitzmyer, *First Corinthians,* 409–11. See also Conzelmann, *1 Corinthians,* 184, 186; Craig S. Keener, *Paul, Women, and Wives: Marriage and Women's Ministry in the Letters of Paul* (Grand Rapids: Baker, 1992), 34; Blomberg, *1 Corinthians,* 209; Dale B. Martin, *The Corinthian Body* (New Haven: Yale University Press, 1995), 232; Witherington, *Conflict and Community in Corinth,* 237; Malina and Pilch, *Social-Science Commentary on the Letters of Paul,* 106; Ciampa and Rosner, *The First Letter to the Corinthians,* 508–9.

61. Wayne A. Grudem, "Does Kephalē ('Head') Mean 'Source' or 'Authority over' in Greek Literature: A Survey of 2,336 Examples," *Trinity Journal* 6, no. 1 (1985): 38–59, at 46–59.

120

the term in Greek literature, he quotes approximately forty-nine cases in which κεφαλή signifies authority and leadership.[62]

2) κεφαλή, *head as the source of life or beginning.* This interpretation was proposed in the 1950s by Stephen Bedale who, however, also admitted its connotations associated with authority.[63] Jerome Murphy-O'Connor argued much more radically for the meaning of "source," claiming that in the LXX κεφαλή is not the expression by which Hebrew ראש in the sense of power would be translated.[64] Exegetes accepting κεφαλή as "source" pointed to Paul's argumentation on the origin of a woman from a man, analogical to the Father–Son relation, in which the former would be the source of the divine or salvific work of the latter (1 Cor 11:8), or to the role of the Son as the giver of life in 1 Cor 8:6.[65] Robin Scroggs argued that Paul, who in Gal 3:27–28 advocates the unity of a man and a woman, cannot speak of subjecting her again to a man in 1 Cor

62. On the polemic with Grudem and his methodology, see Richard S. Cervin, "Does Kephalē Mean 'Source' or 'Authority over' in Greek Literature: A Rebuttal," *Trinity Journal* 10, no. 1 (1989): 85–112. The author claims that only in 4 out of 49 cases mentioned by Grudem κεφαλή may signify "authority". Grudem answered criticism and maintained his position in the subsequent publications: Wayne A. Grudem, "The Meaning of Kephalē ('Head'): A Response to Recent Studies," *Trinity Journal* 11 (1990): 3–72; Wayne A. Grudem, "The Meaning of Kephalē ('Head'): An Evaluation of New Evidence, Real and Alleged," *Journal of the Evangelical Theological Society* 44 (2001): 25–65.

63. Stephen Bedale, "The Meaning of κεφαλή in the Pauline Epistles," *Journal of Theological Studies* 5 (1954): 211–15.

64. Murphy-O'Connor, "Sex and Logic in 1 Corinthians 11:2–16," 491–94, esp. 492. See also B. Mickelsen and A. Mickelsen, "What Does Kephalē Mean in the New Testament?," 97–110 in *Women, Authority & the Bible,* ed. Alvera Mickelsen (Downers Grove, IL: InterVarsity, 1986) (with responses).

65. Barrett, *The First Epistle to the Corinthians,* 248; Scroggs, "Paul and the Eschatological Woman," 299–301; Robin Scroggs, "Paul and the Eschatological Woman: Revisited," *Journal of the American Academy of Religion* 42, no. 3 (1974): 532–37, at 534; Meier, "On the Veiling of Hermeneutics (1 Cor 11:2–16)," 217–18; Morris, *1 Corinthians,* 149; Fee, *The First Epistle to the Corinthians,* 503; C. C. Kroeger, "The Classical Concept of 'Head' as 'Source,'" 267–83 in *Equal to Serve,* ed. G. Gaebelein Hull (London: Scripture Union, 1987), at 267–77; Ben Witherington, *Women in the Earliest Churches* (Cambridge. Cambridge University Press, 1988), 84–85; T. Radcliffe, "Paul and Sexual Identity: 1 Cor 11:2–16," 62–72 in *After Eve: Women, Theology and the Christian Tradition,* ed. J. M. Soskice (London: Collins/Marshall, 1990), 66; Jervis, "'But I Want You to Know . . .,'" 240; Schrage, *Der erste Brief an die Korinther,* 2:501–4; Hays, *First Corinthians,* 184; Richard A. Horsley, *1 Corinthians,* ANTC (Nashville: Abingdon, 1998), 153; Collins, *First Corinthians,* 405; M. Gielen, "Beten und Prophezeien mit unverhüllten Kopf?: Die Kontroverse zwischen Paulus und der korinthischen Gemeinde um die Wahrung der Geschlechtsrollensymbolik in 1 Kor 11,2–16," *Die Zeitschrift für die Neutestamentliche Wissenschaft und die Kunde der älteren Kirche* 90 (1999): 220–49, at 240.

MARCIN KOWALSKI

11:3.[66] These positions were questioned by Wayne Grudem who, having examined over two thousand cases in which κεφαλή appears in Greek literature, contended that it does not occur in the sense of "source" or "beginning."[67] Additionally, the meaning of "source" is not included in dictionaries such as BDAG, TDNT, EDNT, Louw-Nida, Moulton-Milligan, or the *Patristic Greek Lexicon* by Lampe.[68]

3) κεφαλή *denoting the most important part of the body, a metaphor derived from the position of the head in the body.* Galen believed that the head (brain) was the most important body organ. Seneca, in a letter to Nero, wrote about the head as the source of health for the whole body.[69] This interpretation is gaining a broader circle of supporters who read κεφαλή as a synonym for the most important part of the body, deserving a special respect.[70]

Where is the discussion of the meaning of κεφαλή taking us? This debate on the importance of κεφαλή has recently turned into a dispute about the qualification of specific cases where the word appears in Greek literature. Statistics are not convincing as they frequently depend on the commentators' point of view and clearly indicate that the term usually occurs in a literal sense. In such

---

66. Scroggs, "Paul and the Eschatological Woman," 288, 291–93.

67. Grudem, "Does Kephalē ('Head') Mean 'Source' or 'Authority over' in Greek Literature," 38–46. Cervin, "Does Kephalē Mean 'Source' or 'Authority over' in Greek Literature," 89–94, 112, although criticizing Grudem, also rejects the thesis that κεφαλή denotes "source" in 1 Cor 11:2–16.

68. BDAG, "κεφαλή," 541–42; H. Schlier, "κεφαλή," TDNT 3:673–82; M. Lattke, "κεφαλή," EDNT 2:284–86; Moulton and Milligan, *The Vocabulary of the Greek Testament*, 342; Johannes P. Louw and Eugene A. Nida, *Greek-English Lexicon of the New Testament: Based on Semantic Domains* (New York: United Bible Societies, 1996), 738. See also Thiselton, *The First Epistle to the Corinthians*, 818. "Authority" does not appear in LSJ, "κεφαλή," 945, where one finds "source" instead.

69. Seneca, *Clem.* 2.2.1 (LCL).

70. Delobel, "1 Cor 11:2–16: Toward a Coherent Explanation," 378–79; Cervin, "Does Kephalē Mean 'Source' or 'Authority over' in Greek Literature," 112; Victor Hasler, "Die Gleichstellung der Gattin: Situationskritische Reflexionen zu 1 Kor, 11,2–16," *Theologische Zeitschrift* 50, no. 3 (1994): 189–200; Andrew C. Perriman, "The Head of a Woman: The Meaning of Kephalē in 1 Cor 11:3," *Journal of Theological Studies* 45, no. 2 (1994): 602–22; Horrell, *The Social Ethos of the Corinthian Correspondence*, 171; Gundry-Volf, "Gender and Creation in 1 Cor 11:2–16," 159; Linda L. Belleville, "Κεφαλη and the Thorny Issue of Headcovering in 1 Corinthians 11:2–16," 215–31 in *Paul and the Corinthians: Studies on a Community in Conflict. Essays in Honour of Margaret Thrall,* ed. Margaret E. Thrall, Trevor J. Burke and J. K. Elliott, NT.S 109 (Leiden: Brill, 2003), 229; Garland, *1 Corinthians*, 508, 516; Johnson, *1 Corinthians*, 192 (2 and 3); Heil, *The Rhetorical Role of Scripture in 1 Corinthians*, 179; Thiselton, *The First Epistle to the Corinthians*, 820. According to Thiselton, this meaning is linked with the argumentative context in 1 Cor 11:2–14:40.

a case, the key to understanding the term is the cultural context and the logic of Paul's argumentation in 1 Cor 11:2–16. Given the cultural context, it appears difficult to escape the notions of hierarchy and subordination which remain deeply ingrained in the Latin *caput*, Greek κεφαλή, and Hebrew שׁרׁ.[71] Does Paul emphasize this aspect, aiming at maintaining the subordination of women to men in the Corinthian church? It does not seem to be the point he makes in 1 Cor 11:10–12, where he stresses the equality of both sexes. Wire claims the contrary, accusing Paul of sanctioning the existing social order and sealing it with a theological explanation.[72]

Rather than that, in 1 Cor 11:2–16 Paul seems to relativize the existing social order. In his thesis in 1 Cor 11:3, it is not the power but the precedence of a man before a woman that resonates. The model of their relationship is based on the relationship between the Father and the Son: "God is the head of Christ." The Father and the Son give themselves to each other in mutual respect and freedom. They base their relationship on priority, which is not forced but is a gift and is accepted as such. The same is true of the relationship between a man and a woman. John Chrysostom emphasized the same aspect, opposing the simple subordinationist reading of the term κεφαλή in 1 Cor 11:3. If Paul had wanted to speak about subjecting, he would have used the analogy with a slave, not the image of a husband and wife. According to Chrysostom, the husband–wife relation reflects the hierarchy understood as the gift of self, freedom, and respect for one's own individuality, which characterize the communication between the Father and the Son.[73] Christ appears in 1 Cor 11:3 in connection with the theology of creation as the One who is the source of life, who confirms the order of the first creation and is the protagonist of the "new creation" (1 Cor 11:11). The general nature of the statement underlying Paul's arguments and the metaphorical meaning of κεφαλή in v. 3 leads us to the conclusion that the apostle is concerned with something more than just the matter of order and dress code during prayer gatherings. He uses these problems to show the Corinthians the true nature of the relationship between a man and a woman in Christ.[74]

---

71. Seneca, *Clem.* 1.4.3 (LCL); Jorunn Økland, *Women in Their Place: Paul and the Corinthian Discourse of Gender and Sanctuary Space,* JSNTSup 269 (London: T&T Clark, 2004), 175.

72. Wire, *The Corinthian Women Prophets,* 21, 24–25, 29–30, 33, 37–38, 116–34.

73. John Chrysostom, *Hom. 1 Cor.* 26.3. Likewise, Thiselton, *The First Epistle to the Corinthians,* 819.

74. On the universal character of Paul's argument in 1 Cor 11:2–16, see Økland, *Women in Their Place,* 194–95; B. L. Merkle, "Paul's Arguments from Creation in 1 Corinthians 11:8–9 and 1 Timothy 2:13–14: An Apparent Inconsistency Answered," *Journal of the Evangelical Theological Society* 49 (2006): 527–48, at 527–38; Taylor, *1 Corinthians,* 254–55.

MARCIN KOWALSKI

Cultural Argument (1 Cor 11:4–6)

After having presented his thesis, Paul begins the argumentative section with the discussion on male behavior during prayer. He forbids men to pray and prophesy with their heads covered because in this way they cover themselves with shame. The beginning makes us realize that the problem in Corinth did not only concern women but men and women equally.[75] The opposite view is held by Fee and other exegetes who support his view, arguing that problems were caused by women, while men appear in Paul's discourse only to balance the argument.[76] This is contradicted by the thesis put forward by the apostle in v. 3, where a man is described as the head of a woman and Christ as the head of a man. The Christological component would be unnecessary if the issue concerned women only. For both men and women, clothing and appearance are not exclusively external signs, but also reveal attitudes and values and, more importantly, have an impact on the community. What, then, was the motivation of men for covering their heads during prayer? Given the ambiguous expression that describes "something hanging down from the head" (κατὰ κεφαλῆς ἔχων), numerous interpretations arise. They can be essentially subsumed into two categories:[77]

1) Men pray, covering their heads, as the ancient Romans used to do.[78] The Greeks, by contrast, prayed with their heads uncovered. Ancient art and texts, as Oster and many others after him argued, present evidence of men covering their heads in a cultic context.[79] Perhaps, as Gill claims, the Corinthians

---

75. Murphy-O'Connor, "Sex and Logic in 1 Corinthians 11:2–16," 483; Murphy-O'Connor, "1 Cor 11:2–16 Once Again," 266–67; BeDuhn, "'Because of the Angels,'" 296; Thiselton, *The First Epistle to the Corinthians*, 805, 825–26; Winter, *After Paul Left Corinth*, 121; Heil, *The Rhetorical Role of Scripture in 1 Corinthians*, 178.

76. Robertson and Plummer, *A Critical and Exegetical Commentary*, 229; Morris, *1 Corinthians*, 148–49; Fee, *The First Epistle to the Corinthians*, 494–95, 505; Collins, *First Corinthians*, 400, 402; Gielen, "Beten und Prophezeien mit unverhüllten Kopf?," 222, 228; Garland, *1 Corinthians*, 507–8, 517; Fitzmyer, *First Corinthians*, 405, 412; Ciampa and Rosner, *The First Letter to the Corinthians*, 512–13, 537; Edsall, "Greco-Roman Costume and Paul's Fraught Argument in 1 Corinthians 11.2–16," 138–39; Taylor, *1 Corinthians*, 257.

77. See Thiselton, *The First Epistle to the Corinthians*, 822–25.

78. Thus Cornelius à Lapide, *The Great Commentary of Cornelius à Lapide: I Corinthians* (Edinburgh: John Grant, 1908), 261 with reference to Tertullian. Similarly, Robertson and Plummer, *A Critical and Exegetical Commentary*, 229. On the head covering without any specific identification of the custom, see further Barrett, *The First Epistle to the Corinthians*, 249; Conzelmann, *1 Corinthians*, 184; Morris, *1 Corinthians*, 150.

79. Richard Oster, "When Men Wore Veils to Worship: The Historical Context of 1 Corinthians 11:4," *New Testament Studies* 34, no. 4 (1988): 481–505, at 493–505; Richard E. Oster, "Use, Misuse and Neglect of Archaeological Evidence in Some Modern Works on 1 Corinthians

Changing Gender Roles and the Unchanging Message of 1 Corinthians 11:2–16

imitated Roman social elites when praying.[80] Some scholars also see here the influence of Jewish customs, but there are no grounds for the claim that in the first century Jews would cover their heads with tallits during prayer.[81]

2) Men wear long hair which falls on their shoulders.[82] Murphy-O'Connor identifies them directly as homosexuals who preside over the liturgy, which is unacceptable to Paul. Long hair, braided into elaborate hairstyles by homosexual men, was a mark of provocative behavior and promiscuity.[83]

(1 Cor 7,1–5, 8,10, 11,2–16, 12,14–26)," *Die Zeitschrift für die Neutestamentliche Wissenschaft und die Kunde der älteren Kirche* 83, nos. 1–2 (1992): 52–73, at 68–69. See also Cynthia L. Thompson, "Hairstyles, Head-Coverings, and St Paul: Portraits from Roman Corinth," *Biblical Archaeologist* 51, no. 2 (1988): 99–115, at 101–5; David W. J. Gill, "The Importance of Roman Portraiture for Head-Coverings in 1 Corinthians 11:2–16," *Tyndale Bulletin* 41, no. 2 (1990): 245–60, at 246–51, 258–60; Witherington, *Conflict and Community in Corinth*, 232–34; Preston T. Massey, "The Meaning of κατακαλύπτω and κατὰ κεφαλῆς ἔχων in 1 Corinthians 11.2–16," *New Testament Studies* 53, no. 4 (2007): 502–23; Mark Finney, "Honour, Head-Coverings and Headship: 1 Corintians 11.2–16 in Its Social Context," *Journal for the Study of the New Testament* 33, no. 1 (2010): 31–58, at 35–41; Preston T. Massey, "Veiling among Men in Roman Corinth: 1 Corinthians 11:4 and the Potential Problem of East Meeting West," *Journal of Biblical Literature* 137, no. 2 (2018): 501–17.

80. Gill, "The Importance of Roman Portraiture for Head-Coverings in 1 Corinthians 11:2–16," 260. Similarly, Winter, *After Paul Left Corinth*, 122–23; Finney, "Honour, Head-Coverings and Headship," 47.

81. Robertson and Plummer, *A Critical and Exegetical Commentary*, 229; Oster, "When Men Wore Veils to Worship," 487; Malina and Pilch, *Social-Science Commentary on the Letters of Paul*, 106–7. On later customs of covering heads during prayer in Jewish culture, see Hermann L. Strack and Paul Billerbeck, *Kommentar zum Neuen Testament aus Talmud und Midrasch*, 2nd ed., vol. 3 (München: Beck, 1956), 424–26; John Lightfoot, *A Commentary on the New Testament from the Talmud and Hebraica: Matthew–1 Corinthians*, vol. 4, *Acts–1 Corinthians* (Bellingham, WA: Logos Bible Software, 2010), 229–30.

82. Hurley, "Did Paul Require Veils or the Silence of Women," 199, 202, 204; Murphy-O'Connor, "Sex and Logic in 1 Corinthians 11:2–16," 484–87; Alan Padgett, "Paul on Women in the Church: The Contradictions of Coiffure in 1 Corinthians 11:2–16," *Journal for the Study of the New Testament* 6, no. 20 (1984): 69–86, at 69–71; Murphy-O'Connor, "1 Cor 11:2–16 Once Again," 267–68; Blomberg, *1 Corinthians*, 210; Horsley, *1 Corinthians*, 153–54; Collins, *First Corinthians*, 406–7; Johnson, *1 Corinthians*, 192; Heil, *The Rhetorical Role of Scripture in 1 Corinthians*, 180; A. P. Brown, "Chrysostom and Epiphanius: Long Hair Prohibited as Covering in 1 Corinthians 11:4, 7," *Bulletin for Biblical Research* 23, no. 3 (2013): 365–77.

83. Epictetus, *Diatr.* 3.1.25–31; Philo, *Spec.* 3.37–38; Ps.-Phoc., 210–14; James H. Charlesworth, ed., *The Old Testament Pseudepigrapha*, vol. 2, *Expansions of the "Old Testament" and Legends, Wisdom and Philosophical Literature, Prayers, Psalms, and Odes, Fragments of Lost Judeo-Hellenistic Works* (Garden City, NY: Doubleday, 1985), 581; Collins, *First Corinthians*, 396–99; Winter, *After Paul Left Corinth*, 132–33.

MARCIN KOWALSKI

The first interpretation seems to contain the highest grade of probability. If the issue had concerned long hair and homosexual orientation, Paul's reaction would have been much more severe and he would not have resorted to the praise of the Corinthians in 1 Cor 11:2. Togas, with which the Romans covered their heads during cultic ceremonies, constitute a convincing cultural context for the behavior of the Corinthians.[84] The images of Emperor Augustus, like the one from the Basilica Iulia, who offered sacrifice with his head covered, were probably deeply rooted in the collective imagination of the Corinthians.[85] Massey, in his latest study, also shows a wealth of contexts in which men covered their heads, motivated by desire to avoid shame, to defend against unfriendly omens, to display their status, and to dedicate themselves to gods.[86]

Regardless of the differences in the interpretation of the expression κατὰ κεφαλῆς ἔχων, the exegetes generally agree on the significance of Paul's argument. By making a prophetic speech or teaching with a covered head, a man becomes like a woman and thus disgraces his head, which can be understood as a reference to his own person (*synecdoche*) but also to Christ who is his head. In Roman culture, as Bruce Malina and many other commentators point out, honor is the basic capital of a man.[87] In a collective society, the game of honor is never an individual matter, but should be perceived in a wide network of social connections. If Christ is the head of a man, in a culture in which the honor of the patron was reflected in his clients and vice versa, the man's shame also falls on Christ. In a similar way, every woman who prays or prophesies with her head uncovered disgraces her head, both physical and metaphorical, namely, a man.[88] Paul describes this situation as synonymous

84. Contra Garland, *1 Corinthians*, 517.

85. Gill, "The Importance of Roman Portraiture for Head-Coverings in 1 Corinthians 11:2–16," 246–48.

86. Massey, "Veiling among Men in Roman Corinth," 505–17.

87. Bruce J. Malina, *The New Testament World: Insights from Cultural Anthropology*, 3rd ed. (Atlanta: John Knox, 2001), 27–57. See also Halvor Moxnes, "Honor, Shame and the Outside World in Paul's Letter to the Romans," 207–18 in *The Social World of Formative Christianity and Judaism: Essays in Tribute to Howard Clark Kee,* ed. Howard C. Kee and Jacob Neusner (Philadelphia: Fortress, 1988); Carlin A. Barton, *Roman Honor: The Fire in the Bones* (Berkeley: University of California Press, 2001); Mark T. Finney, *Honour and Conflict in the Ancient World: 1 Corinthians in Its Greco-Roman Social Setting,* LNTS 460 (London: T&T Clark, 2012). See the application of honor and shame categories to 1 Cor 11:2–16 in: Finney, "Honour, Head-Coverings and Headship," 44–53.

88. On the female status being reflected in men, see Sarah B. Pomeroy, *Goddesses, Whores, Wives, and Slaves: Women in Classical Antiquity* (New York: Schocken Books, 1995), 182–85; Collins, *First Corinthians*, 410; Finney, "Honour, Head-Coverings and Headship," 50–51.

Changing Gender Roles and the Unchanging Message of 1 Corinthians 11:2–16

with being shaved. What does the exposed female head refer to? It can be interpreted as:[89]

1) Rejection of the custom of the Jewish head covering which Paul introduced at Corinth.[90]

2) Lack of head covering or loose hair as a sign of freedom and equality demonstrated by *pneumatikoi* or enthusiasts at Corinth, blurring gender differences.[91]

3) Loose hair as a mark of the free prophetic spirit, akin to pagan cults.[92]

The first interpretation is problematic because female head coverings were not a specifically Jewish custom but a practice commonly known in antiquity.[93] Ciampa and Rosner draw attention to the fact that this usage may not have been commonplace in the western part of the Empire, but they admit that

89. Collins, *First Corinthians*, 407–9.

90. Annie Jaubert, "Le voile des femmes, I Cor 11:2–16," *New Testament Studies* 18, no. 4 (1972): 419–30; Scroggs, "Paul and the Eschatological Woman," 290–91; A. Feuillet, "La dignité et le rôle de la femme d'après quelques textes pauliniens: Comparison avec l'Ancien Testament," *New Testament Studies* 21, no. 2 (1975): 157–91, at 160–61; Watson, *Agape, Eros, Gender,* 53 (Eastern, Asian custom).

91. Hurley, "Did Paul Require Veils or the Silence of Women," 201; Wayne A. Meeks, "Image of the Androgyne: Some Uses of a Symbol in Earliest Christianity," *History of Religions* 13, no. 3 (1974): 165–208, at 202–3; Robertson and Plummer, *A Critical and Exegetical Commentary*, 230; Meier, "On the Veiling of Hermeneutics (1 Cor 11:2–16)," 217; Murphy-O'Connor, "Sex and Logic in 1 Corinthians 11:2–16," 488–90; Fee, *The First Epistle to the Corinthians*, 497; Dennis R. MacDonald, "Corinthian Veils and Gnostic Androgynes," 276–92 in *Images of the Feminine in Gnosticism,* ed. Karen L. King (Philadelphia: Fortress, 1988); Jervis, "'But I Want You to Know . . .,'" 235–39; Blomberg, *1 Corinthians*, 211; Horrell, *The Social Ethos of the Corinthian Correspondence*, 170; Hays, *First Corinthians*, 183–84; Gundry-Volf, "Gender and Creation in 1 Cor 11:2–16," 154; BeDuhn, "'Because of the Angels,'" 316–17; Merkle, "Paul's Arguments from Creation in 1 Corinthians 11:8–9 and 1 Timothy 2:13–14," 533.

92. Abel Isaksson, *Marriage and Ministry in the New Temple: A Study with Special Reference to Mt. 19.13–12 [i.e. 19.3–12] and 1. Cor. 11.3–16,* ASNU 24 (Lund: Copenhagen: CWK Gleerup; E. Munksgaard, 1965), 166; Gail P. Corrington, "The 'Headless Woman': Paul and the Language of the Body in 1 Cor 11.2–16," *Perspectives In Religious Studies* 18, no. 3 (1991): 223–31, at 228–31; Schüssler Fiorenza, *In Memory of Her*, 227–28; Witherington, *Conflict and Community in Corinth,* 236, Birgitte G. Hjort, "Gender Hierarchy or Religious Androgyny?: Male-Female Interaction in the Corinthian Community—a Reading of 1 Cor. 11,2–16," *Studia Theologica* 55, no. 1 (2001): 58–80, at 72–75 (combination of 2 and 3); Philip B. Payne, *Man and Woman, One in Christ: An Exegetical and Theological Study of Paul's Letters* (Grand Rapids: Zondervan, 2009), 44–47. One of the first scholars writing on the influence of pagan cults in Corinth was S. Lösch, "Christliche Frauen in Corinth: Ein neuer Lösungsversuch," *Theologische Quartalschrift* 127 (1947): 216–61.

93. Witherington, *Conflict and Community in Corinth*, 235 rightly emphasizes the Greco-Roman character of Corinth.

MARCIN KOWALSKI

women with uncovered heads quite commonly raised social critique.[94] This conclusion is also supported by the detailed study of Massey which, based on the inscriptions from Andania and Lycosura and a series of ancient texts, proves the widespread use of head coverings by women.[95] Regarding interpretations 2) and 3), we do not know if there was a group of the so-called spiritual people (*pneumatikoi*) at Corinth which also included women.[96] It remains a hypothesis whether they claimed the right to equality with men. It is also a pure conjecture whether there were prophetesses who uncovered their heads and let their hair loose while prophesying to emphasize their gift of the Spirit. Forbes convincingly criticized the pagan parallels to the cult of Dionysus and Isis as unrelated to the situation of the Christian community at Corinth.[97]

Contrary to those who in 1 Cor 11:5 perceive the loose hair of women, we argue in favor of the lack of the female head coverings during the prayer meetings. What motivated women to take them off? The answers given to this question can be only tentative and hypothetical. As Paul's argument is conducted at the cultural and theological level, the behavior of women at Corinth was probably motivated both by cultural and theological reasons. Perhaps the Pauline teaching on the equality between a man and a woman, such as the one contained in Gal 3:28, prompted women to put it into effect during their prayer meetings.[98] Women could also have uncovered their heads because worship took place in their own households. Paul basically orders the Corinthians to treat the households in which they pray as if they were a public sphere. At Corinth, men and women worshiped in one place, so the only differences between them were clothing and behavior.[99] Ultimately, we do not have enough clues to answer the question of the motives driving the behavior of the Corinthian women.

Based on historical data, ancient literature, and cultural anthropology,

94. Ciampa and Rosner, *The First Letter to the Corinthians*, 515–16 with reference to Ramsay MacMullen, "Women in Public in the Roman Empire," *Historia* 29 (1980): 208–18.

95. P. T. Massey, "Dress Codes at Roman Corinth and Two Hellenic Sites: What Do the Inscriptions at Andania and Lycosura Tell Us about 1 Corinthians 11,2–16," *Journal of Greco-Roman Christianity and Judaism* 11 (2015): 51–81.

96. It is suggested by Fee, *The First Epistle to the Corinthians*, 498.

97. See Christopher Forbes, *Prophecy and Inspired Speech in Early Christianity and Its Hellenistic Environment*, WUNT II/75 (Tübingen: Mohr Siebeck, 1995), 103–217.

98. Gielen, "Beten und Prophezeien mit unverhüllten Kopf?," 235; Edsall, "Greco-Roman Costume and Paul's Fraught Argument in 1 Corinthians 11.2–16," 142–44.

99. Garland, *1 Corinthians*, 507, 521; Ciampa and Rosner, *The First Letter to the Corinthians*, 519–20. On the public and private sphere in relation to gender and ritual in antiquity, see Økland, *Women in Their Place*, 31–38, 58–77, 124–30, esp. 173–95 (on 1 Cor 11:2–16).

we can say that their behavior blurs differences between the sexes and harms the reputation of the community members.[100] Covering the head with a veil or hood signified a respectable female status. Horace described a married woman (*matrona*) showing only her face because other parts of the body were concealed by a large robe. Pliny was happy that his wife listened to his works *discreta velo*, "hidden behind the veil."[101] The wife of Emperor Augustus, Livia, was presented with a head covering as an official model of piety and virtue.[102] A head without cover was a sign of promiscuity and sexual availability.[103] According to Philo, a woman accused of adultery was to be judged without a head covering, a symbol of modesty (*Spec.* 3.56). Following the cultural customs of his time, Paul claims that prayer with an uncovered head disgraces a woman, as much as having a shaved head (1 Cor 11:6). In the latter image John Chrysostom saw a rhetorical device, *reductio ad absurdum*, but more serious cultural connotations seem to be concealed here.[104] In ancient times, the shaved head was a punishment reserved for adulterous women (Dio Chrysostom, *2 Fort.* 64.3) and mothers whose sons grew up to be bad citizens (Aristophanes, *Thesm.* 838). It entailed public stigma, loss of respect, and the status of a dissolute woman. It was also linked to disgrace and loss of femininity.[105] Thus, according to the

100. Murphy-O'Connor, "Sex and Logic in 1 Corinthians 11:2–16," 491–98; Fee, *The First Epistle to the Corinthians*, 510–11; Thiselton, *The First Epistle to the Corinthians*, 832; Orr and Walther, *I Corinthians*, 260; Fitzmyer, *First Corinthians*, 413.

101. Horace, *Sat.* 1.2.80–108; Pliny the Younger, *Ep.* 19.4 (LCL).

102. Gill, "The Importance of Roman Portraiture for Head-Coverings in 1 Corinthians 11:2–16," 252.

103. On women's head coverings in antiquity and on their links with honor, shame, culture and medicine, see Thompson, "Hairstyles, Head-Coverings, and St Paul," 105–13; Gill, "The Importance of Roman Portraiture for Head-Coverings in 1 Corinthians 11:2–16," 251–56; Keener, *Paul, Women, and Wives*, 22–31; Martin, *The Corinthian Body*, 233–39; Thiselton, *The First Epistle to the Corinthians*, 801–2, 828–33; Winter, *After Paul Left Corinth*, 127–30; A. Rousselle, "Body Politics in Ancient Rome," 296–337 in *A History of Women in the West*, vol. 1, *From Ancient Goddesses to Christian Saints*, 7th ed., ed. Pauline Schmitt Pantel (Cambridge, MA: The Belknap Press of Harvard University Press, 2002), 314–15; Økland, *Women in Their Place*, 189–92; Kelly Olson, "Matrona and Whore: Clothing and Definition in Roman Antiquity," 186–204 in *Prostitutes and Courtesans in the Ancient World*, ed. Christopher A. Faraone and Laura McClure, Wisconsin Studies in Classics (Madison, WI: University of Wisconsin Press, 2006); Ciampa and Rosner, *The First Letter to the Corinthians*, 515–17; Edsall, "Greco-Roman Costume and Paul's Fraught Argument in 1 Corinthians 11.2–16," 133–41; Massey, "Dress Codes at Roman Corinth and Two Hellenic Sites," 51–81.

104. John Chrysostom, *Hom. 1 Cor.* 26.4.

105. Winter, *After Paul Left Corinth*, 128–29; Garland, *1 Corinthians*, 520–21; Ciampa and Rosner, *The First Letter to the Corinthians*, 520–21.

MARCIN KOWALSKI

apostle, the behavior of men and women at Corinth, in which the difference between the sexes is blurred, ultimately leads to their loss of honor and social identity.

The Theology of Creation Argument and Its Evangelical Qualification (1 Cor 11:7–10; 11–12)

The cultural argument can be considered a fragile foundation for building an early Christian understanding of sexuality because culture as such is subject to constant changes. Thus, the second step in the Pauline discourse involves the argument from the theology of creation, which accentuates and explains the necessity of keeping the differences between men and women. The apostle refers to Gen 1:26–27, where humanity is described as created in God's image (εἰκών) and likeness. A man, according to Paul, should not cover his head because he is the image and glory of God (εἰκὼν καὶ δόξα θεοῦ) (1 Cor 11:7a). A woman, in turn, is the glory of a man (ἡ γυνὴ δὲ δόξα ἀνδρός ἐστιν) (11:7b). Paul, passing to Gen 2:21–24, explains his position with a reference to the order of creation according to which a woman was made from a man, not a man from a woman, and for this reason "a woman ought to have an authority over her head because of the angels" (διὰ τοῦτο ὀφείλει ἡ γυνὴ ἐξουσίαν ἔχειν ἐπὶ τῆς κεφαλῆς διὰ τοὺς ἀγγέλους) (11:10). This text abounds with problems of an exegetic and anthropological-theological nature. Does Paul sanction the submission of women to men here? What is the meaning of the "authority" (ἐξουσία) that a woman must have on her head? How is it related to the presence of the angels?

Let us begin with the statement on a man who is "the image and glory of God" (1 Cor 11:7b). The key term εἰκών appears in Gen 1:26–27, where God creates humankind in his image to rule over all creation in his name.[106] The power over the created world seems to be the closest to the context of the Book of Genesis as regards the meaning of the divine "image and likeness" within us. In Gen 1:27, it is granted to both man and woman, who are the crown of creation. Both of them were created in the image and likeness of God, of which the apostle is perfectly aware.[107] According to Thiselton, in Paul's appeal to the authority of the Scriptures, the emphasis falls not on power but rather on the

---

106. On the term εἰκών which encompasses the ideas of image and representation, and their place and theological significance in the Old and New Testament, see BDAG, "εἰκών," 281–82; TDNT 2:381–97 (multiple authors); H. Kuhli, "εἰκών," EDNT 1:388–91; C. Spicq, "εἰκών," TLNT 2:412–19; Conzelmann, 1 Corinthians, 187–88.

107. Against Kuhli, "εἰκών," EDNT 1:390, who claims that Paul indirectly denies the concept of "image" to a woman.

reciprocity underlying the concept of image (εἰκών). Man and woman, with all their differences and individuality, were both created to reveal God's presence and rule over the created world.[108] This interpretation is supported by the context of the Book of Genesis. Paul, aware of the truth about the same dignity and vocation of a woman and a man, rooted in Gen 1:27, certainly does not deny women the status of God's image. If in 1 Cor 11:7 he assigns the title of εἰκών directly only to a man, it is because he should take more responsibility for his attitude, in which God's image and glory are to be manifested.

The concept of "image" (εἰκών) naturally leads to the "glory" (δόξα θεοῦ) of God, also applied to a man (11:7a).[109] Glory is an element which accompanies God's manifestation in the created world.[110] A man as "God's glory" manifests God's presence in creation, revealing through words and actions who God is and what he is like. A woman, called the glory of a man (δόξα ἀνδρός) (11:7b), in turn, reveals a man's true nature. In other words, just as God needs a man to reveal himself to the world, so a man needs a woman who reveals the true identity of a man, allows him to understand himself, and motivates him to act. He needs her as different from him and, at the same time, as being closely related to him. The distinction between man and woman, so deeply inscribed in the theology of creation, has a revelational, cognitive, and relational significance.

Let us emphasize once again that Paul does not speak of a woman as an image of a man (εἰκών) but as his glory (δόξα ἀνδρός). The woman is, after all, created in the image of God. The difference between them is expressed not in the language of subordination and servitude but in the language of glory (δόξα), which brings to mind revelation and honor. The difference between

---

108. Thiselton, *The First Epistle to the Corinthians*, 834.

109. Spicq, "εἰκών," TLNT 2:419. According to Barrett, *The First Epistle to the Corinthians*, 252; Fee, *The First Epistle to the Corinthians*, 515, Paul is mostly interested in the presentation of a man as God's glory and not as God's image, Cornelius à Lapide explains the image and glory as hendiadys—a man is a glorious image of God; see *The Great Commentary of Cornelius À Lapide: I Corinthians*, 360. G. von Rad and G. Kittel, "δόξα," TDNT 2:237, and Ciampa and Rosner, *The First Letter to the Corinthians*, 523 perceive the terms "image" and "glory" as synonymous. Further on the relation of these two terms in Judaism, see J Jervell, *Imago Dei: Gen 1, 26f. im Spätjudentum, in der Gnosis und in den paulinischen Briefen*, FRLANT 58 (Göttingen: Vandenhoeck & Ruprecht, 1960), 110–14.

110. On the term δόξα, and its association with revelation and honor, see BDAG, "δόξα," 256–58; von Rad and Kittel, "δόξα," TDNT 2:233–53; H. Hegermann, "δόξα," EDNT 1:344–48; A. Feuillet, "Homme 'gloire de Dieu' et la femme 'gloire de l'homme,'" *Revue biblique* 81, no. 2 (1974): 161–82; Ciampa and Rosner, *The First Letter to the Corinthians*, 525–26. The authors emphasize not only the revelational character of "glory" but also its association with cult, in particular referring to 1 Cor 11:2–16.

MARCIN KOWALSKI

a woman and a man determines their honor.[111] It also reflects the glory of the Creator and allows them to fulfill their life roles in revealing God and helping each other to discover their deepest identity. The gender differences, which belong to the inner structure of a person, are the foundation of relationship between a man and a woman.[112] They are not presented in conflict and they do not serve to perpetuate the patriarchal culture, because they are anchored in God's plan of creation (1 Cor 11:7–9) and salvation (1 Cor 11:11) of mankind. Paul calls men and women to embrace their sexuality as God's gift, accepting the differences and reading them as full of purpose in the process of discovering each other's identity. This call takes the form of a simple plea for men not to cover their heads in prayer meetings, while women are to cover them. The related language of Genesis, referring to the theology of creation together with the ideas of God's image and glory, make us see in this gesture something more than just a mere teaching on the proper headgear during the liturgy. Paul, in a way characteristic to him, efficiently navigates between the contextual and universal dimensions of his teaching.[113] Thus, respect for diversity and gender differences, which finds its specific expression in head coverings and dress, becomes tantamount to respect for the will of God contained in the work of creation.

If Paul does not imply subordinating a woman to a man, what is the "authority" that a woman should have on her head (ἐξουσίαν ἔχειν ἐπὶ τῆς κεφαλῆς)?[114] The traditional association of the image with a man's authority over a woman is no longer accepted. From the end of the nineteenth century on, scholars have been arguing for the woman's power and her control over her head in 1 Cor 11:10.[115] This does not imply simply leaving a woman free to

111. Fee, *The First Epistle to the Corinthians*, 516–17; Gundry-Volf, "Gender and Creation in 1 Cor 11:2–16," 157; Fitzmyer, *First Corinthians*, 415.

112. John Paul II, General Audience (November 7, 1979), in *Man and Woman He Created Them: A Theology of the Body*, trans. Michael Waldstein (Boston: Pauline Books & Media, 2006), 8:1, p. 157.

113. See 1 Cor 8:1–11:1 (the problem of *eidolothyta* which allows Paul to formulate a universal teaching on love and self-abandonment that edifies the community); 1 Cor 11:17–34 (the problem of the Eucharist in Corinth and its universal meaning as "the Lord's banquet"); 1 Cor 12–14 (the issue of spiritual gifts, their hierarchy and the principle of building up the community); 1 Cor 15 (a universal teaching on the resurrection in Corinth, which raises the problems that the Corinthians had with understanding it).

114. On the meaning of ἐξουσία, see Thiselton, *The First Epistle to the Corinthians*, 837–39.

115. Thomas C. Edwards, *A Commentary on the First Epistle to the Corinthians* (New York: Armstrong, 1886), 277; Allo, *Saint Paul premiere epitre aux Corinthiens*, 266–67; Morna D. Hooker, "Authority on Her Head: An Examination of 1 Cor 11:10," *New Testament Studies* 10,

Changing Gender Roles and the Unchanging Message of 1 Corinthians 11:2–16

choose whether to cover her head or not.[116] It is about being in control of one's head, treating it with reverence, which ultimately suggests covering it,[117] Mitchell rightly points out that Paul's argument resembles his reasoning from 1 Cor 8.1–11.1, where the theme was also the ἐξουσία and resignation from it for the good of the community.[118] The ecclesial framework of 1 Cor 11:2–16 suggests that a woman should use her authority over her head for the good and order of the Church at Corinth. As in 1 Cor 11:7 Paul expected a man to uncover his head ("a man ought not to have his head veiled"), so in 1 Cor 11:10 he expects a woman to cover it ("she ought to have an authority over her head"). The parallel construction with ὀφείλω in vv. 7 and 10 signifies the equality of women and men and their freedom to implement Paul's teaching. This, in turn, strengthens our interpretation that in 1 Cor 11:10 Paul refers to the authority that a woman exercises over her head.

Paul also adds that she should have control over her head because of the angels (διὰ τοὺς ἀγγέλους). This motivation, which at first glance does not fit the Pauline argument, may be interpreted in at least seven ways:[119]

1) Because of priests and bishops (Ephrem the Syrian, Ambrosiaster),

2) Because of the fallen angels, to protect herself from their lust (Tertullian),[120]

3) Because of angelic beings who also participate in the liturgy of the Church (Augustine, Peter Lombard, Thomas Aquinas),[121]

no. 3 (1964): 410–16, at 415–16; Robertson and Plummer, *A Critical and Exegetical Commentary*, 232–34; Morris, *1 Corinthians*, 151; BeDuhn, "'Because of the Angels,'" 302–3.

116. Thus Padgett, "Paul on Women in the Church," 72.

117. Robertson and Plummer, *A Critical and Exegetical Commentary*, 232; Fee, *The First Epistle to the Corinthians*, 521; David R. Hall, "A Problem of Authority," *Expository Times* 102, no. 2 (1990): 39–42; Blomberg, *1 Corinthians*, 212; BeDuhn, "'Because of the Angels,'" 303–4; Garland, *1 Corinthians*, 525; Fitzmyer, *First Corinthians*, 417; Ciampa and Rosner, *The First Letter to the Corinthians*, 533.

118. Mitchell, *Paul and the Rhetoric of Reconciliation*, 262.

119. BeDuhn, "'Because of the Angels,'" 304–8; Thiselton, *The First Epistle to the Corinthians*, 839–40; Garland, *1 Corinthians*, 526–29; Fitzmyer, *First Corinthians*, 417–19; Ciampa and Rosner, *The First Letter to the Corinthians*, 529–31.

120. Meier, "On the Veiling of Hermeneutics (1 Cor 11:2–16)," 220–22; Martin, *The Corinthian Body*, 243–49; Lambertus J. Lietaert Peerbolte, "Man, Woman, and the Angels in 1 Cor 11:2–16," 76–92 in *The Creation of Man and Woman*, ed. Gerard P. Luttikhuizen (Leiden: Brill, 2000), 87–91.

121. H. J. Cadbury, "A Qumran Parallel to Paul," *Harvard Theological Review* 51, no. 1 (1958): 1–2; Joseph A. Fitzmyer, "A Feature of Qumran Angelology and the Angels of 1 Cor 11:10," *New Testament Studies* 4, no. 1 (1957): 48–58; Robertson and Plummer, *A Critical and Exegetical Commentary*, 233 (also option no. 5); Hays, *First Corinthians*, 188; Collins, *First Corinthians*, 412;

MARCIN KOWALSKI

4) Because of guardian angels (Theodoret),

5) Because of the angels who cover their faces before God (Isa 6:3),[122]

6) Because of the angels who are the witnesses of the order of creation (Gen 1),[123]

7) Because of outsiders who could report to the authorities that the community is disturbing the social order.[124]

Contemporary commentators often select options 3 and 6, referring, like Fitzmyer, to the Qumran testimonies, where the angels participating in the liturgy are mentioned (1QM 7:4–6; 1QS 2:3–11). This suggestion is entirely appropriate and is further strengthened by the liturgical context of 1 Cor 11:2–16. The sixth interpretation is also consistent with the argument based on the theology of creation in 1 Cor 11:7–12. In Gen 1:26–27, God creating humankind speaks in plural, "let us make," turning, as Philo claims, to the surrounding angelic court.[125] It can be assumed, therefore, that the apostle, in accordance with the Jewish tradition, refers to the angels perceived not only as participants in the liturgy of the Church but also witnesses of the order of creation.[126] However, this is not the end of the argument. The emphatic πλήν in v. 11 introduces an important comment which qualifies Paul's earlier statement.[127] The chronological precedence and the creation of a woman for and from a man does not mean that he has control over her.[128] This statement further strengthens the interpretation of the

Garland, *1 Corinthians*, 528–29; Økland, *Women in Their Place*, 184; Fitzmyer, *First Corinthians*, 418–19; Cecilia Wassen, "'Because of the Angels': Reading 1 Cor 11,2–16 in Light of Angelology in the Dead Sea Scrolls," 735–54 in *The Dead Sea Scrolls in Context: Integrating the Dead Sea Scrolls in the Study of Ancient Texts, Languages, and Cultures,* ed. Armin Lange, Emanuel Tov and Matthias Weigold, VT.S 140 (Leiden, Boston: Brill, 2011).

122. Payne, *Man and Woman, One in Christ*, 51–53.

123. Hooker, "Authority on Her Head," 412–13; Barrett, *The First Epistle to the Corinthians*, 254; Witherington, *Women in the Earliest Churches*, 236 (3 and 6); Thiselton, *The First Epistle to the Corinthians*, 841 (3 and 6); Orr and Walther, *I Corinthians*, 261 (3 and 6).

124. Winter, *After Paul Left Corinth*, 133–38.

125. Philo, *Conf.* 168–72 (LCL). See also Gordon J. Wenham, *Genesis 1–15,* WBC 1 (Dallas: Word, 1998), 27–28.

126. BeDuhn, "'Because of the Angels,'" 308–13 suggests an original, albeit improbable, thesis that the angels are not witnesses but creators of the woman.

127. Fitzmyer, *First Corinthians*, 420: "Paul introduces the qualification with the conj. particle *plēn*, 'however,' to conclude his discussion and stress what is essential (BDF §449.2)." Johnson, *1 Corinthians*, 184, speaks of "qualified patriarchalism." According to the author, vv. 11–16 break with the patriarchal subordination of women to men. At the same time, Paul maintains cultural practices related to clothing, issues of honor and shame, so as not to impede the proclamation of the Gospel.

128. John Chrysostom, *Hom. 1 Cor.* 26.5.

Changing Gender Roles and the Unchanging Message of 1 Corinthians 11:2–16

woman's authority over her head and her right to decide about it. At the same time, it introduces an important aspect of gender equality and complementarity placed in the Christian perspective. A woman without a man is nothing, just like a man is nothing without a woman, in the Lord (ἐν κυρίῳ), says Paul (11:11).[129].

This radical statement means that only Christ reveals the full meaning and depth of the relationship between a man and a woman. Paul goes back to the thesis he put forward in 1 Cor 11:3, which presents the relationship between the Father and the Son as a model for male-female relationships. Divine love and dedication are to be imitated by a man and a woman who in their daily lives become a gift offered for each other in respect and freedom. There is no room for a mere submission or praise of male domination in 1 Cor 11:11. In this light the expression ἐν κυρίῳ can signify an order objectively established by God or a bond which gains a significance in Christ. Thiselton and Gundry-Volf see here a reference to the Gospel and the eschatological dimension of the argumentation introduced by Paul.[130] According to the Gospel, there is no longer male or female, for all are one in Christ (Gal 3:28). The Good News preached by the apostle emphasizes more strongly than the Book of Genesis the equality between man and woman, which Paul also underlines in the conjugal relationship in 1 Cor 7:3–5.[131] At the same time, the Gospel does not negate gender differences. Neither a man nor a woman mean anything without each other, but they must remain truly themselves—a woman and a man faithful to God's plan determining their identity.[132] In 1 Cor 11:11–12, there is a close connection between equality and diversity, the Gospel and the order of creation, as Paul, speaking of Christ, remains still within the Book of Genesis 2:18–25 and 3:20. The new creation does not obliterate the old one.[133]

---

129. On the parallel regarding the expression "neither is the man without the woman, neither the woman without the man" in *Genesis Rabbah* 8:9, see Ciampa and Rosner, *The First Letter to the Corinthians*, 524, 534. For more on the Jewish tradition associated with Paul's argumentation, see R. D'Angelo, "The Garden: Once and Not Again: Traditional Interpretations of Genesis 1:26–27 in 1 Corinthians 11:7–12," 7–41 in *Genesis 1–3 in the History of Exegesis: Intrigue in the Garden*, ed. Gregory A. Robbins, SWR 27 (Lewiston, NY: Edwin Mellen, 1988).

130. Gundry-Volf, "Gender and Creation in 1 Cor 11:2–16," 169; Thiselton, *The First Epistle to the Corinthians*, 842. Similarly Murphy-O'Connor, "Sex and Logic in 1 Corinthians 11:2–16," 497–98; Fee, *The First Epistle to the Corinthians*, 523n41; Ciampa and Rosner, *The First Letter to the Corinthians*, 536.

131. Collins, *First Corinthians*, 403 rightly observes in 1 Cor 11:11–12 a parallel to 1 Cor 7 where Paul also acknowledges the equality of men and women.

132. Witherington, *Conflict and Community in Corinth*, 240; Collins, *First Corinthians*, 403.

133. Økland, *Women in Their Place*, 183, 187; Ciampa and Rosner, *The First Letter to the Corinthians*, 510, 534. According to Økland, in his theology of the old and new creation, Paul

MARCIN KOWALSKI

One can repeat after Watson that the old creation is the prophetic anticipation of the new one.[134] This does not signify a simple tolerance for the order set by the first creation until the new one comes to abolish completely the old one, as Scroggs, Meeks, or DeBuhn argue.[135] Gender differences are not an accidental condition from which man will be freed in the world to come. They constitute the essence of woman and man, and as such, they will be transformed but kept in a glorified afterlife. Theology of creation with evangelical qualification opens up a space for yet another argument originating from the world of nature, which also postulates unity in diversity between a woman and a man.

The Natural Law Argument (1 Cor 11:13–15)

In this short argument, the apostle asks the addressees to judge on their own once again whether it is appropriate for a woman to pray with her head uncovered. The imperative Ἐν ὑμῖν αὐτοῖς κρίνατε refers to the audience's reasoning abilities and defines the character of this argument. From the observation of nature (φύσις) it can be concluded that for a man long hair is a cause for shame, whereas for a woman it is a source of glory (1 Cor 11:13–14). "For her hair is given to her for a covering" (1 Cor 11:15). To understand the importance of this argument, it is necessary to answer first the question of what Paul has in mind when he speaks of nature (φύσις). Thiselton lists the most important interpretative options:[136]

1) φύσις as an intuitive, innate sense of what is good and right,

2) φύσις as a way in which people were created,

3) φύσις as a physical reality reflecting the order of the universe,

4) φύσις as norms and customs accepted in a given society.

Out of these four options, Thiselton advocates for the last one, claiming that Paul refers to the state of affairs he encountered in the culture and society

---

delegates women to the margins of sacred space, masculinizing it (188). Female head covering serves as a determinant of the border between the sexes in which there is no equality (191–94).

134. Watson, *Agape, Eros, Gender,* 79.

135. Scroggs, "Paul and the Eschatological Woman," 302; Meeks, "Image of the Androgyne," 203; BeDuhn, "'Because of the Angels,'" 319.

136. Thiselton, *The First Epistle to the Corinthians,* 844–46; Malina and Pilch, *Social-Science Commentary on the Letters of Paul,* 108. On φύσις in Greek philosophy and possible interpretations of this term in 1 Cor 11:14, see Thiselton, *The First Epistle to the Corinthians,* 844–46; Malina and Pilch, *Social-Science Commentary on the Letters of Paul,* 108.

136

Changing Gender Roles and the Unchanging Message of 1 Corinthians 11:2–16

of his time.[137] Long hair was not acceptable for men at that time.[138] However, such an interpretation seems to correspond only partially to the content of vv. 13–15. Hair and clothing still remain part of the symbolic language used by the apostle arguing for gender differences. The personified nature speaks here in the language of God's creation. In this case, the third interpretation seems to be the most appropriate. The apostle refers to the nature which reflects the order and purpose of the world created by God.[139]

Such an understanding of nature was also popular among the ancients.[140] The question of nature evolved in Greek philosophy and thought in two directions: the structure and the origins of all things.[141] The Pre-Socratics (Heraclitus) defined it as a real and unchangeable structure of things which enabled reality to be understood through the universal laws that governed it. Plato described it as the immaterial essence of things, and Aristotle perceived in it the form and power animating the created reality which determined its purpose, usefulness, and beauty.[142] Hellenistic philosophy, especially the Stoics, equated universal nature with deity in different ways. For the Stoics, φύσις was the cosmic principle of life which permeated the entire universe, guarding its order.[143] The Stoics, speaking of the order and beauty of every being guaranteed by nature, also used the example of hair and beard. A man's removal of his hair was interpreted as acting against nature, an act of rejection of the male identity.

---

137. Thiselton, *The First Epistle to the Corinthians*, 845. Similarly Köster, "φύσις," TDNT 9:272–73; Fee, *The First Epistle to the Corinthians*, 527; Hays, *First Corinthians*, 189; Garland, *1 Corinthians*, 530; Fitzmyer, *First Corinthians*, 420 with reference to Oda Wischmeyer, "Physis und ktisis bei Paulus: Die paulinische Rede von Schöpfung und Natur," *Zeitschrift für Theologie und Kirche* 93 (1996): 352–75.

138. On hairstyles of men and women in antiquity and the importance of this cultural element, see Collins, *First Corinthians*, 396–99.

139. Barrett, *The First Epistle to the Corinthians*, 256; Meier, "On the Veiling of Hermeneutics (1 Cor 11:2–16)," 222; Malina and Pilch, *Social-Science Commentary on the Letters of Paul*, 108; Merkle, "Paul's Arguments from Creation in 1 Corinthians 11.8–9 and 1 Timothy 2:13–14," 535; Böhm, "1 Kor 11,2–16," 231; Ciampa and Rosner, *The First Letter to the Corinthians*, 539; Taylor, *1 Corinthians*, 266. See also John Chrysostom, *Hom. 1 Cor.* 26.4. Keener, *Paul, Women, and Wives*, 45, leaves the matter unresolved.

140. See H. Köster, "φύσις," TDNT 9:251–71; Thiselton, *The First Epistle to the Corinthians*, 844–45.

141. Köster, "φύσις," TDNT 9:256.

142. Plato, *Crat.* 389b–c; *Phaed.* 87e; *Phaedr.* 270c; Aristotle, *Met.* 5.4, 1014b–1015a (LCL).

143. Chrysippus, SVF 2:912, 2:945; following Hans von Arnim and Roberto Radice, *Stoici antichi, tutti i frammenti: Testo greco e latino a fronte. Introduzione, traduzione, note e apparati a cura di Roberto Radice*, Il pensiero occidentale (Milano: Bompiani, 2002).

MARCIN KOWALSKI

Hair as such proclaims: I am a man.[144] The Stoics cultivated the ideal of life in harmony with nature, which reflected the divine *logos*, the rational principle governing the whole world.[145] From here came the concept of natural law (*lex naturae*) which we can find, for example, in the works of Cicero.[146]

A similar idea of nature also frequently appears in the works of Philo and Josephus Flavius.[147] The former describes it in a personified form as the creator and power sustaining the world and endowed with the divine features of uncreatedness and immortality.[148] Nature endows humankind with its gifts and shapes its being.[149] For Philo, the law of nature is closely related to God's law, which is the same for all and stands at the origins of creation.[150] Thus, it can be said that Abraham fulfilled all the commandments of the Law, not the written ones, as they did not exist at that time, but the unwritten ones revealed in nature and inscribed in the human heart.[151] For a complete picture, in the LXX, the term φύσις appears in the Books of Wisdom and 3–4 Maccabees, signifying creatures (3 Macc 3:29), corporeality, physical aspect (4 Macc 1:40), nature as a gift giver (4 Macc 5:8–9), the order of things instituted by God (4 Macc 5:25), the foundation of brotherly and parental bonds (4 Macc 13:27; 15:13, 25; 16:3), the characteristics of creatures (Wis 7:20), physical qualities of the constituent elements of the universe (Wis 19:20), and the structure of humankind open to knowing God (Wis 13:1).

In spite of some researchers' suggestions, it is hard to say that in his understanding of nature Paul pursues a specific philosophical school, e.g., stoicism.[152] Instead, he follows the common elements found in the Greco-Roman and Jewish milieu which suggest linking nature with deity. Regardless of whether it was defined as a material or spiritual element, nature was permeated with the divine rational spirit (*logos*), obedience to which was the key to a happy life. Leaving aside the materialism and pantheism characteristic of Greco-Roman thought, the law and order binding the created world with its divine referent are

144. Epictetus, *Diatr.* 3.1.27–30; 1.16.9–14 (LCL).

145. Epictetus, *Diatr.* 1.11.6–12 (LCL). On the understanding of nature and *logos* by the Stoics, see Köster, "φύσις," TDNT 9:264–65.

146. Cicero, *Off.* 3.6.27 (LCL).

147. Köster, "φύσις," TDNT 9:267–71.

148. Philo, *Sacr.* 98–100 (LCL).

149. Philo, *Spec.* 1.172, 266 (LCL).

150. Philo, *Opif.* 13, 143.

151. Philo, *Abr.* 275.

152. Thus Köster, "φύσις," TDNT 9:273; Fee, *The First Epistle to the Corinthians*, 526–27. Contra Conzelmann, *1 Corinthians*, 190; Collins, *First Corinthians*, 413.

Changing Gender Roles and the Unchanging Message of 1 Corinthians 11:2–16

definitely close to Paul. Thus it can be said that, according to the apostle, nature itself testifies to God's intended differentiation between man and woman.

Conclusions

A variety of strategies were proposed to explain Paul's argument in 1 Cor 11:2–20. According to Wire, a classic representative of the hermeneutics of suspicion, Pauline discourse has a manipulationist character.[153] The apostle calls the Corinthian prophetesses to order and reminds them of their subordination to men, which is typical of the patriarchal culture. However, we have pointed out that Paul in his arguments in 1 Cor 11:2–16 does not stress the subordination of a woman to a man and even relativizes it with his reference to the Gospel (1 Cor 11:11–12). According to Watson, the apostle's argument serves to defend women who cannot and should not be subject to attacks or lust on the part of men.[154] Thus, according to the strategy dominating in 1 Corinthians, the apostle also cares for order in the community. Murphy-O'Connor, Collins, and Thiselton stress, in turn, how important for Paul is the gender distinction which he defends in 1 Cor 11:2–16.[155] Blurring it, either by clothing, appearance, or behavior, is disastrous for the individual as well as for the whole community and society. Finally, the document of the Pontifical Biblical Commission strongly emphasizes the aspect of defending the Christian community against the pagan world surrounding it, in which a man holds a privileged role. Public removal of men from their position in society would threaten young churches, which could be easily accused of subverting the social order, and would lead to sanctions and persecution.[156] In other words, the Church was able to fulfill her mission only by surrendering to certain cultural norms of the time. Gundry-Volf rightly perceives here a strategy aiming at the transformation of contemporary culture or, as Vernon Robbins puts it, at creating an "alternative culture."[157]

---

153. Wire, *The Corinthian Women Prophets.*

154. Watson, *Agape, Eros, Gender*, 41. See also Hooker, "Authority on Her Head," 415.

155. Murphy-O'Connor, "Sex and Logic in 1 Corinthians 11:2–16"; Collins, *First Corinthians*, 393–416; Thiselton, *The First Epistle to the Corinthians*, 800–99.

156. *The Inspiration and Truth of Sacred Scripture*, §132. See also Robertson and Plummer, *A Critical and Exegetical Commentary*, 230–31: "In Corinth anything questionable in Christian wives was specially dangerous, and the Gospel had difficulties enough to contend against without shocking people by breaches of usage."

157. Gundry-Volf, "Putting the Moral Vision of the New Testament into Focus," 285–86; Vernon K. Robbins, *The Tapestry of Early Christian Discourse: Rhetoric, Society, and Ideology* (London: Routledge, 1996), 168–70.

MARCIN KOWALSKI

To some extent, all these interpretations, apart from the manipulationist scenario, can be found in 1 Cor 11:2–16. The most important for us is, however, the inspired character of the Pauline text and the unchanging message coded here which concerns the relationship between a woman and a man. Under the seemingly trivial dispute over clothing during prayer meetings, a very import-ant, multi-layered, early Christian understanding of gender relations is con-cealed. They are expressed through dress code and external appearance that are, as Roland Barthes or Umberto Eco observe, a universal language through which we communicate our identities.[158] The dress code and head coverings used by the Corinthians blurred the differences between a man and a woman which, according to Paul, are fundamental to the functioning of the individual, the Christian community, and the society.

The truth about the necessity and purposefulness of the distinction between men and women, as well as their mutual interaction, can be called the fundamental and unchanging message of 1 Cor 11:2–16. The way in which this distinction is manifested may vary from era to era. What does not change is the thesis that Paul puts forward at the very beginning of his argumentation in 1 Cor 11:3: the relationship between a man and woman consists in imitating the relationship between the Father and the Son. In this relationship, both equality and the diversity of participants are important. Similarly to the Father and the Son, a man and a woman share an equal dignity and glory, but they differ in the way they act and behave. They need to keep this difference in order to help each other in discovering their own identity and fulfilling their mission in the world. Paul perceives the relationship between a man and a woman as an area of imitation of the inner life of God. Just as the Son gives himself to the Father in freedom and love, so are men and women to give themselves to one another. Just as the Father is the head of the Son, the first and the one to give him life and mission, in the same way a man is to take care of his wife. Paul's metaphor of the head does not point at authority and subordination, or at least they are not the most important aspects of the image. Rather, it speaks of service, love, and care on the image of the Father and the Son; it promotes honor and respect granted freely and on the basis of mutual consent. Today, the functions of the family head are also performed by a woman, which was much rarer in Paul's days. Yet, it does not render the Pauline metaphor and teaching invalid. Both

158. Roland Barthes, *Elements of Semiology*, Cape Editions (London: Cape, 1967), 13–28; Umberto Eco, "Social Life as a Sign System," 57–72 in *Structuralism*, ed. D. Robey (Oxford: Clarendon, 1973), 59; following Thiselton, *The First Epistle to the Corinthians*, 802.

Changing Gender Roles and the Unchanging Message of 1 Corinthians 11:2–16

male and female performance of the function of the head aims at imitating the interior life and relationships of the Holy Trinity.

Interpreting the gift of sexuality, Paul begins with the broadest cultural level that defines the honorable and shameful (1 Cor 11:4–6.) The categories of honor and shame change over the centuries and many of the things Paul mentions in 1 Cor 11:2–16 are no longer relevant for us today. These include undoubtedly uncovering the head by women in a place of prayer or in a public space. Nowadays, women's honor cannot be reduced to their roles as wives and mothers, just as men's honor is not solely defined by their business and public interactions. The understanding of power and authority in the family, which today are shared between a man and a woman, has also changed. Nevertheless, the essential message of Paul from the first cultural argument (1 Cor 11:4–6) is still valid. By questioning their own sexuality, men and women lose their socio-cultural footing and cannot fulfill their roles in society. This is what the universal language of honor and shame in 1 Cor 11:4–6 points at.

What also still remains relevant is the message related to the central part of Paul's argument, drawing on the theology of creation and its evangelical qualification (1 Cor 11:7–12). On the level of the theology of creation, the blurring of differences between the sexes or negation of them leads to the questioning of the order established by the Creator. Men and women then lose their identity and cannot perform their roles of witnesses to God's creative love and presence in the world. They cease to be of help to each other in discovering their own identities. At the same time, the communion between them is lost because it is based on differences searching for completion and on unity in diversity (1 Cor 11:7–12).

At the level of the natural law argument, we encounter many problems related to the fact that numerous modern commentators reduce it to a cultural factor or simply deny its existence. Hairstyles and head coverings are undoubtedly a cultural element, subject to change over time. However, Paul's message in 1 Cor 11:13–15, linking sexuality with the law of nature and stressing the necessary distinction between man and woman, remains unchanged. On the level of nature, binary gender differentiation is a fact which is empirically observable and constitutes an object of philosophical reflection. It is testified by the ancient Greco-Roman and Jewish authors such as Plato, Seneca the Younger, Dio Chrysostom, Pseudo-Lucian, Philo, Josephus, and Pseudo-Phocylides. They strongly associated the binary nature of the sexes with the divine plan, inscribed in nature and serving procreation.[159] In the postmodern era, the con-

---

159. See Plato, *Tim.* 91A-D; *Leg.* 838E; Seneca the Younger, *Ep.* 122.7–9; Dio Chrysostom, *Or.* 7.134, 136, 149; Ps-Lucian, *Am.* 19; Philo, *Abr.* 136–37; *Contempl.* 62; *Spec.* 1.325; 3.37–39;

MARCIN KOWALSKI

cept of binary genders is criticized and treated as the cause of marginalization of "non-normative" sexual minorities. An attempt to eliminate it from contemporary discourse and replace it with a fluid or constructivist idea of sexuality, however, meets resistance not only in the circles of Christian thinkers, but also in the field of evolutionary biology and natural selection, where gender differentiation is a fact.[160] Paul calls us additionally to reflect upon it and to discover that the particulars of human nature have their purpose and reveal the divine plan inscribed there (1 Cor 11:13–15).

At the end, reverting to the criteria of inspiration as laid out in the document *The Inspiration and Truth of Sacred Scripture*, let us draw a general picture of biblical inspiration that emerges from 1 Cor 11:2–16. First, Paul's teaching contained here is placed in an ecclesial framework and firmly grounded in the tradition of the Church. Both at the beginning and at the end of his argumentation, Paul refers to the praxis of the numerous communities he founded, to the praxis of the Church, which helps to discern and evaluate new customs introduced by the Corinthians (1 Cor 11:2, 16). The Apostle, as the document of the Pontifical Biblical Commission emphasizes, roots his teaching in the tradition (παράδοσις) of the Church and regards himself its debtor.[161] His Gospel aims at building and strengthening the Church community, which testifies to its inspiration.

Second, according to the document by the Pontifical Biblical Commission, the Good News of the Crucified and Risen Lord forms the core of the Pauline Gospel and determines the inspired character of his letters. In 1 Cor 11:2–16, the apostle refers to Christ in his thesis (11:3) and in the central argument based on the theology of creation with its evangelical qualification (11:11). The Father and the Son are presented to human couples as a model relationship governed by love, mutual respect, self-offering, and care (11:3). By referring to the Book of Genesis in 1 Cor 11:7–10, Paul recognizes the inspired character and truth of the Old Testament and shows its significant development in Christ. The Gospel stresses even more the dignity and equality of men and women who from now

Josephus, *C. Ap.* 2.199; 2.273.275; Pseudo-Phocylides, 175–76. See also Bernadette J. Brooten, *Love Between Women: Early Christian Responses to Female Homoeroticism,* The Chicago Series on Sexuality, History, and Society (Chicago: University of Chicago Press, 1996), 270 and 271 with n12 on the bibliography related to the concept of natural law and its application in the Bible.

160. See Malcolm O. Slavin, "An Evolutionary Biological-Postmodern Dialogue About Sex and Gender: A Discussion (As Imagined Conversation) of Articles by D Kriegman (1999) and D Schwartz (1999)," *Psychoanalytic Psychology* 16, no. 4 (1999): 565–87.

161. *The Inspiration and Truth of Sacred Scripture,* §92.

Changing Gender Roles and the Unchanging Message of 1 Corinthians 11:2–16

on participate in and imitate the internal life of the Holy Trinity (1 Cor 11:11–12). The creative work of the Father and the redeeming work of the Son bind together the old and the new creation, as well as the Old and the New Testament.

According to *Dei verbum*, the revelation concerning the nature of God and the salvation of man constitutes the fundamental truth contained in Sacred Scripture.[162] It also lies at the heart of Paul's argument in 1 Cor 11:2–16. As stated at the beginning, this truth cannot be divorced from historical and socio-cultural circumstances. In 1 Cor 11:2–16, Paul interestingly combines theology with cultural and philosophical arguments (honor and shame and the natural law). The apostle must have been well aware of their relative and subsidiary role in relation to the ecclesial and theological message he was communicating. However, this combination testifies to the inspired character of his letters, deeply rooted in human history, society, and culture. The variability of these elements does not invalidate the Pauline teaching. On the contrary, it stresses its authenticity based on the historical event of Christ and concerned with the language through which the divine truth can be communicated to the world.[163] Human history, culture, and philosophy become thus the bearers of the Good News and cannot be easily separated from it. Of that fact we are reminded also by the teaching of Benedict XVI. According to the Pope, the Gospel presupposes culture; it never replaces it, but it does leave its mark on it. The Christian message addresses the culture by using its inroads open to faith, by purifying and healing it, and eventually by transforming it from within.[164] Christian faith, according to the Pope, is open to all that is great, pure, and true in world culture. It can be perceived as bridge-building: we accept what is good, but we become the sign of opposition to whatever in culture is evil and corrupt.[165] That is exactly the strategy of Paul in 1 Cor 11:2–16. The Apostle assumes the gender roles current in his culture to transform them from inside in the spirit of Christ's Gospel. That is also why 1 Cor 11:2–16 can be called inspired and inspiring for people of all cultures and times.

---

162. *Dei verbum*, §§1–6. See also *The Inspiration and Truth of Sacred Scripture*, §§63–64.

163. On the criterion of historicity as marking off the ingenuity of the biblical revelation, see Joseph Ratzinger, *Principles of Catholic Theology: Building Stones for a Fundamental Theology*, trans. M. F. McCarthy (San Francisco: Ignatius, 1987), 326–67.

164. Joseph Ratzinger, *On the Way to Jesus Christ*, trans. M. J. Miller (San Francisco: Ignatius, 2005), 42–52, esp. 44–48; following Vincent Twomey, "Ratzinger on Modern Culture, Truth and Conscience," *Forum Teologiczne* 13 (2012): 155–70, at 157–58.

165. Joseph Ratzinger, *Truth and Tolerance: Christian Belief and World Religions*, trans. H. Taylor (San Francisco: Ignatius, 2004), esp. Chapter 2, "Faith, Religion and Culture"; following Twomey, "Ratzinger on Modern Culture, Truth and Conscience," 158–59.

7. The Old Testament as an Earthly Translation of an Inner-Trinitarian Dialogue: Implications for Inspiration

Kelly Anderson

Introduction

This essay seeks to answer two questions: first, how do the New Testament authors arrive at the idea that the Old Testament is, at least in part, an earthly translation of a dialogue between the persons of the Trinity; and second, how can this understanding of the Old Testament impact our understanding of inspiration.

To examine these questions, I will first illustrate how two New Testament authors, those of the Gospel of Mark and the letter to the Hebrews, consider the Old Testament to be reflective of an inner-Trinitarian dialogue. I will then explore how that idea developed, specifically by looking at God's creation of the world in Genesis 1–2 wherein God creates his sanctuary by speaking (1:3, 6, 9, 11, 14, 20, 24, 26). I will show how that paradigmatic speech and dialogue is foundational in the construction of the tabernacle (Exod 25–40), and the temple (1 Kgs 6–9), and then how that idea is developed in the Song of Songs. The conclusion is that the Wisdom of God, the one to whom God speaks in Genesis, is instantiated in the builders of the tabernacle/temple as well as in Solomon in the Song of Songs. These people are privy to God's inner dialogue, and they are thus capable of creating sacred space fit for liturgy, as God himself does in Genesis 1–2.

If the above argument can be demonstrated, then the implications for inspiration become clear. Sacred Scripture is a record of the dialogue between the persons in God, which is expressed and concretized in liturgical spaces. Scripture is both a record of the establishment of liturgical spaces, as well as the rubric for how liturgy is to be carried out.

The Old Testament as an Earthly Translation of an Inner-Trinitarian Dialogue

I will begin to answer the above questions by establishing that the authors of Mark and Hebrews view the Old Testament, at least in part, to be an earthly translation of a divine dialogue.

I. The Old Testament as an Earthly Translation of an Inner-Trinitarian Dialogue

The Gospel of Mark begins with a scriptural citation wherein God announces that he will send his messenger before "you," and he identifies this "you" as the Lord, the one coming to redeem his people.[1] Although the narrator attributes the quote to Isaiah, it is a combination of three Old Testament passages: Exodus 23:30, Malachi 3:1, and Isaiah 40:3. The Gospel thus begins with God speaking to the Son using personal terms from the Old Testament: "I send" (ἀποστέλλω), and "you" (σου).[2]

The end of the Gospel recounts Jesus' final words in his earthly life (15:34) which he addresses to God the Father. Jesus' cry of dereliction appears to be a transliteration of Psalm 22:1 in Aramaic, while the Greek translation reflects the LXX.[3] Just as God does in 1:2–3, here too Jesus employs terms from the Old Testament to communicate to his Father. Thus, the Gospel is enclosed by dialogue between the Father and the Son, a dialogue which deploys terms from the Old Testament.[4]

A similar phenomenon is found in the Letter to the Hebrews. The author

---

1. The content of the word κύριος is debated. According to Daniel Johansson the term indicates the divinity of Jesus (*"Kyrios* in the Gospel of Mark," JSNT 33 [2010]: 101–24). For a similar idea, see Paul Danove, "The Rhetoric of the Characterization of Jesus as the Son of Man and Christ in Mark," *Biblica* 84 (2003): 16–34, at 21. Others maintain that the term refers to the messiah to whom God speaks in Psalm 110.

2. Max Botner argues that the Markan narrative depicts God as the central actor in the prologue who summons and commissions the *dramatis personae* to enact his will. Botner states: "The gospel begins with God speaking to Jesus (1:2). In doing so, the Evangelist is able to show his audience that the ἀρχή of the gospel of Jesus Christ [Son of God] takes root not in the emergence of the Baptist in 1:4, but in a conversation that took place between two persons – 'I' and 'you'," and Botner later adds, "Mark locates a conversation taking place between God and the Christ, wherein the divine 'I' dictates the roles of the *dramatis personae* (Jesus and John) within the theodrama" ("Prophetic Script and Dramatic Enactment in Mark's Prologue," *Bulletin for Biblical Research* 26 [2016]: 369–80, at 370, 375).

3. R. T. France, *The Gospel of Mark: A Commentary on the Greek Text*, NIGTC (Grand Rapids: Eerdmans, 2002), 652. Mark follows the LXX while omitting πρόσχες μοι and replaces ἵνα τί with εἰς τί.

4. The two scriptural quotations are further connected by the word βοάω, a term employed only in these two instances in the Gospel (1:3, 15:34).

demonstrates the superiority of the Son to the angels by a string of seven Scripture quotations (1:5–14). The citations from the LXX include five texts from the Psalms (2:7; 103:4; 44:7–8; 101:26–28; 109:1) as well as two others from 2 Samuel 7:14 and Deuteronomy 32:43. Through these quotes, the author reveals the relationship and intention of God vis–à–vis his Son and the angels. According to the author, God has spoken *to* and *about* the Son and the angels in the Old Testament.[5] Thus, the author views the Old Testament, at least in part, as reporting God's speech to his Son.

Therefore, at least two New Testament authors view part of the Old Testament as an earthly translation of a heavenly dialogue, or even an earthly translation of an inner-Trinitarian dialogue. God is speaking to Christ employing the words of the Old Testament, and Jesus speaks to the Father also employing the Old Testament.

As previously stated, this view of the Old Testament raises two questions: first, where does this idea come from? And second, what implications, if any, does such an understanding of the Old Testament have for the Church's teaching on inspiration?

To answer these, I will examine the first time God speaks in the Old Testament, that is, in the creation account in Genesis 1–2. I will then demonstrate how the pattern established in Genesis is carried out in the "creation" of the tabernacle by Bezalel, and then again in the temple by Solomon. I will also consider the figure of Solomon as portrayed in the Song of Songs. I will then offer some conclusions as I return to the two questions at hand.

II. The Establishment of Sacred Space and Liturgy

The best place to begin is Genesis 1–2. Creation in seven days is portrayed as a liturgy, and the cosmos itself is created for liturgical purposes. God speaks and creates the cosmos, that is, through his word he orders and structures the cosmos, rendering it fit for worship. Mankind is God's culminating work in creation, and they are to function as leaders of the worship. God blesses them and gives them dominion over the world. Finally, he creates the seventh day, the Sabbath, the day he sanctifies.

In Genesis 2:4 the creation of days ceases, and the narrative depicts the activity of God on the seventh day. God forms a garden, places the man in the garden, and gives him the command to work and guard the garden, that is,

---

5. God speaks to the Son in Heb 1:5 and implicitly in 1:13. He speaks about the Son in 1:6, 8–9, 10–11, and about the angels in 1:7.

The Old Testament as an Earthly Translation of an Inner-Trinitarian Dialogue

Adam is to be a priest of the garden.[6] Thus, Adam is presented as king and priest. God then brings forth Eve from the side of Adam, and she is to be a helper (עֵזֶר) to Adam, one who can stand before him. To be a helper means to engage in activity usually reserved for God, that is, the woman appears to have a divine quality instantiated in her which gives her a certain force or power.[7] This divine quality is meant to be used to bring about the flourishing of the man, but Eve perverts this capacity and uses it against Adam, and thus he falls.

To summarize: In the Genesis creation accounts, the cosmos is created/ordered by God through his word which renders it fit for liturgy. God's action of creation is itself portrayed as a liturgical procession, with the highpoint being the establishment of men and women for sacred purposes.[8]

---

6. For an overview of the argument that Adam is depicted as a primordial priest serving in God's sanctuary, see Steven C. Smith, *The House of the Lord: A Catholic Biblical Theology of God's Temple Presence in the Old and New Testaments* (Steubenville: Franciscan University Press, 2018), 81–89.

7. The verb עזר conveys the notion of protection, and God is frequently its subject. In the noun form, God is the help, and the help that he gives is essential to the life and well-being of the one who needs his help. In the secular world, the help can also be for military purposes (see H. J. Fabry "עֵזֶר," TDOT 11:13–16). A helper can be negative in that pagan gods/demons have those who help them (Job 9:13; Isa 30:7; 41:5–7). The fact that the woman is called a helper to and for the man means that she is essential to his flourishing and well-being. No other person, neither man nor woman, is designated as a helper by God. It appears that a woman's particular power, likened to a divine power, is to be used for the flourishing of the man (Prov 31:10–31), but it can be exercised for his downfall. This destructive power of the woman is best seen in Delilah who uses her charm to lure Samson to "tell her all that was in his heart" (Judg 16:17), and when she discovers his secret, she turns him over to her wicked overlords who bind him, torture him, and mock him. Another example may be Lady Folly who lures the man into her house where she presents him as her sacrifice to her lords of Sheol (Prov 7:14–15, 27). Eve unfortunately exercises this power for Adam's doom.

8. Many scholars have noted that creation is depicted as a cosmic liturgy. Further, many have noted that the garden is depicted as a sanctuary of God and have delineated the intertextual connections between Genesis 1–2, the tabernacle, and the temple, illustrating how the tabernacle and temple are to be seen as successors to the garden of Eden. Finally, scholars have also illustrated how the three major parts of the tabernacle/temple (courtyard, Holy Place, Holy of Holies) correspond to the three parts of the cosmos (earth/sea, heavens, highest heavens). Since these arguments are so well documented, I will not repeat them here. See P. J. Kearney, "Liturgy and Creation: The P Redaction of Exodus 25–40," *Zeitschrift für Alttestamentliche Zeitschrift* 89 (1977): 375–87; Michael Fishbane, *Text and Texture: Close Readings of Selected Biblical Texts* (New York: Schocken Books, 1979), 9–13; Gordon Wenham, "Sanctuary Symbolism in the Garden of Eden Story," 399–404 in *I Studied Inscriptions from Before the Flood: Ancient Near Eastern, Literary, and Linguistic Approaches to Genesis 1–11*, Proceedings of the Ninth World Congress of Jewish Studies, eds. R. S. Hess and D. T. Tsumara (Winona Lake, IN: Eisenbrauns, 1994); Craig R. Koester, *The Dwelling of God: The Tabernacle in the Old Testament*,

147

III. The Establishment of the Tabernacle/Temple: Liturgy and Wisdom

The builders of the tabernacle and temple imitate God's actions in creation: that is, they construct sacred spaces meant for liturgy. These are Bezalel, Solomon, and Solomon as portrayed in the Song of Songs. I will briefly examine each of these.

A. Bezalel

Bezalel and his assistant Oholiab are imbued with attributes of the divine which enable them to act as God does in the establishment of the cosmos.[9] They arrange the material world in a way which renders it fit for liturgy.

Bezalel's name means "shadow of God," and twice it is said that he is given

Intertestamental Jewish Literature, and the New Testament, CBQMS 22 (Washington, DC: Catholic Biblical Association of America, 1989), 6–22; Joseph Ratzinger, '*In the Beginning . . .': A Catholic Understanding of the Story of Creation and the Fall*, trans. Boniface Ramsey (Grand Rapids: Eerdmans, 1995), 19–39; G. K. Beale, *The Temple and the Church's Mission: A Biblical Theology of the Dwelling Place of God* (Downers Grove, IL: InterVarsity, 2004), 29–80; Jack Kilcrease, "Creation's Praise: A Short Liturgical Reading of Genesis 1–2 and the Book of Revelation," *Pro Ecclesia* 21 (2012): 314–25; Robert Hinckley, "Adam, Aaron, and the Garden Sanctuary," *Logia* (2013): 5–12; Smith, *House of the Lord*, 35–94.

9. The concept of divinization which enables one to command the cosmos is well attested in the Old Testament. A few examples can be provided to illustrate this point. In Ps 114, Judah and Israel became God's sanctuary and domain, that is, they became imbued with his divine presence, and creation reacted to them the way it reacted to God: the sea fled, the Jordan flowed upstream, the mountains and hills jumped. When asked why, the psalmist responds using an imperative that the earth tremble/dance/writhe before the Lord (חיל). Thus, creation fears God's creatures who are imbued with the divine, and the psalmist commands creation much in the way God does.

More than any other figure, Elijah is presented as an embodiment of God, or as a theophany of God. He engages in godlike activities: he raises from the dead, a capacity only God has (Deut 32:39; 1 Sam 2:6; Tob 4:19; Wis 16:13), he does not die, and he rides on God's divine chariot. The niphal of the verb ראה is used as the subject for Elijah, a verbal form usually reserved to God or angels, thus Elijah appears as God does in a theophany. For further details see Nicholas P. Lunn, "Prophetic Representations of the Divine Presence: The Theological Interpretation of the Elijah–Elisha Cycles," *Journal of Theological Interpretation* 9 (2015): 49–63.

Divinized people can construct divinized things. Psalms 46 and 48, two psalms of Korah, describe how God is in Jerusalem and how his attributes of omnipotence and eternity are communicated to the city. Jerusalem is portrayed as a sacrament of God whose enemies are impotent before it. Gary Anderson explores how the temple furnishings are also imbued with the divine and "possessed something of the very being of the God of Israel" ("Towards a Theology of the Tabernacle and Its Furniture," 159–94 in *Text, Thought, and Practice in Qumran and Early Christianity,* eds. Ruth Clements and Daniel R. Schwartz [London: Brill, 2004], at 159).

The Old Testament as an Earthly Translation of an Inner-Trinitarian Dialogue

a divine spirit (רוּחַ אֱלֹהִים; 31:3; 35:31). The exact expression, (רוּחַ אֱלֹהִים), is found in Genesis 1:2 where the spirit of God hovers over the waters prior to the creation of the world (Gen 1:3) and thus Bezalel is imbued with the spirit of God present at creation. He acquires three qualities from the divine spirit: wisdom (חָכְמָה), understanding (תְּבוּנָה), and knowledge (דַּעַת). These are associated with the wisdom tradition and they enable him to build the tabernacle with the same entities used by God in the creation of the world.[10] Thus, Bezalel arranges the material world fit for worship as God did in creation, and he does this through the gift of the divine spirit, rendering the tabernacle a second garden which allows the Israelites to enjoy the presence of God lost after the fall of Adam and Eve.

Bezalel's assistant, Oholiab, is also given all wisdom in his heart: וּבְלֵב כָּל־חֲכַם־לֵב נָתַתִּי (חָכְמָה; 31:6), and later Exodus says that both Bezalel and Oholiab have been given wisdom in their inner being (חָכְמַת־לֵב; 35:35). Others are given wisdom for particular works, such as the women who spin the goat hair (35:25), and the artisans who work with Bezalel and Oholiab (36:1–2). Thus, Bezalel who has the divine spirit leads a team of wise men and women who have wisdom from God to build the tabernacle (35:35). They are given the divine capacity to arrange the material elements in such a way as to make it proper for worship, each in his or her own way.

But what exactly is this gift of wisdom that Bezalel and Oholiab receive? According to the wisdom tradition, Wisdom is acquired (קנה) or created (κτίζω) by God prior to the creation of the world (Prov 8:22; Sir 24:8) and serves as the architect/craftsman of the cosmos (אָמוֹן), and thus of liturgy (Prov 8:30). Wisdom rests or dwells in Jerusalem and serves in the liturgy (Sir 24:10–11), where it functions as a tree of life to all who come to it (Prov 3:18; 9:5; Sir 24:12–19), the tree of which Adam and Eve presumably would have eaten had they fulfilled their vocations as priest/king and helper. Those who are imbued with wisdom attain its knowledge of the cosmos, and thus can arrange the world in a way which renders it fit for the worship of God. Bezalel, given the gift of a divine spirit of wisdom, is endowed with the necessary competency to construct the tabernacle which is patterned upon the heavenly tabernacle.

Given the above discussion as well as the intertextual connections between the creation of God's primordial sanctuary and the creation of the

---

10. See, for example, Prov 3:19–20, where the three terms are placed together in the context of creation: "The LORD by wisdom (חָכְמָה) founded the earth, established the heavens by understanding (תְּבוּנָה); By his knowledge (דַּעַת) the depths break open, and the clouds drop down dew." See also Ps 104:24: "How many are your works, O Lord, by wisdom (חָכְמָה) you have made them all" (see also Jer 10:12; 51:15).

149

KELLY ANDERSON

tabernacle (see footnote 8), it is possible to conclude that God's conversation in Genesis 1:26 is directed to Wisdom who has been discovered in creation[11] and has been the means by which God creates the world for liturgy.[12] Wisdom

---

11. According to Bruce Vawter, God discovers Wisdom in his act of creation in Job 28 and Prov 8 ("Prov 8:22: Wisdom and Creation," *Journal of Biblical Literature* 99 (1980): 205–16, at 206.

12. While literary dependency between Gen 1:1–2:4a and Prov 8:22–31 cannot be established, there are nevertheless three basic similarities which are noteworthy. First, there are several words which overlap between the two accounts. The first two verses of Gen 1 have five common words with Prov 8:22–31 (רֵאשִׁית Gen 1:1/Prov 8:22; אֶרֶץ Gen 1:1/Prov 8:23, 26, 29, 31; מַיִם Gen 1:2/Prov 8:24; שָׁמַיִם Gen 1:2/Prov 8:27; תְּהוֹם Gen 1:1/Prov 8:24, 27, 28). Beyond that there are several further lexical similarities: יוֹם Prov 8:30/Gen 1:5, et al; אָדָם Gen 1:26, 27/Prov 8:31; עשׂה Gen 1:7/Prov 8:26. Scholars are quick to point out that these words are so common that no relationship can be determined, but the fact remains that eight words from Gen 1:1–26 appear in a passage of nine verses, two of which are not all that common (תְּהוֹם, רֵאשִׁית).

Second, both accounts are connected to the *Enuma Elish*. Alan Lenzi has demonstrated the unique lexical similarities between Prov 8:22–31 and the *Enuma Elish* 1:79–108 ("Prov 8:22–31: Three Perspectives on Its Composition," *Journal of Biblical Literature* 125 [2006]: 687–714), while Victor Avigdor Hurowitz says, "Describing the unformed universe negatively, in terms of what did not yet exist, is comparable to the beginning of the J creation account in Gen 2,4 and the Babylonian creation myth *Enuma elish*" ("Nursling, Advisor, Architect?: אמון and the Role of Wisdom in Proverbs 8,22–31," *Biblica* 80 [1999]: 391–400, at 393). Scholars have long noted the similarities between the first creation account and the *Enuma Elish* (for an overview see Babatunde A. Ogunlana, "Inspiration and the Relationship between Genesis 1:1–2:4a and *Enuma Elish*," *BTSK Insight* 13 [2016]: 87–105).

Third, there are several theological parallels. First, the role of God's word and Wisdom in Prov 8:22–31 are identical. According to Leo G. Perdue, the first creation account is "a cosmological portrayal of origins, God creates the heavens and the earth primarily by means of the divine word that orders and structures the cosmos" (*Wisdom and Creation: The Theology of Wisdom Literature* [Nashville: Abingdon, 1994], 90). This is the exact role Wisdom plays in Prov 8:22–31. Gail Yee notes, "Creation is the divine establishment of order in the cosmos for the purposeful existence of human beings and other living things. . . . Through the mediation of Woman Wisdom . . . God and humanity become co-creators in the ongoing task of keeping the created world order stable" ("Theology of Creation in Proverbs 8:22–31," 85–96 in *Creation in the Biblical Traditions*, eds. Richard J. Clifford and John J. Collins, CBQMS 24 [Washington, DC: Catholic Biblical Association of America, 1992], 93, 94). The term נסך found in Prov 8:23 can have the meaning of "installed," and this seems to be the function of the word which is imprinted upon the cosmic order. Also, Prov 8:24–26 offers a negative way of describing reality prior to creation (when there was no, v. 24; before, v. 25; not made, v. 26) which shows that creation was not out of nothing, but "that life was shaped out of an unformed, lifeless chaos," similar to the first creation account (Perdue, *Wisdom and Creation*, 90), Further, Prov 8:27–29 envisions a three-dimensional cosmos: the earth, the deep, and the skies, as does the first creation account.

While any of these singularly is unpersuasive, taken together they present a formidable argument to show at least some crossover between the first creation account and Prov 8:22–31.

150

The Old Testament as an Earthly Translation of an Inner-Trinitarian Dialogue

is instantiated in Bezalel and his associates who likewise respond positively to God's commands and build a sanctuary patterned after the heavenly sanctuary and the garden established in Genesis. The tabernacle and all its accoutrements become the concrete expressions of the work of Wisdom. Thus, Bezalel and his associates are drawn into the dynamic, dialogical process of creation between God and Wisdom, and the tabernacle is the concrete expression of that process.

B. Solomon in Kings and Chronicles

The pattern illustrated above is replicated in Solomon who builds the temple. Solomon asks for and is given the gift of wisdom. This renders him wiser than those who compose the psalms for worship (1 Kgs 4:11), and able to ascertain and speak the truth (1 Kgs 4:12). He can render justice and judgment (1 Kgs 3:15–28). He knows the mysteries of the created world (1 Kgs 4:13) and is thus able to arrange it in a way to render it fit for liturgy, similarly to how God arranged the world and made it fit for worship. His words are carried off to other kings (1 Kgs 5:14), and thus his words of wisdom spread far over the earth like the water flowing from Eden. He offers seven petitions on behalf of the people, the perfect prayer of repentance, similar to Wisdom who builds her seven columns (Prov 9:1). Wisdom, therefore, imbues him with the capacity to act as God does.

The portrait of Solomon in 1 Kings 3–11 varies from his portrayal in 2 Chronicles 1–9. I will first examine him in 1 Kings, and then the Chronicler.

How might that have happened? One theory suggests that the first creation account and Prov 8:22–31 arose from a similar milieu (George M. Landes, "Creation Tradition in Proverbs 8:22–31 and Genesis 1," 279–93 in *A Light Unto My Path: Old Testament Studies in Honor of Jacob M. Meyers*, ed. Howard N. Bream et al., GTS 4 [Philadelphia: Temple University Press, 1974]). Some scholars have suggested that Gen 1 is dependent upon Prov 8, a theory which seems improbable (Matthew McAffee, "Creation and the Role of Wisdom in Proverbs 8: what can we Learn?," *Southeastern Theological Review* 10 [2019]: 31–67). But it may also be that Gen 1:26 was redacted into the text by wisdom authors. The three plurals throughout Gen 1–11 (1:26; 3:22; 11:4–7) do not align with the traditional JEPD divisions, and so these may have been purposely inserted into the narrative by wisdom sages. If that is the case, then it is possible that "the 'us/our' in v26 is God's deliberation with *Wisdom*" (B. M. D. McNamara, "A Theology of *Wisdom* as the *imago Dei*: A Response to *When God Talks Back*," *Evangelical Quarterly* 87 [2015]: 151–68, at 156; [italics in original]); cf. Claus Westermann who considers that Gen 1:26–30 is an independent unit integrated into the narrative (*Genesis 1–11: A Commentary* [Minneapolis: Augsburg Publishing House, 1984], 156–57; cf. Walter Brueggemann, *In Man We Trust: The Neglected Side of Biblical Faith* [Atlanta: John Knox, 1972], 61). This seems to be the understanding of the text in the Targum Neofiti, "From the beginning with wisdom the *Memra* of the Lord created and perfected the heavens and the earth" (Martin McNamara, *Targum Neofiti 1: Genesis*, ArBib 1A [Edinburgh: T&T Clark, 1992], 52, as quoted in McNamara, "Theology of Wisdom," 156).

151

KELLY ANDERSON

In 1 Kings, Solomon hires Hiram of Tyre to fashion the items in the temple made from bronze. Hiram is endowed with the same gifts as Bezalel before him, that is, with wisdom (חָכְמָה), understanding (תְּבוּנָה), and knowledge (דַּעַת 1 Kgs 7:14). With these capacities, he establishes the bronze of the temple: two bronze columns (vv. 15–22), the sea (vv. 23–26), and ten basin stands (vv. 27–40). The columns recall the foundations of the earth while the sea may recall the water from which creation emerged (Gen 1); thus Hiram, like God, is depicted as shaping and forming the world for liturgical purposes.[13]

Solomon's weakness, however, is foreign women, and, like Adam before him, he is led astray by his wives. The visit of the queen of Sheba (1 Kgs 10:1–13) indicates that Solomon's heart is not inclined toward the wise woman. The queen exhibits some similarities to the woman of Psalm 45. Both are foreign women, and if the daughter of Tyre forgets her people and father's house, the king will desire her beauty (Ps 45:12). Thus, she is beautiful in as much as she is exclusive to the king. The queen of Sheba's speech indicates that she recognizes the God of Israel and his intentions toward Solomon (1 Kgs 10:6–9), a quality which renders her wise, and, if expressed in relationship with Solomon, would make her beautiful and desirable. She brings a large amount of wealth, anticipating the prophecy of Isaiah that the nations will bring their wealth (Isa 60:5–7). The word for her wealth (חַיִל) is used to describe the wise woman of Proverbs (31:10) and Ruth (3:11); thus her vast riches indicate both her wisdom and her capacity to bless the man as Wisdom promises to do (Prov 8:18). It seems Solomon should have asked this wise, wealthy woman to marry him, but instead he does not. He is drawn to women who turn his heart to other gods, and they become his downfall.

Thus, Solomon is endowed with the wisdom of God, a divine quality which enables him to act as God does in judging, ruling, and building the temple for liturgy. Nevertheless, like Adam before him he is brought down by his wives,

13. Marvin A. Sweeney considers that the name of the right column means "he establishes," and the left column means "in strength." He concludes, "When read from right (north) to left (south), the names produce the phrase 'in strength he establishes,' which suggests that the columns symbolize the foundations of the earth and the stability of creation (Mic 6:2; Isa 24:18; Jer 31:37; Ps 82:5; Prov 8:29; cf. 'foundations of the world' in Ps 18:16; 2 Sam 22:16; 'foundations of the mountains' in Deut 32:22; Ps 18:8; 'foundation of heaven' in 2 Sam 22:8; 'foundations of generation and generation' in Isa 58:12; 'pillars of the earth' in Job 9:5; Ps 75:4; and 'pillars of heaven' in Job 26:11)." He later adds, "It (the sea) might also serve a symbolic function, perhaps to depict the sea from which creation emerged (Gen 1) or the sea through which Israel passed on the way from Egypt to the land of Israel (Exod 14–15)" (*I and II Kings: A Commentary*, OTL [Louisville: Westminster John Knox, 2007], 122).

The Old Testament as an Earthly Translation of an Inner-Trinitarian Dialogue

in this case foreign women who turn his heart from God. His reticence toward the wise woman of Sheba and his passion for foreign, unwise women may be an indication of his lack of love toward the temple, which can be seen as embodied wisdom. He spends more time building his palace than the temple (1 Kgs 6:38–7:1), he gives Hiram twenty cities in the land of Galilee (1 Kgs 9:11), and he conscripts the people to engage in forced labor (1 Kgs 9:21). All these show his lack of love for his people and the land which he as priest and king ought to protect and nourish, and his lack of love is mirrored in his indifference to the wise woman, the queen of Sheba.

The Chronicler explicitly presents Solomon and Huram-abi as the second or new Bezalel and Oholiab. Bezalel is only mentioned outside Exodus in the Chronicler (2 Chr 1:5). Solomon and Bezalel are both from the tribe of Judah (Exod 31:2), while Oholiab and Huram-abi are both from the tribe of Dan (Exod 31:6; 2 Chr 2:13). Both Solomon and Bezalel receive wisdom from God for the task of building, and Huram-abi, like Oholiab, is endowed with wisdom and understanding (אִישׁ־חָכָם יוֹדֵעַ בִּינָה; 2 Chr 2:12). Solomon seeks God at the altar built by Bezalel and is then given the gift of wisdom which enables him to construct the temple, embodied wisdom (2 Chr 1:5–12). Hiram appears only to cast the bronze for the temple (1 Kgs 7:13–47), but Huram-abi was involved in the building construction from the beginning, as was Oholiab. Huram-abi acts as a liaison between Hiram of Tyre and Solomon (2 Chr 2), and his skills are similar to those of Bezalel and Oholiab (2 Chr 2:13/Exod 31:1–6; 35:30–36; 38:22–23).[14]

Thus, in both Kings and the Chronicler Solomon and Hiram/Huram-abi are drawn into the dynamic process of creation as first explicated in Genesis and repeated in Bezalel, Oholiab, and their associates. They are given Wisdom through whom the world is created, and thus their respective creations become embodied Wisdom, expressions of the primordial dialogue between God and Wisdom.[15]

---

14. Raymond B. Dillard, *2 Chronicles*, WBC 15 (Waco, TX: Word, 1987), 4–5.

15. See Michaela Bauks who argues that God's blessing and his command to be fertile and multiply, fill the earth and subdue it (Gen 1:28) is provisionally fulfilled in the tent of meeting where God dwells with the Israelites, blessing them and giving them life, and then definitively fulfilled in the building of God's dwelling place in Jerusalem ("Genesis 1 als Programmschrift der Priesterschrift (P^g)," 333–45 in *Studies in the Book of Genesis: Literature, Redaction and History*, ed. André Wénin, BETL 155 [Leuven: Leuven University Press, 2001]).

KELLY ANDERSON

C. Solomon in the Song of Songs

The Song of Solomon offers a poetic description of a man and woman who are respectively referred to as Solomon and the Shulammite.[16] The man in the poem is therefore identified with the wise king who built the temple.[17] Given

16. I employ a spiritual exegesis in the reading of the Song. Spiritual exegesis considers that the writers of Scripture infuse historical entities with symbolism, enlarging their potential meaning. According to Paul Ricœur, "Literary texts involve potential horizons of meaning, which may be actualized in different ways. This trait is more directly related to the role of the secondary metaphoric and symbolic meanings. . . . The secondary meanings, as in the case of the horizon, which surrounds perceived objects, open the work to several readings. It may even be said that these readings are ruled by the prescriptions of meaning belonging to the margins of potential meaning surrounding the semantic nucleus of the work" (*Interpretation Theory: Discourse and the Surplus of Meaning* [Fort Worth: Texas Christian University Press, 1976], 78; see also Claudio Ciancio, "Il tema teologico nell'orizzonte del pensiero ermeneutico," *Teologia: Rivista della Facoltà Teologica dell'Italia Settentrionale* 45 [2020]: 307–28, at 311). The "potential meanings" of Scripture are accessed by deciphering symbols purposely employed by the sacred authors.

The tendency to spiritualize or symbolize in Sacred Scripture is rooted in the hermeneutic of the sacred authors who have a "predominant concern for the great mystery of the whole body," that is, the entire history of salvation and how it affects all humanity (Henri de Lubac, *Catholicism: Christ and the Common Destiny of Man*, trans. Lancelot C. Sheppard and Elizabeth Englund [San Francisco: Ignatius, 1988], 197). This concern prompts the sacred authors in the postexilic period to attempt wholistic syntheses using symbols, particularly human beings who become symbolic entities. For example, the Chronicler portrays David as an amalgamation of Adam, Moses, Abraham, and Melchizedek whose life has implications for all of humanity (Scott Hahn, "Liturgy and Empire: Prophetic Historiography and Faith in Exile in 1–2 Chronicles," *Letter and Spirit* 5 [2009]: 13–50). Likewise, Judith is portrayed as a synthesis of the greatest figures of Israel, and her defeat of Holofernes frees the pagan world around her (Irene Nowell, "Judith," 845–57 in *The Collegeville Bible Commentary,* eds. Dianne Bergant and Robert J. Karris [Collegeville, MN: Liturgical Press, 1989]). This hermeneutic is adopted by the NT authors, who also present historical realities in a spiritualized or symbolic manner (see de Lubac, *Catholicism*, 197–99).

Symbolic reading encompasses both allegorical and typological reading, for typology is a peculiar fusion of symbol with a historical event, while allegory can be utilized in the service of symbols (Glenn W. Olsen, "Allegory, Typology, and Symbol: The *sensus spiritalis*; Part II: Early Church through Origen," *Communio* 4 [1977]: 357–84, at 383); Henri de Lubac, *Exégèse Médiévale: Les Quatre Sens de L'Écriture,* vol. 2 [Paris: Aubier, 1964], 179). There is a "special appropriateness of symbol to express the inexhaustibility and illimitability of God" (Olsen, "Allegory," 383). Thus, I will presume that the man and woman in the Song could be historical beings, but also most certainly symbolic realities.

17. Ludger Schwienhorst-Schönberger argues that the sacred author intended the poem to be read allegorically. He points out that the beloved is called "my beloved" (דּוֹדִי) exactly 26 times, the numerical value of God's personal name, YHWH. The song has thus honored the command of God not to pronounce his name, and yet indicated the identity of her beloved. The central passage 8:6 mentions the flames of *Yah* (שַׁלְהֶבֶתְיָה) where *Yah* serves as an abbreviation of

154

The Old Testament as an Earthly Translation of an Inner-Trinitarian Dialogue

the Solomonic depiction expressed in 1 Kings 3–11, his relationship with the woman will be the curious aspect of the Song. There are three instances in the Song wherein the activity or essence of the man is described (2:8–9; 3:6–10; 5:10–16), and they are all in relation to the woman.

In Song 2:8–9 the woman hears the voice of the man who is then described as springing across the mountains and leaping across the hills to arrive at her house. His voice which resounds across the hills and his physical prowess are supra-human; human voices do not carry that far, nor do humans leap over mountains with ease. God's voice is the one heard across great distances (Ps 29:3–9), and he treads the heights (Mic 1:3). He enables the person to go upon the heights (Hab 3:19), and thus this man is imbued with divine energy and force which enables him and his voice to traverse the earth as God does![18]

Song 3:6–10 is one of the most enigmatic poems of the Song. It is basically a description of a litter or palanquin Solomon built, but given the various and multiple allusions, the poem invites us to consider Solomon's construction in light of other aspects of God's revelation.

The section beings with a question: Who is this (זֹאת) coming up from the desert? The pronoun "this" is feminine, and the question mirrors the questions of 6:10; 8:5 where the answer is the woman. The answer to the question of 3:6 seems to come in v. 7 (the litter), but given the similarities to the other questions, it could also be that the woman is likened to the litter.[19]

---

the divine name. If the beloved represents God, then the female voice represents God's people as a woman ("Traces of an Original Allegorical Meaning of the Song of Songs," 317–30 in *"When the Morning Stars Sang": Essays in Honor of Choon Leong Seow on the Occasion of his Sixty-fifth Birthday*, ed. Scott C. Jones and Christine Roy Yoder, BZAW 500 (Berlin: de Gruyter, 2018), 322).

18. Ludger Schwienhorst-Schönberger notes that the male figure is portrayed as king and shepherd, and these are two conventional metaphors for God in both exilic and postexilic texts. Further, the woman is presented along with images of the city of Jerusalem, and descriptions of the land ("Der Theologische Charakter des Hoheliedes: Evidenzen und Konsequenzen," 269–86 in *The Song of Songs in Its Context: Words for Love, Love for Words*, ed. Pierre van Hecke, BETL 310 [Leuven: Peeters, 2020], 272, 282.

19. Some scholars consider that the pronoun (זֹאת) refers to the palanquin, but it may be the poem intends to place the woman and tabernacle on the same plane, and to invite the audience to consider them together. According to Marvin H. Pope, "The key to understanding the present verse has to be seen in the identical line in 8:5a, and there it is clear from the succeeding line that the one who comes up from the desert is none other than the Bride" (*Song of Songs: A New Translation with Introduction and Commentary*, AncB 7C [Garden City, NY: Doubleday, 1977], 424). Julio Trebolle Barrera examines how the phrase "Who is this?" is used in Job, Isaiah, and the Song, and concludes that the question refers to a mysterious, cosmic supra-human figure whose presence advances the action ("Paralelismos de género en la poesía hebrea bíblica: la mujer del Cantar de los Cantares y el hombre del libro de Job," *Revista de Ciencias de las*

Her arrival is compared to a column of smoke (3:6). The word column (תִּימָרָה) is derived from the root תמר, a palm. The walls, doors, and bronze stands of Solomon's temple are festooned with palms (1 Kgs 6:29, 32 [2x], 35; 7:36), and thus the author describes the one coming from the desert with an allusion to the palms of Solomon's temple. In 7:8, 9 the woman is directly compared to a palm (תָּמָר). Further, given that column (תִּימָרָה) also functions as a synonym of "עַמּוּד/pillar," which is used in 3:10, her arrival also recalls the pillars of fire and cloud which function as a theophany of the presence of God who preceded the Israelites in the desert (Exod 13:21, 22; 14:19, 24; Neh 9:12, 19).[20]

The verse continues by saying that she is perfumed (קטר) with myrrh and frankincense. These spices are used in anointing and sacrifices (Exod 30:23, 34), and the verb קטר is used numerous times for the burning of sacrifices.[21] The clouds of smoke and incense ascending from the offerings recall the offerings in the tabernacle and the temple.[22]

The text then exclaims that it is the bed/litter (מִטָּה) of Solomon (3:7), "the bed which is to Solomon," similar to "my vineyard which is to me" (8:12), indicating possession.[23] Though this bed "comes up" from the desert, it is nevertheless presented as a fixed structure with pillars. The bed is surrounded by sixty warriors, and these terms are applied to David's elite guard (2 Sam 10:7; 23:9, 16, 17, 22; 1 Kgs 1:8).

The litter is described further in 3:9–10. Wood from Lebanon recalls the temple (1 Kgs 5:20), while gold was present in the garden (Gen 2:11–12) and used extensively in the tabernacle and the temple (1 Kgs 6:21). The pillars recall God's presence in the wilderness (Exod 13:21) as well as the pillars for the

---

Religiones 10 [2005]: 225–47, esp. 240). Donatella Scaiola also argues that three queries refer to the woman and mark a shift in the narrative of the poems ("מי זאת—Who Is She?: The Query Refrain in the Song of Songs," 523–31 in *The Song of Songs in Its Context: Words for Love, Love for Words*, ed. Pierre van Hecke, BETL 310 (Leuven: Peeters, 2020).

20. Pope, *Song of Songs*, 426.

21. These include Exod 9:13, 18, 25; 30:7, 8, 20; 40:27; Lev 1:9, 13, 15, 17; 2:2, 9, 11, 16; 3:5, 11, 16; 4:10, 19, 26, 31, 35; 5:12; 6:5, 8, 15; 7:5, 31, among many others.

22. Pope, *Song of Songs*, 426. Victor Avigdor Hurowitz notes that oils are used in the dedication of a temple in order to entice the god to enter his temple. Likewise, the tabernacle and all its cultic equipment are anointed at the time of dedication (Exod 40:9–16; Lev 8:10–11). The oil was made with fragrant spices (Exod 30:22–33). While the function of attracting the god to enter the temple may not be present, nevertheless, it is possible to conclude that hints of the dedication of the tabernacle remain in the background, especially in light of the sacrificial term (see footnote 21) (*I Have Built You an Exalted House: Temple Building in the Bible in Light of Mesopotamian and Northwest Semitic Writings*, JSOTSup 115 [Sheffield: JSOT Press, 1992], 278–79).

23. Pope, *Song of Songs*, 431.

The Old Testament as an Earthly Translation of an Inner-Trinitarian Dialogue

tabernacle (26:31–32; 36:36). Purple was used in the decorations of the tabernacle (Exod 26:1, 36; 27:16), the vestments of the high priest (Exod 28:5, 6, 8, 15, 33), and the veil of Solomon's temple (2 Chr 3:14).

Given these allusions, the author is depicting the wise Solomon as constructing a palanquin, but the poem presents the construction of a palanquin as the construction of the tabernacle/temple.[24] Further, the question of 3:6 is parallel to 6:10; 8:5, creating an allusion to the woman.[25] Finally, the references to procession depict the movement of the ark through the desert, but given that the context is a wedding, the palanquin/ark moves to Solomon, the bridegroom.[26] Thus, the text combines images of the palanquin, the temple/tabernacle, and the woman on her wedding day, all of which are constructed by Solomon, effectively putting sacred places and sacred people on the same

24. See Ellen Davis who argues that the Song is putting forth a theology of a third sacred space, the first being Eden and the second being the tabernacle/temple. "[T]he garden of the lovers is the third important garden in the Bible. Both the second and the third gardens are related to the first, to Eden. The second garden is the Temple, which, as both its décor and its hymnody show, is the stylized Garden of God. The columns of the Temple were crowned with lilies and festooned with hundreds of pomegranates (1 Kgs.7:18–20), symbols of fertility and life. Its great gold menorah was shaped like an almond tree in full bloom (Ex.37:17–24). The walls were carved and gilded with palm trees and flower and cherubim, those guardians of Eden. Lions lurked under the lavers, along with more cherubim, and oxen (1 Kgs.7:29). The inside of the building smelled like the woods; the whole building was lined with cedar, 'not a stone was seen' (1 Kgs.6:18). On that dry stony hill in Jerusalem, Solomon had created a second Lebanon, the majestic and myth-laden mountains of the North. The whole Temple was a sensuous and at the same time a spiritual triumph over what would seem to be the limits of nature and geography. . . . So pilgrimage to the Temple was conceived as a return to Eden, to life as it was meant to be, for a few days each year. But the story of the second garden, like the first, ends with exile. So I believe that the third garden of the lovers takes up the 'story line' that proceeds from the other two, and effects—or envisions—a resolution of the abiding problem of humanity's exile from the Garden of God" ("Reading the Song Iconographically," *The Journal of Scriptural Reasoning* 1 [2001] at https://jsr.shanti.virginia.edu/back-issues/vol-1-no-1-august-2001/reading-words-the-song-of-songs-and-the-path-of-love/reading-the-song-iconographically/)

25. Jan Holman notes that in the Sumerian text Lu-dingir-ra there is a double metaphor of chariot and litter for a woman. The goddess Inanna, disguised as a woman, is compared to a wagon and a litter, both of which smell sweetly. Holman, pointing to Song 6:12 where the chariot clearly stands as a metaphor for the woman, is able to conclude that the litter of 3:7, and subsequently the palanquin of 3:9, are also able to be metaphors for the bride of Solomon ("A Fresh Attempt at Understanding the Imagery of Canticles 3:6–11," 303–9 in *"Lasset uns Brücken bauen . . .": Collected Communications to the XVth Congress of the International Organization for the Study of the Old Testament*, BEATAJ 42 [New York: Lang, 1998]).

26. According to Gianni Barbiero, the woman's appearance is like that of the Ark of the Covenant ("Die Liebe der Töchter Jerusalems: Hld 3,10b MT im Kontext von 3,6–11," *Biblische Zeitschrif* 39 [1999]: 96–104, at 102).

KELLY ANDERSON

plane. The result of this is not only to equate sacred space and sacred people, but also to communicate that Solomon is the builder of all of it.

Nina Sophie Heereman offers a penetrating analysis of this pericope where she ties these many allusions together:

> The scene telescopes the history of Israel, centered around the Ark, from the Exodus to its installation in "its place," the Temple of Jerusalem, by King Solomon. . . . According to Israel's understanding of its divinely appointed kingship, Solomon is Yhwh's proxy in the consummation of his covenant marriage with Israel on the day of the Ark's installation. Solomon's wedding is, in fact, Yhwh's wedding with Israel as he enters into his Temple (as the divine presence takes possession of the Temple). While the Lord takes possession of his Temple, his symbolic bride, Solomon receives Israel in marriage; that is, he receives the crown by which his kingship is established.[27]

Jewish and Christian authors generally agree with this interpretation. The Targum sees Solomon's bed as the Temple and the sixty heroes as the priests, Levites, and all the tribes of Israel equipped with the words of the Torah.[28] Christian interpreters saw the woman coming up from the desert as the Church rising from the wilderness, or the soul making such spiritual progress that even the angels marvel:[29] "The Church, or the holy soul, dwells in the wilderness of the world, in exile from the kingdom, but not deserted by her Spouse."[30] The bed, likewise, is seen as the Church, the soul, or the sanctified womb of the Virgin Mother.[31] Thus Solomon constructs his bride, so to speak, in the making of the palanquin, and then marries her.

The third moment (5:10–16) is a description of the man. There are several similarities between the description of the man and the litter which he makes for himself: myrrh (מֹר; 3:6/5:13); Lebanon (לְבָנוֹן; 3:9/5:5); gold (זָהָב; 3:10/5:14); pillar (עַמּוּד; 3:10/5:15), this final word being used only these two times in the Song. Thus, the man has constructed an icon of himself in 3:6–10.[32]

---

27. Nina Sophie Heereman, "Recuperating the Song of Songs as Religious Poetry: Building a Bridge from Composition to Canon," 219–70 in *The Song of Songs in Its Context: Words for Love, Love for Words*, ed. Pierre van Hecke, BETL 310 (Leuven: Peeters, 2020), 252–53.

28. *The Targum of Canticles: Translated with a Critical Introduction, Apparatus, and Notes*, ArBib 17A, trans. Philip S. Alexander (Collegeville, MN: Liturgical Press, 2003), 124–28.

29. Richard Frederick Littledale, *A Commentary on the Song of Songs from Ancient and Medieval Sources* (New York: Pott and Amery, 1869), 124.

30. Pope, *Song of Songs*, 430.

31. Littledale, *Song of Songs*, 124–40.

32. Gen 2:22 says God built (בנה) the rib from the man into the woman. When God is the subject of the verb "to build," he builds his chambers in the upper heavens, his sanctuary, Jeru-

The Old Testament as an Earthly Translation of an Inner-Trinitarian Dialogue

Likewise, the depictions of the man bear several similarities to sacred spaces. Three times the man is compared to gold (5:11, 14, 15), and as noted above, gold was used extensively in the tabernacle and temple. He is likened to spices and myrrh, and this recalls the incense and sacrifices in the tabernacle/temple. His arms are rods of gold (5:14), and rods of gold recall the poles which carried the ark (Exod 25:28). His body of ivory recalls the throne of Solomon (1 Kgs 10:18), while the pillars, golden pedestals, and Lebanon cedars are all evocative of the tabernacle and temple (see above).

Four basic conclusions can be drawn from this description. First, the man appears to be the embodiment of wisdom, but also of the tabernacle/temple, and of God himself. He is a theophany of God who creates an icon of himself in 3:6–10.[33] Second, the divinized person who constructs the tabernacle/temple is set on par with that constructed sacred space; the man and the woman are viewed as sacred spaces comparable to tabernacle and temple. In putting these human beings on the same plane as liturgical spaces, the human person is presented as having a dignity and respect worthy of that which God himself requires in the tabernacle/temple.[34] Third, the pericope depicts not only the wedding of Solomon, but the wedding of God himself to his people, Israel. Fourth, the Song puts forth the idea of restoration between man and woman. Unlike Eve, the Shulammite seeks after Solomon to give him her good fruits and she is exclusive to him, and unlike Solomon in 1 Kings 3–11, the man in the Song constructs and builds her lovingly (Song 3:10), ensures her protection (3:7–8), and is exclusive to her (7:11).

---

salem, and "builds" (establishes) his steadfast love forever (Ps 89:3) (see Siegfried Wagner, "בָּנָה," TDOT 2:173). Gen 2:22 is unique in that God is said to build a specific person from the body of another. This usage may indicate how the author of the Song can see the woman as a symbolic entity of the city of Jerusalem, an entity also built by God (Ps 78:69; 147:2), and how Solomon, portrayed as a theophany of God, can construct an icon of himself. Ben Sira describes the virtuous woman in similar terms, "Golden columns on silver bases are her shapely limbs and feet" (Sir 26:18), showing that the depictions of the man can be attributed to the woman (this reference to Ben Sira was found in Roland E. Murphy, *The Song of Songs: A Commentary on the Book of Canticles or the Song of Songs*, Hermeneia [Minneapolis: Augsburg Fortress, 1990], 172).

33. See Sir 50:5–13 where the appearance of the priest is likened to a theophany of God.

34. The human person is compared to sacred space. According to the Old Testament, accessing sacred space is dangerous, and thus God provides liturgical rites which enable holy people to enter what is holy without danger. Sacred space in the Song is both the tabernacle/temple and the human person, and this teaching corresponds to the two sacraments of vocation: Holy Orders and Holy Matrimony. "Access" to a holy realm or a holy person ought not to be done prior to a liturgical activity.

The Song thus portrays the ideal of what Solomon and the Shulammite should be, and what the construction of sacred spaces entails by the divinized man. Thus, the pattern established in Genesis and carried out by Bezalel and his associates, as well as Solomon and Hiram/Huram-abi, serves as the backdrop for the Song. Now, however, instead of creating a tabernacle/temple, Solomon, the divinized man, constructs an icon of himself which reflects both the tabernacle/temple and his bride.

IV. Synopsis

At the beginning of the essay, I posed two questions: how is it that the authors of Mark and Hebrews consider the Old Testament to be an earthly translation of an inner-Trinitarian dialogue, and whether this understanding has any implications for the doctrine of inspiration. I am now in a better position to answer these questions. I will begin with the first, and then address the second.

God creates the cosmos by speaking, that is, through his word which structures and orders the cosmos, rendering it fit for liturgical purposes. In Genesis 1:26, a certain dialogue proceeds the creation of mankind. There is good reason to think that God is speaking here to Wisdom as is portrayed in Proverbs 8:22–31 (see footnote 12). Thus, God's creation is portrayed as a dialogical process.

Wisdom is instantiated in Bezalel and Solomon who can then act as God does by arranging the world, rendering it fit for liturgical purposes. Bezalel and Solomon both have someone like a "wingman," a helper, or an architect (Oholiab, Hiram/Huram-abi), who help them in their creation, just as God employed his word, and then Wisdom. Thus, they engage in a dialogical process similar to that of God. It is interesting that when God creates Adam as priest and king, he gives him a "helper," divine assistance that is needed for him to function as a priest and king.

The Song of Songs looks back upon Israel's history and envisions a divinized man, a theophany of God himself who creates a litter/palanquin/ark, portrayed as a supra-human woman whom he marries. So, this man who is a theophany of God can construct something like himself which is likewise godlike.

Thus, Wisdom who is in dialogue with God is instantiated in men who build the tabernacle/temple. Those who have Wisdom within them are privy to the dialogical experience of God's creation. The creation of the cosmos/tabernacle/temple is recorded and actualized in liturgy, and Sacred Scripture becomes the record and blueprint of that liturgy. Therefore, some New Testament authors see the Old Testament as God's word to man, but also, at

The Old Testament as an Earthly Translation of an Inner-Trinitarian Dialogue

times, as God's word to Wisdom, who is understood to be the Logos in the New Testament.[35]

Could this have any implications for inspiration?

It seems to me that Bezalel, Solomon, and the theophanic man in the Song could give an insight into the writing of Sacred Scripture. Perhaps there is an analogy between the creation of liturgical space, and the creation of text which is a blueprint and record of that liturgical process.

To re-summarize the findings so far: Wisdom is instantiated in certain people, and when God speaks, these men are privy to that cosmic, heavenly dialogue. That dialogue within them enables them to create the world fit for liturgy, as God does. Each of them employs others in their building, engaging in their own forms of "dialogue." Just as God creates with his word/Wisdom, so Bezalel creates with Oholiab, and Solomon creates with Hiram/Huram-abi. Further, others are employed in their constructions: in Exodus, others who are also endowed with wisdom serve as artisans, and Solomon makes use of the men of Tyre for building.

Now, the establishment of liturgy also entails the establishment of a written work which serves as both a record and guide of that creation. Sacred Scripture is the expression of the liturgical cult which is being created, a blueprint and record of liturgical spaces. So, the liturgical event is first, and the writing of that event takes place after the event is actualized in liturgy.[36]

But who is the author who can construct such a liturgical text? Can our understanding of the creation of sacred spaces aid in our understanding of the "creation" of biblical texts?

---

35. "In the form of reason and word, the source of wisdom becomes a hypostatic personification in Philo's thought and associated with the Son of God as the *logos* of the Gospel of John." R. S. Hess, "Wisdom Sources," 894–901 in *Dictionary of the Old Testament: Wisdom, Poetry and Writings*, IVP Bible Dictionary Series, ed. Tremper Longman III and Peter Enns (Downers Grove, IL: IVP Academic, 2008), 901.

36. The book of Esther mirrors such an understanding of liturgy and inspiration. The book recounts the *event* of God's salvation for his people, how this event is to be *remembered* (Esth 9:20–23), and then how Mordecai and Esther *compose the rubrics* for this liturgical rite (9:29–32). In this case, the revelatory *event* is the salvation God wrought through Esther, the wise woman. Her wisdom enables her to direct King Ahasuerus during two banquets to save her people from the wicked Haman. God's act of salvation is *actualized in liturgy* which is ordered by Mordecai the Jew and savior (9:20–24). The Jews agree to follow the rubrics established by Mordecai (9:26–28), and Esther the wise woman *writes and confirms the establishment of the feast and its prescriptions* (9:29–32). The book of Esther, which is composed and formed in the liturgical cult, is the record of God's saving act and the rubric of how that salvific event is to be actualized in liturgy.

It seems that an analogy can be drawn with the theophanic man from the Song. Unlike God in the first creation account, Bezalel, or Solomon, this man is not helped by anyone. Here, the helper and the created entity seem to be merged in this depiction of the woman who is likewise sacred space and an icon of the man. And so, it seems best to view the writer of Scripture as analogous to the divinized man from the Song who creates something of his own being. The writer is imbued with the divine force he receives, possibly from his own encounter in the liturgy, and with that he "builds" a liturgical text which also reflects himself. In some way, then, we can say that *Scripture is a liturgical icon*. The writer is not like Bezalel or Solomon in that he has a wingman, but he is more like the theophanic man in the Song who creates something of himself which is also godlike in his writing.

But, like Bezalel and Solomon, it does seem that this writer is privy to a cosmic dialogue in a way which enables him to construct this text. To be able to write the words of God means that he in some way has heard them first. Further, this writer will have helpers from the wider community. In fact, source criticism has shown that the sacred texts have been reworked over time, and this has been difficult to reconcile with inspiration. But perhaps this is where Bezalel and Solomon can help. Bezalel is helped by artisans and women who spin goat hair. Finally, Solomon employs the men of Tyre to help. All this shows that certain other ancillary figures can aid in the construction of liturgical spaces, and thus also the liturgical icon which is Sacred Scripture. It may be best to see inspiration as flowing from one divinized font around whom other ancillaries are gathered and employed, according to the divine help given to them.

Conclusion

In this essay, I sought to examine how certain New Testament authors came to see the Old Testament as, at least in part, a Trinitarian dialogue. I began with Genesis 1 where God speaks, and then speaks directly to someone in Genesis 1:26 whom he involves in his created work. I suggest that this one to whom he spoke was Wisdom, inserted into the tradition by later wisdom sages who composed Proverbs 8:22–31.

I then examined how Bezalel and Solomon construct liturgical spaces, and how these two men are patterned after God who constructed the cosmos in a liturgical process for liturgical purposes. After that, I sought to investigate the figure of Solomon in the Song who is portrayed as a theophany of God, a divinized man who creates an icon of himself, who is likewise a divinized

The Old Testament as an Earthly Translation of an Inner-Trinitarian Dialogue

woman and sacred space. Finally, I noted that Sacred Scripture is a blueprint and record of these liturgical activities.

Given all that, I was able to conclude that the New Testament authors saw in the creation account a dialogue between God and his word, and between God and Wisdom. Bezalel and Solomon follow this pattern, and thus in the writing of their respective "creations," the sacred author not only recorded God's word to mankind, but also, on occasion, God's word to Wisdom, who in the New Testament is seen as the Logos.

The implications for inspiration are that the builder of the sacred spaces may be seen as analogous to the creators of sacred texts. I suggested that the man in the Song provides the best analogy for the writers of Sacred Scripture, as he creates a divine image of himself, a *liturgical icon*! But Bezalel and Solomon can also serve as analogies, for they are instantiated with Wisdom and are privy to God's dialogue in creation. In some way the sacred author also knows the divine word, for he writes the word of God. Likewise, as Bezalel and Solomon are helped by others in their work and the wider community aids in the establishment of the text, each according to the divine assistance received.

Considering the sacred texts as liturgical icons flowing from liturgical activity may aid in the continual study of inspiration.

Contributors

KELLY ANDERSON, Saint Charles Borromeo Seminary, Wynnewood, PA

MATTHEW C. GENUNG, Mount St. Mary's Seminary & School of Theology, Cincinnati, OH

MARCIN KOWALSKI, John Paul II Catholic University, Lublin, Poland

MICHAEL K. MAGEE, Saint Charles Borromeo Seminary, Wynnewood, PA

ANTHONY PAGLIARINI, University of Notre Dame, South Bend, IN

AARON PIDEL, SJ, Marquette University, Milwaukee, WI

LUIS SÁNCHEZ-NAVARRO, DCJM, Ecclesiastical University San Dámaso, Madrid, Spain

KEVIN ZILVERBERG, The Saint Paul Seminary School of Divinity of the University of St. Thomas, St. Paul, MN

Index of Names and Subjects

Adam, 34n25, 147, 149, 152, 160
allegory, 154n16, 154n17
Ambrosiaster, 112, 133
angels, 44, 82, 116, 133–34, 146, 148n9, 158
Aristotle, 112n23, 113n28, 115n35, 117, 118n47, 137
Augustine, 75n24, 76n27, 81–82, 133
authorship, 35–46, 49–50, 76, 87–88, 109, 143

Babylon, 70, 72, 77, 82–83
Benedict XVI, Pope. *See* Ratzinger, Joseph/Pope Benedict XVI
Bezalel, 148–51, 152, 153, 160–62
Bonaventure, 17

canon, biblical, 9–10, 15, 43, 68, 79n32
captatio benevolentiae, 113
Christ. *See* Jesus Christ
Chronicler, 153, 154n16
Church
    ecclesial aspect of inspiration, 17–21, 33, 87–88
    ecclesial framework of 1 Cor 11:2–16, 112, 113, 116, 118–20, 133, 139, 142

Magisterium, 23–25, 32
prefigured in Old Testament, 82, 158
Ratzinger's test of ecclesial reception, 89–91, 98–99, 102–4
Cicero, 112n23, 113n28, 114n31, 118n47, 138
Clement of Alexandria, 98–99
cloud, 55, 58, 60–61, 65
Congregation for the Doctrine of the Faith, 9, 13, 22
Covenant Code, 52n5, 55, 56, 64
creation
    argument from theology of creation in 1 Cor 11:2–16, 115–17, 130–36, 141, 142
    of cosmos for liturgy, 146–47, 150n12
    imitated by builders of the tabernacle/temple, 148–53
    imitated by divinized man in Song of Songs, 154–63
    interpretive issues regarding Genesis account, 33, 34, 44, 91
    role of divine Wisdom in, 149–51, 153, 160–63

David, 82, 154n16, 156
Decalogue, 57, 59, 64–65

167

INDEX OF NAMES AND SUBJECTS

Dei verbum
  on anthropomorphic language for
    God, 51n3
  criteria for inspiration, 14
  drafting of, 35n28, 37–40, 104n80
  on historicity of the Gospels, 85–86,
    102–4, 105
  on human authors of Scripture,
    85–86, 103–4, 109, 143
  on inerrancy, 10, 26, 32–40, 104
  and methodology of *Jesus of
    Nazareth,* 92
  on providential shape of history,
    74–75, 82
  Ratzinger as guide to intentions of,
    104, 105
  on relation of inspiration and revela-
    tion, 17
  relation to *The Inspiration and Truth
    of Sacred Scripture,* 24–26, 31, 43,
    48, 49
demythologization, 88–90
derivatio, 113
Devil, 88–90, 94
dispositio, 111–12
Divino afflante Spiritu (Pius XII), 8,
  26–27, 28, 32, 35n28, 39
Documentary Hypothesis, 57, 150n12
Dominus Iesus, 9

Eden, Garden of, 51n3, 72n14, 146–47,
  149, 151, 156, 157n24
Elijah, 148n9
emotivist hermeneutics, 10–15, 18
Enuma Elish, 150n12
Ephrem the Syrian, 133
Essenes, 94, 95
Esther, 161n36
Eucharist, 19, 84, 109, 118n49. *See also*
  Last Supper chronology
Eve, 147, 149, 159, 160
exile, 70–74, 76, 77, 81–83

Exodus 19
  both permanent and open to con-
    tinuing revelation, 63–68
  cultic symbols in, 59–63, 66–67, 68
  exegesis of redacted text, 51–53,
    65–68
  redactional character of, 53–59
exordium, 112–13, 114, 118
Ezekiel. *See* Temple Vision

Farkasfalvy, Denis, 15, 28n9, 29, 35, 36,
  41, 43, 46, 49
Father–Son relation. *See* Trinity
1 Corinthians 11:2–16
  in broader context of 1 Corinthians,
    109–11
  Christological-theological thesis, 112,
    115–17, 120–23, 142
  critiqued as patriarchal, 108–9, 119,
    123, 132, 134n127, 139
  cultural argument, 115–16, 124–30,
    139, 141
  ecclesial framework, 112, 113, 116,
    118–20, 133, 139, 142
  inspired text with a universal mes-
    sage, 109, 123, 132, 140–43
  natural law argument, 112, 117,
    136–39, 141–42, 143
  referenced in *The Inspiration and
    Truth
    of Sacred Scripture,* 107–8, 139
  rhetorical structure of, 111–18
  theology of creation argument,
    115–17, 130–36, 141, 142
Fortschreibung, 57–59
fundamentalism, 30–31, 41, 44, 48

gender roles. *See also* 1 Corinthians
  11:2–16
  Father–Son relation as model for,
    121, 123, 135, 140–41, 142–43
  idealized in Song of Songs, 159

Index of Names and Subjects

and natural law, 112, 117, 136–39, 141–42, 143

and patriarchy, 108–9, 119, 123, 132, 134n127, 139

in Paul's cultural context, 115–16, 124–30, 139, 141

and theology of creation, 115–17, 130–36, 141, 142, 147

woman's role as helper, 147, 149, 152, 160

glory (δόξα), 112, 116, 130–32, 136

Gnosticism, 7, 13, 84

Gospels. *See* Last Supper chronology

Haag, Herbert, 88–90

Haggai, Book of, 79n32

hairstyles, 116, 117, 125–28, 136–38

head

Christ as, 112, 114, 116, 120, 126

covering of, 115, 116, 117, 119, 124–30, 132–33, 140, 141

hairstyles, 116, 117, 125–28, 136–38

meaning of κεφαλή, 114–15, 120–23

woman's authority over, 132–35

helper (עֵזֶר), 147, 149, 160

Heraclitus, 137

Hiram, 152, 153, 160, 161

historicity. *See* Last Supper chronology; tests of faith and reason (Ratzinger)

history, theology of, 74–76, 81–83

holiness, 76, 81, 83

Holy Spirit, 17, 20

homosexuality, 125–26

honor/shame, 116, 126, 130, 131–32, 134n127, 141, 143

Horace, 41, 129

Huram-abi, 153, 160, 161

illocution, 76–77, 83

image (εἰκών), 130–31

inerrancy, 10–11, 26–28, 30, 32–40, 43–45, 47–48, 87, 104

inspiration and truth of Scripture

analogy to divine creative dialogue, 160–63

and canonicity, 9–10, 15, 43, 68, 79n32

and cultural context of human author, 109, 123, 140–43

ecclesial aspect of inspiration, 17–21, 33, 87–88

and emotivist hermeneutics, 10–15, 18

and historical-critical reductionism, 31, 35, 74–75

ignored by mainstream postconciliar exegesis, 8–10

and inerrancy, 10–11, 26–28, 30, 32–40, 43–45, 47–48, 87, 104

not clarified by *The Inspiration and Truth of Sacred Scripture*, 22–23, 28–29, 48–50

and providential shape of history, 74–83

relation between divine and human authors, 35–40, 44–46, 49–50, 76, 87–88, 109, 143

relation to revelation, 17–19, 34

Scripture's internal testimony to its inspiration, 16–17, 41–43

significance for Christian life, 9, 19–20

Vatican II's discussion of, 32–40

whether it applies to all or only parts of Scripture, 24–28, 38–40, 42–45, 49, 87–88

Irenaeus of Lyons, 90

Israel. *See* Exodus 19; Temple Vision

Jaubert, Annie, 94, 95, 97, 98–99

Jeremias, Joachim, 93, 95, 98n58, 99

Jesus Christ. *See also* Last Supper chronology; Trinity; Wisdom of God

Christological-theological thesis of 1 Cor 11:2–16, 112, 115–17, 120–23, 142

INDEX OF NAMES AND SUBJECTS

emotivist interpretations of, 13–15
fullness of revealed truth, 18–19
guides Church's interpretation of
Scripture, 88
as head of a man, 112, 114, 116, 120,
126
incarnation analogy for inspiration,
45–46, 49–50
prefigured in Psalm 137, 82
John, Gospel of. *See* Last Supper
chronology
John Chrysostom, 51n3, 113, 123, 129
John Paul II, Pope, 19–20, 132n112
Josephus, Flavius, 118, 120, 138, 141
Judith, 154n16

kabod, 71, 80

Last Supper chronology
discrepancies between Synoptic and
Johannine accounts, 93–94
and Gospels writers' attitude toward
historicity, 84–87
and Pitre's Passover Hypothesis, 94,
100, 101–2, 105–6
Ratzinger's tests of faith and reason,
91–92, 94–106
law. *See* Mosaic Law
Leo XIII, Pope. *See Providentissimus
Deus* (Leo XIII)
literary criticism, 28, 30
litter, 154–58, 160
liturgy
construction of the tabernacle/
temple, 148–53
cosmos and Eden as liturgical
spaces, 146–47
sacred spaces and sacred people,
158–59
Scripture as liturgical icon, 160–63
Loretz, Oswald, 10–11, 20, 28n8, 34n26,
40n42, 47–48
Luz, Ulrich, 11–12, 14–15

Magisterium, 23–25, 32
Meier, John, 93, 94, 97, 99–101, 103
men and women. *See* gender roles
midrash, 81, 82, 116n41
modernity, 9, 12–15, 18, 74–75
Mosaic Law, 52n5, 55, 56, 64, 77–81, 96,
138
Moses
author of scripture, 52, 63, 65
mediator in Exodus 19, 51, 53–63, 65–67
relation to Ezekiel, 73, 77–79, 81
mountain. *See* Sinai, Mount

natural law, 112, 117, 136–39, 141–42, 143
nature (φύσις), 136–37
neo-Scholasticism, 35–37, 39–40, 87

Oholiab, 148–49, 153, 160, 161

palanquin, 154–58, 160
Passover. *See* Last Supper chronology
Passover Hypothesis, 94, 100, 101–2,
105–6
patriarchy, 108–9, 119, 123, 132, 134n127,
139. *See also* gender roles
patristic exegesis, 7, 15, 27, 36, 49,
98–99, 112
Paul. *See* 1 Corinthians 11:2–16
Pelagianism, 13
peroratio, 118
Peter Lombard, 112, 133
Philo, 118, 120, 125n83, 129, 134, 138, 141,
161n35
Pitre, Brant, 94, 97n56, 100, 101–2, 105–6
Pius XII, Pope. *See Divino afflante Spiri-
tu* (Pius XII)
Placuit Deo, 13
Plato, 137, 141
pleonasm, 113
Pliny, 129
Pontifical Biblical Commission. *See The
Inspiration and Truth of Sacred
Scripture*

170

Index of Names and Subjects

positivism, 31, 32

postmodernity, 12, 74–75, 141

preaching, 33, 35

prophets/prophecy, 14, 16, 20, 72–73.
   See also Temple Vision

propositio, 113–16, 120

Providentissimus Deus (Leo XIII),
   26–27, 32

queen of Sheba, 152–53

Qumran, 94, 95, 134

Rahner, Karl, 29, 35–37, 39, 40

Ratzinger, Joseph/Pope Benedict XVI.
   See also tests of faith and reason
   (Ratzinger)
   attitude toward the Gospels' histo-
      ricity, 84–85, 91–92, 94–106
   Bonaventurian model of inspiration,
      17–18
   Christological analogy for inspira-
      tion, 45–46
   on culture, 143
   and drafting of *Dei verbum*, 37, 38,
      104, 105
   on triple authorship of Scripture,
      87–88

redaction
   and evolutionary models of exegesis,
      100, 101
   exegesis of, 51, 55, 63–66
   of Ezekiel's Temple Vision, 71n10, 73
   of Last Supper chronology, 103–4
   redactional character of Exodus 19,
      53–59
   redactional expansion (*Fortschrei-
      bung*), 57–59

Revelation, Book of, 76n27

rhetoric, 111–18

Sabbath, 96. *See also* Last Supper
   chronology

Schökel, Luis Alonso, 15, 29

Second Vatican Council. *See* Vatican II

senses of Scripture, 27–28, 154n16

sexuality. *See* 1 Corinthians 11:2–16;
   gender roles

shofar, 56, 59, 62, 66

sin, 14–15, 88–89

Sinai, Mount, 54–63, 66–67, 68, 78

sola Scriptura, 32

Solomon
   and construction of the temple,
      151–53, 158, 159, 162
   divinized man in Song of Songs,
      154–60, 162

Song of Songs, 154–63

spiritual exegesis, 154n16

stasis, 114

Stoics, 137–38

structural sin, 88–89

symbolism, 154n16

Synod of Bishops 12th Ordinary
   General Assembly (2008), 22–29

Synoptic Gospels. *See* Last Supper
   chronology

tabernacle
   cultic symbols in Exodus 19, 59–63
   parallels with Eden, 147n8
   symbolized in Song of Songs, 156–60
   in Temple Vision imagery, 73, 77
   Wisdom instantiated in builders of,
      140–51, 160–61

Tatian, 17

temple. *See also* Temple Vision
   cultic symbols in Exodus 19, 59–63, 67
   as embodied wisdom, 153
   God's entrance into, 66, 158
   and Jewish festal calendar, 95–96,
      100n69
   parallels with Eden, 147n8, 153n15
   patterned after Genesis creation
      account, 147n8, 151–53
   symbolized in Song of Songs,
      156–60

INDEX OF NAMES AND SUBJECTS

Wisdom instantiated in builders of, 151–53, 160–61

Temple Vision
conveys transcendent message through historical imagery, 76–83
as "failed" prophecy, 70–74, 77, 83
and providential shape of history, 74–76, 81–83
within structure of Book of Ezekiel, 69–70

Tertullian, 124n78, 133

tests of faith and reason (Ratzinger)
consistency with *Dei verbum*, 85–86, 102–4, 105
in "Farewell to the Devil?," 86–91
and Last Supper accounts, 91–92, 94–106
test 1 (relationship between Testaments), 89, 91n33, 94–95
test 2 (New Testament portrait of Christ), 89, 91n33, 95–98
test 3 (ecclesial reception), 89–91, 98–99, 102–4
test 4 (scholarly reason), 90, 93–94, 99–102, 105

The Inspiration and Truth of Sacred Scripture
Commission's understanding of its task, 29–32, 41–42
in context of discussion at Vatican II, 32–40
in context of discussion by 2008 Synod of Bishops, 22–29
criteria for inspiration, 142
critique of, 22–23, 28–29, 41–50
drafting and methodology of, 41–43, 48, 49
focuses on fundamentalism, 30–31, 41, 44, 48
on historicity of the Gospels, 86
on inerrancy, 43–45, 47–48
on the Pauline letters, 107–8, 139

on relation between divine and human authors, 43–46, 48–49
relation to *Dei verbum*, 24–26, 31, 43, 48, 49
on significance of Exodus 19, 51–53

Theodoret, 112, 134

Thomas Aquinas, 36n33, 79n31, 104n78, 112, 133. *See also* neo-Scholasticism

tradition, 18, 48, 118–19, 142

Trent, Council of, 32, 33n23, 103

Trinity
Father is revealed in Jesus, 19
Father–Son relation as model for gender roles, 121, 123, 135, 140–41, 142–43
Holy Spirit, 17–20
inner-Trinitarian dialogue, 145–47, 150–51, 153, 160–63
and work of salvation, 13

truth. *See* inerrancy; inspiration and truth of Scripture

typology, 154n16

Vatican I, 32, 33n23

Vatican II. *See also Dei verbum*
discussion of inspiration and inerrancy, 32–40, 87
rupturist interpretation of, 10

Verbum Domini (Benedict XVI), 19, 45–46

Wiederaufnahme, 58

Wisdom of God
helps to create the cosmos, 149–51, 153
instantiated in builders of tabernacle/temple, 148–53, 160–61
participates in inner-Trinitarian dialogue, 149–51, 153, 160–63

women. *See* 1 Corinthians 11:2–16; gender roles

yôbel, 56

Index of Scripture References

Genesis

1	134
1–2	117, 144
1:1	150n12
1:1–2:4a	150n12
1:1–26	150n12
1:2	149, 150n12
1:3	144, 149
1:5	150n12
1:6	144
1:7	150n12
1:9	144
1:11	144
1:14	144
1:20	144
1:24	144
1:26	144, 150, 150n12, 160
1:26–27	116n40, 130, 134
1:26–30	150n12
1:27	116n41, 130–31, 150n12
1:27–28	116n41
1:28	153n15

1:31	116n40
2	116n41
2:4	146
2:11–12	156
2:18	116n40, 116n41
2:18–25	116, 135
2:20–23	116n40
2:21–24	116n41, 130
2:22	158n32
3:8	51n3
3:16	116n40, 116n41
3:20	135
3:22	150n12
5:1	116n40
9:6	116n40
11:4–7	150n12
35:2	62n32

Exodus

3:12	60
4:22	78
9:13	156n21
9:18	156n21
9:25	156n21
13:21	60n23, 156

13:22	60n23, 156
14:19	60n23, 156
14:24	60n23, 156
19:1	54
19:2	54
19:3	54, 55
19:3b–8	63–64
19:4	67
19:5	63n34, 65–66, 67
19:5–6a	64
19:5b	64
19:6	58
19:7	55
19:7–11	54
19:8	57, 55, 64
19:8–9	55
19:9	55, 58, 60–61, 61, 65–66
19:10–12	58
19:10–13	62
19:11	55
19:12–13	54, 58
19:12–13a	56
19:13b	55, 56
19:14	55, 58

173

INDEX OF SCRIPTURE REFERENCES

19:16	61	26:30	61	**Leviticus**	
19:16–17	54	26:31–32	157	1:1	61, 61n24
19:16–19	59, 62	26:36	157	1:9	156n21
19:17	54, 56	27:16	157	1:13	156n21
19:18	54, 55, 59	28:5	157	1:15	156n21
19:19	51, 52, 54, 66–67	28:6	157	1:17	156n21
19:20	55	28:8	157	2:2	156n21
19:20–24	54, 55, 56–57, 58, 66	28:15	157	2:9	156n21
		28:33	157	2:11	156n21
19:20–25	58–59	29:36–37	73	3:5	156n21
19:21	54	30:7	156n21	3:11	156n21
19:22	56, 66	30:8	156n21	3:16	156n21
19:23	57, 58	30:20	156n21	4:10	156n21
19:24	66	30:22–33	156n22	4:19	156n21
19:25	55, 57	30:23	156	4:26	156n21
19:25–20:1	55, 57, 59	30:34	156	4:31	156n21
20:1–17	57, 59, 64	31:1–6	153	4:35	156n21
20:18	54, 59	31:2	153	5:12	156n21
20:18–20	54	31:3	149	6:5	156n21
20:18–21	57	31:6	149, 153	6:8	156n21
20:21	55	31:18	52n4	6:15	156n21
20:22–23:33	52n5, 55, 64	32:16	52n4	7:5	156n21
		32:26–29	58	7:31	156n21
23:30	145	33:9–10	61	8:10–11	156n22
23:32	52n5, 63n34	34:1	52n4	15	62n30
24:1	55, 56, 66	34:28	52n4	18	62n30
24:3	64	35–40	80	19:2	78, 80, 81
24:3–8	63	35:25	149		
24:4	52	35:30–36	153	**Numbers**	
24:4a	65	35:31	149	11:18	62n31
24:7	52, 52n5, 63n34, 65	35:35	149	12:5	61
		36:1–2	149	14:14	60n23
24:7b	67	36:36	157	28:9–15	80
24:8	63n34	37:17–24	157n24		
24:9–8	66	38:22–23	153	**Deuteronomy**	
24:9–11	56	40:9–16	156n22	4:5–8	80
24:11	66	40:27	156n21	4:13	52n4
24:12	52n4	40:34	61	5:4–5	57
25–31	80	40:34–35	60	9:10	52n4
25–40	144	40:35	61n24	10:3	52n4
25:28	159			10:4	52n4
26:1	157			31:15	61

Index of Scripture References

32:22	152n13	4:12	151	**Nehemiah**	
32:29	73	4:13	151	9:12	60n23, 156
32:39	148n9	5:14	151	9:19	60n23, 156
32:43 LXX	146	5:20	156		
32:52	73	6:18	157n24	**Tobit**	
		6:21	156	4:19	148n9
Joshua		6:29	156		
3:5	62n31	6:32	156	**Esther**	
7:13	62n31	6:35	156	9:20–23	161n36
		6:38–71	153	9:20–24	161n36
Judges		6–9	144	9:26–28	161n36
5:4–5	61n25, 67n37	7:13–47	153	9:29–32	161n36
16:17	147n7	7:14	152		
		7:15–22	152	**3 Maccabees**	
Ruth		7:18–20	157n24	3:29	138
3:11	152	7:23–26	152		
		7:27–40	152	**4 Maccabees**	
1 Samuel		7:29	157n24	1:40	138
2:6	148n9	7:36	156	2:13	119
7:10	62n27	8	66	5:8–9	138
21:1	34	8:6–11	61	5:25	138
21:5–6	62n31	9:11	153	6:13	119
		9:21	153	13:22	119
2 Samuel		10:1–13	152	13:27	119, 138
6:2	62	10:6–9	152	15:13	138
6:14–15	62	10:18	159	15:25	138
7:14 LXX	146			16:3	138
10:7	156	**2 Kings**			
12:20	62n32	10:22	62n32	**Job**	
22:8	152n13			9:5	152n13
22:8–20	61n25, 67n37	**1 Chronicles**		9:13	147n7
22:16	152n13	13:8	62n29	26:11	152n13
23:9	156	13:18	62n29	28	150n11
23:16	156				
23:17	156	**2 Chronicles**		**Psalms**	
23:22	156	1–9	151	2	61n25
		1:5	153	2:7 LXX	146
1 Kings		1:5–12	153	7:6	116n40
1:8	156	2	153	8:6	116n40
3–11	151, 155	2:12	153	18:8	152n13
3:15–28	151	2:13	153	18:8–20	61n25, 67n37
4:11	151	3:14	157	18:8–29	61n25

175

INDEX OF SCRIPTURE REFERENCES

18:14	62n27	8:27–29	150n12	7:26	80
18:16	152n13	8:28	150n12	13:1	138
22:1	145	8:29	150n12, 152n13	16:13	148n9
29	67n37	8:30	149, 150n12	19:20	138
29:3–5	62n27	8:31	150n12		

Sirach

29:3–9	155	9:1	151	17:3	116n40
44:7–8 LXX	146	9:5	149	24	80
45:12	152	11:16	116n40	24:3–6	80n33
46	148n9	31:10	152	24:8	80n33, 149
48	148n9	31:10–31	147n7	24:10–11	149
50:1–3	61n25, 67n37	31:30–31	116n40	24:12–19	149
68:8–9	61n25, 67n37			24:23	80n33
68:16–18	67n37	**Ecclesiastes**		26:18	158n32
75:4	152n13	3:11	116n40	36:1	116n40
78:69	158n32			50:5–13	159n33
82:5	152n13	**Song of Songs**			
85:12	12	2:8–9	155	**Isaiah**	
89:3	158n32	3:6	155, 156, 157, 158	2:2–4	67
99:7	60n23	3:6–10	155–58, 159	4:5	67n37
101:26–28 LXX	146	3:7	155, 156, 157n25	6	62
103:4 LXX	146	3:7–8	159	6:3	134
104:24	149n10	3:9	157n25, 158	24:18	152n13
109:1 LXX	146	3:9–10	156	29:6	62n27
110	145n1	3:10	156, 158, 159	30:7	147n7
114	148n9	5:5	158	30:30–31	62n27
137:8–9	82	5:10–16	155, 158–59	40:3	145
147:2	158n32	5:11	159	40:6–8	116n40
		5:13	158	41:5–7	147n7
Proverbs		5:14	158, 159	45:7	116n40
3:18	149	5:15	158, 159	58:1	62
3:19–20	149n10	6:10	155, 157	58:12	152n13
7:14–15	147n7	6:12	157n25	60:5–7	152
7:27	147n7	7:8	156		
8	150n11	7:9	156	**Jeremiah**	
8:18	152	7:11	159	10:12	149n10
8:22	149, 150n12	8:5	155, 157	10:13	62n27
8:22–31	150n12, 160	8:6	154n17	31:37	152n13
8:23	150n12	8:12	156	51:15	149n10
8:24	150n12				
8:24–26	150n12	**Wisdom**		**Ezekiel**	
8:25	150n12	2:23	116n40	1:1	70, 82
8:26	150n12	7:20	138	8:3	70
8:27	150n12	7:22–30	80		

Index of Scripture References

11:16	71, 77
12:25	76
12:26–28	76
34 36	72
37	72
37:11	76
38:16	71
40–42	72
40:1	70
40:1–43:13	79
40:2	70, 73
40:38–43	72
40:45–46	72
43:1–5	71
43:6	73
43:10	71
43:10–11	77
43:11	71
43:12	78
43:13–46:24	79
43:18–27	72, 73
46:4–7	80
47:1–48:35	79
48:35	70, 71

Joel

4:16	62n27

Amos

1:2	62n27
5:8	116n40

Micah

1:3	155
3:1	71n10
4:1–3	67
6:2	152n13

Habbakuk

3:3–15	61n25, 67n37
3:19	155

Malachi

3:1	145

Matthew

1:22	16
12:8	96
15:2	119
15:3	119
15:6	119
23	13–15
27:9	34

Mark

1:2	145n2
1:2–3	145
1:4	145n2
1:5–14	146
2:26	34
2:28	96
7:3	119
7:5	119
7:8	119
7:9	119
7:13	119
14:1	97
14:1a	101
14:12	93
14:12–16	101
14:12a	97
15:34	145

Luke

6:5	96

John

1:14	19, 83
1:18	19
1:29	97
10:35	16, 74
13–17	93
14:6	18
14:9	19
18:28	93, 101

18:39	119
19:14	93, 102
20:31	21

1 Corinthians

1:10	110, 112n21
5:7	97
7	135n131
7:3–5	135
7:12	107n3
7:17	107n3
7:25	107n3
8:1–11:1	109, 110, 111, 132n113, 133
8:6	121
8:7	119
10:4	82n44
11:2	109, 112–13, 118–19, 126, 142
11:2–14:40	112n21, 122n70
11:2–16	109–11
11:2–34	110, 111, 112n21
11:3	108, 112, 114, 115, 115n37, 117, 120–23, 124, 135, 140, 142
11:4	115, 116
11:4–6	108, 112, 116, 124–30, 141
11:5	115, 116, 128
11:6	116, 129
11:7	108, 115, 130–31, 133
11:7–9	132
11:7–10	112, 114, 116, 130–36, 142
11:7–12	115n37, 117–18, 134, 141
11:7a	130, 131
11:7b	130, 131
11:7c	116
11:8	121
11:8–9	108, 116

INDEX OF SCRIPTURE REFERENCES

11:10	115, 115n37, 117, 130, 132, 133	7:2–4	107n3	**Titus**	
		10–13	107	2:5	108
11:10–12	123	10:7–8	107n3		
11:11	117, 123, 132, 134, 135, 142	11:1–4	107n3	**Hebrews**	
		11:2–3	120	1:5	146n5
11:11–12	112, 114, 116, 117, 130–36, 139, 143	13:1–10	107n3	1:6	146n5
				1:7	146n5
		Galatians		1:8–9	146n5
11:11–16	134n127	1–2	107	1:10–11	146n5
11:12	117	1:14	118	1:13	146n5
11:13	117	2:7–9	107		
11:13–14	136–39	3:27–28	121	**1 Peter**	
11:13–15	112, 115n37, 117, 136–39, 141	3:28	111, 118n49, 128, 135	1:19	97
11:14	117	6:16	81	**2 Peter**	
11:15	117, 118n48, 136–39			1:20–21	43
		Ephesians		1:21	16
11:16	112, 115n37, 117–18, 119, 142	1:13	1	3:16	17
		2:18	13		
11:17	109, 114	5:22–33	108	**1 John**	
11:17–34	109, 110, 111, 132n113	5:25–27	120	1:1–4	1
		Colossians		**2 John**	
11:23	109, 118n49	2:8	119	4	21
12–14	110, 111, 132n113	3:18	108		
				Revelation	
14:34–38	108	**2 Thessalonians**		5:6	97
15	132n113	2:15	119	17:5	82
15:58	110	3:6–7	119	19:10	20
16:4	110				
16:12	110	**1 Timothy**			
		2:11–15	108		
2 Corinthians					
2:14–17	107n3	**2 Timothy**			
3:1–6	107n3	3:15–16	43		
5:19	13	3:16	1, 16, 74		
5:20	107n3	3:16–17	39		
6:1–2	107n3				

OTHER BOOKS IN THIS SERIES

Augustine's Confessions *and Contemporary Concerns,* ed. David Vincent Meconi, SJ (2022)

In the School of the Word: Biblical Interpretation from the New to the Old Testament, Carlos Granados, DCJM, and Luis Sánchez-Navarro, DCJM (2021)

Piercing the Clouds: Lectio Divina *and Preparation for Ministry,* ed. Kevin Zilverberg and Scott Carl (2021)

The Revelation of Your Words: The New Evangelization and the Role of the Seminary Professor of Sacred Scripture, ed. Kevin Zilverberg and Scott Carl (2021)

On Earth as It Is in Heaven: Cultivating a Contemporary Theology of Creation, ed. David Vincent Meconi, SJ (2016; repr., 2021)

Verbum Domini *and the Complementarity of Exegesis and Theology,* ed. Scott Carl (2015; repr., 2021)